LAND, PEOPLE AND POLITICS

Roy Douglas

LAND, PEOPLE & POLITICS

A History of the Land Question in the United Kingdom 1878-1952

ALLISON & BUSBY, LONDON

First published in Great Britain by Allison & Busby
6a Noel Street, London W1V 3RB

Copyright © Roy Douglas 1976

ISBN 0 85031 147 0

Set in 11pt Lectura, and printed by
Villiers Publications Ltd., Ingestre Road, London NW5 1UL

To
ASHLEY MITCHELL
in appreciation

CONTENTS

ACKNOWLEDGEMENTS

The author has received much assistance in writing this book, and fears that he will fail to give proper acknowledgement to some of those who have helped. He would like to express gratitude to the people who have read and criticised the manuscript: his wife; Dr L. F. Haber of the University of Surrey; and Mr V. H. Blundell, Secretary of the United Committee for the Taxation of Land Values. Thanks are also due to the late Mr Andrew MacLaren, sometime MP for Burslem, who gave personal recollections of the great land battles before the First World War and during the inter-war period; to the Hon. Mrs Helen Bowen Pease, who allowed the author to consult the papers of her father, the first Lord Wedgwood, and gave some very useful sidelights on several of the personalities; to Mr A. J. A. Morris, who was particularly helpful in showing the author extracts from the papers of Sir Charles Trevelyan (of whom he has written a biography, shortly to be published); to Professor T. W. Moody for a helpful discussion, and facilities for the author to give a seminar at Trinity College, Dublin; to Mr Christopher Wrigley, who found some very useful material at the Ulster Record Office: to Mr Ronald Banks for his useful comments; and to Mr Malcolm Hill, without whom the book would probably not have seen the light of day. Two of the author's friends — Mr David K. Mills of London, and Mr Harry Pollard of Tujunga, California — require special mention, for it was they who originally persuaded him of the importance of the Land Question. The author would also thank the University of Surrey for a grant from the Faculty IV Research Fund.

A number of archives have been used, and in all cases the author has good reason for gratitude to the librarians for their kindness and help. These include authorities of the National Libraries of Ireland, Scotland and Wales; the British Library; the Beaverbrook Library; the Bodleian Library; the Library of Christ Church, Oxford; the Public and Scottish Record Offices; the Universities of Birmingham, Edinburgh and Newcastle-upon-Tyne; the National Liberal Club and the United Committee for the Taxation of Land Values. The author wishes to thank those bodies for permission to quote documents in their possession, or in which they have copyright, and also the following copyright owners: the First Beaverbrook Foundation; Mrs M. Ellis; Miss E. Humphreys-Owen; the Marquis of Lothian; Mrs Helen Bowen Pease; Lord Primrose; the (late) Marquis of Salisbury; the Scottish Liberal Party; the United Committee for the Taxation of Land Values.

CHRONOLOGICAL TABLE

1874-80:	Benjamin Disraeli (Lord Beaconsfield) Prime Minister
1878:	Commencement of Irish "Land War"
1879:	Formation of Land League
1880:	W. E. Gladstone's second Ministry (Liberal)
	Publication of *Progress and Poverty in U.K.*
1881:	Irish Land Act
	Land League declared illegal
1882:	Hebridean disturbances begin (Skye)
	National League formed
1883:	Agricultural Holdings Act
	English Land Restoration League formed
1883-5:	*Radical Programme* articles appear
1885:	Lord Salisbury Prime Minister of minority Conservative government
	Ashbourne Land Purchase Act
	(December) General Election
1886:	(February) Gladstone's third Ministry
	Crofters' Act
	(April) Defeat of First Home Rule Bill
	(July) Salisbury's second Ministry
	Welsh Tithe War begins
	(October) Plan of Campaign
1887:	Allotments Act
	Park Raid (Lewis); Mochdre Riots (Flintshire); Mitchelstown incident (Co. Cork)
1889:	National Liberal Federation committed to measure of site value taxing
1891:	Newcastle Programme
	Death of Parnell
1892:	Gladstone's fourth Ministry
1893:	Second Home Rule Bill
1894:	Lord Rosebery Prime Minister (Liberal)
1895:	Salisbury's third Ministry; General Election gives large Unionist majority
1899-1902:	Boer War
1901:	Royal Commission on Local Taxation reports

11

1902:	A. J. Balfour Prime Minister (Conservative)
1903:	Wyndham's Land Purchase Act
	"Tariff Reform" campaign begins
1905:	Balfour resigns; Campbell-Bannerman (Liberal) Prime Minister
1906:	General Election: large Liberal majority
1906-8:	Scottish Land Value Bills
1908:	H. H. Asquith Prime Minister (Liberal)
	Old Age Pensions
1909:	"People's Budget"
1910:	Two General Elections
1911:	Parliament Act
	Pentland Act
1912:	Hanley, etc., by-elections
1913-4:	Land Enquiry Committee reports
	Government Land Campaign
1914-8:	First World War
1915:	First Coalition (Asquith Prime Minister)
1916:	(December) Second Coalition (Lloyd George Prime Minister)
1918:	(December) General Election gives large Coalition majority
1920:	Repeal of Lloyd George land taxes
1922:	Bonar Law Prime Minister (Conservative)
	Irish Free State formed
1923:	Baldwin Prime Minister (Conservative) General Election gives no overall majority
1924:	(January) First Labour Government (MacDonald Prime Minister)
	(October) General Election. Baldwin's second Ministry
1925:	"Green Book"; "Brown Book"
1929:	General Election: Second Labour Government (MacDonald Prime Minister)
1931:	Snowden's Land Taxing Budget
	(August) National Government. MacDonald still Prime Minister (to 1935)
1932:	Liberals and Snowden resign from National Government
1934:	Repeal of Snowden's land valuation and taxation
1939-45:	Second World War

1940:	Coalition Government (Churchill Prime Minister)
1942:	Final Uthwatt Report
1945:	Third Labour Government (Attlee Prime Minister)
1947:	Town and Country Planning Act: Development Charge
1951:	Conservative Government (Churchill Prime Minister to 1955)
1953:	Repeal of Development Charge

1 THE ISSUE

When wilt Thou save the people?
O God of mercy, when?
Not kings and lords, but nations!
Not thrones and crowns but men!

Ebenezer Elliott
(1781-1849)

Because man is a land animal, and the quantity of land available for his use is limited in quantity, disputes of one kind or another over rights to land are as old as history, and probably a great deal older. In that sense, the "land problem" is universal and perennial, and most unlikely to disappear completely so long as man himself survives. At certain times, however, the "land problem" has acquired a degree of urgency, and people who had once been prepared tacitly to accept the *status quo* have begun to demand drastic changes. These occasions have usually occurred at times when the capacity of land to meet human needs has suddenly declined.

Such an occasion arose in the United Kingdom in the late 1870s. Its origin must be sought in a natural calamity, which we shall later need to discuss.

This crisis, however, did not simply lead to a brief period of agrarian distress and turbulence which gradually died away as conditions improved. It set people asking a great many searching and fundamental questions about land. As time went on, these questions were asked not merely in rural areas, but in urban areas as well; and right down to 1914 more and more people in all parts of the United Kingdom began to ask them. The clamour was taken up again at intervals after the end of the 1914-18 War. It continued to exert a substantial and demonstrable effect on politics long after the Second World War, and is far from silent to this day.

As a general rule, the "land problem" in its various manifestations has been treated essentially as an accessory to other stories: the story of Irish Home Rule; the story of the constitutional crisis of 1909-11; the story of British Socialism, and so on. This work is concerned to study the "land problem" in its own right. We shall consider to what extent, and in what ways, the various eruptions of the issue into the newspaper headlines were related to each other, and how a concern with land has influenced the general course of history. It will be seen that this thread, the "land problem", was no mere accessory or decoration, but the thread which tied together a very large part of our economic and political history.

Conditions in the period which immediately preceded the agricultural catastrophe of the late 1870s were exceedingly good, by the standards to which men had previously been accustomed. The *Encyclopaedia Britannica* article on agriculture, published in 1875, concluded a complacent survey with the observation that: "It is gratifying and cheering to reflect that never was this great branch of national industry in a healthier condition, and never was there such solid ground for anticipating for it a steady and rapid advance."[1]

The vast majority of people in all social classes, in town and country alike, could look back on a quarter of a century of steadily advancing prosperity. Of course there was still squalor; still the gloomy prospect of the workhouse for great numbers of British working people; still a scanty and precarious existence for innumerable Irish peasants; still long hours of wretched, monotonous toil for millions of industrial workers, and much worse conditions still for the agricultural labourers.

Yet the present was better than the past, and men had every reason for thinking that the future would be a great deal better still — if not for themselves, then for their children. People believed, and not without reason, in the great ideas of the age: in Free Trade; in Progress; in the Christian religion; in Britain as the preceptress of the world. We talk today of "Victorian smugness", but it is well to remember that men of the middle 1870s had quite a lot of justification for being smug. Although they certainly did not live in the best of all possible worlds, they could easily believe that they were marching along the road which led to that happy destination.

Land, in the eyes of most people, was a species of property essentially like other property; and all property rights were quite literally sacred, for a violation of property rights was an infringement of the Commandment not to steal. To put it less dramati-

16

cally, as one Welsh Liberal landlord wrote to another in 1881: "I look on a landlord with a farm to let as very much in the position of a farmer with a score of bullocks to sell at a fair. He has a perfect right to say whether he will dispose of his property and on what terms."[2]

Yet the possession of land had special attractions over and above the attractions of other kinds of property. The 15th Earl of Derby was a great landowner; he was also a politician who oscillated between the Liberal and Conservative parties. Writing in 1881, he declared: "The objects which men aim at when they become possessed of land in the British Isles may, I think, be enumerated as follows: (1) political influence; (2) social importance, founded on territorial possession, the most visible and unmistakable form of wealth; (3) power exercised over tenantry; the pleasure of managing, directing and improving the estate itself; (4) residential enjoyment, including what is called sport; (5) the money return — the rent."[3]

No doubt other landowners would have set rent in a higher place on the list; but the importance of land ownership for purposes other than financial profit must have meant that the rent collected was frequently far less than could have been drawn if the estate were regulated as a purely economic undertaking. Land had a much greater emotional significance to its owner than did most forms of property. The attractions of land ownership were never greater than in the early and middle 1870s, when agriculture seemed set in a permanent condition of prosperity.

There had been substantial reforms in some features of land ownership and land transfer during the previous twenty or thirty years. Many archaic legal restrictions on land transfer had been removed by the Encumbered Estates Act of 1848. The Agricultural Holdings Act of 1875, proposed by a Conservative duke, gave some sort of acknowledgement to the idea that a tenant who introduced improvements on to land has a title to the value of those improvements when his tenancy ceased. The effects of that Act were a good deal less impressive than many people had hoped; but at least a step in the right direction had been taken. Again, the practice of "enclosure", through which the grazing commons and the great open fields were brought into private hands, had long been an issue of passionate controversy, and had been the subject of many Acts of Parliament; but it was the Commons Act of 1876 which virtually ended the enclosures.

17

Throughout this long period of comparative prosperity, many famous reformers pressed for further land legislation. John Bright called for "free land" in the early 1850s.[4] The same cry was taken up by Cobden, in the last speech which he made, at Rochdale in 1864: "If I were five and twenty or thirty instead of, unhappily, twice that number of years, I would take Adam Smith in hand . . . and I would have a League for free trade in Land just as we had a League for free trade in Corn . . . If you can apply free trade to land and labour too . . . then, I say, the men who do that will have done for England probably more than we have been able to do by making free trade in corn."[5]

The demand for "free land" was raised again, and raised repeatedly, by Joseph Chamberlain in the 1870s. Yet it would be wrong to read too much into the slogan. Chamberlain was immensely self-conscious about his radicalism, and it is doubtful whether many politicians would have gone much further than he did, when he explained his own interpretation of the term in 1873: "I am in favour of freeing the land from all the trammels which press upon its utmost production. I am in favour of promoting by every means its ready sale and transfer. I am in favour of four great reforms. In the first place I would abolish the absurd custom of primogeniture . . . I am in favour of the repeal of those laws of entail by which more than half of the land in this country is tied up . . . for the supposed benefit of less than 150 families. I am in favour in the next place of such a revision of the laws which affect the appropriation of commons as shall secure those that remain for the people, and should provide for their tenancy in small plots direct from the State, on fair and reasonable conditions. And I am in favour, lastly, of a full tenant right, for every farmer, in spite of any conditions in his lease, which shall give him property in the unexhausted improvements he may make . . ."[6]

A few people, however, were prepared to go a good deal further. The Land and Labour League, founded in 1869, campaigned for "nationalisation of land" and "home colonisation". The Land Tenure Reform Association, which was formed in the same year, included such eminent men as John Stuart Mill, Henry Fawcett, Sir Charles Dilke and Thorold Rogers. This body was influential among educated opinion, and Mill at least seems to have accepted some very radical ideas indeed. The Labour Representation League, under whose auspices the first two working men were elected to Parliament in 1874, declared the need for "changes in the tenure and transfer of land".[7]

Thus the political climate of the middle 1870s was favourable to modest reforms in land questions, as in most other matters. The idea of "progress" — in the sense both of technological improvements and the removal of social and legal anachronisms — was very much in the air. Not many people, however, were in a mood to demand any fundamental alteration in the system of land ownership, or to ask any really searching questions about the title through which men owned land.

Then came the crash. A run of wet summers culminated in the fearful year 1879, when grain rotted in the English fields in November, and Ireland was brought to the very verge of famine by failure of the potato crop. About the same time, sheep and cattle were visited by epidemic disease. Thus there was an enormous demand for food for the urban population, which home production could not possibly satisfy. By a remarkable coincidence, the prairie lands of the New World had just been opened up to cultivation, and techniques had recently been devised which made it possible to bring food from the Americas to the British market in great quantities. Agricultural producers found themselves with woefully small crops, but without power to command the high prices of scarcity. This influx of food from abroad did not cease when the weather improved, for land was cheap in the New World, and production costs much lower than in Britain. A few years later, in the 1880s, the stockbreeder suffered a similar threat from abroad, with the development of refrigeration methods which made it possible to bring dairy produce and frozen meat to Britain from anywhere in the world.

Thus did the late 1870s mark the end of an era. Men who suddenly found that everything was going wrong became anxious to secure fundamental changes. The worse their conditions had been before the downswing commenced, the more willing were they to take vigorous and even violent action. As living standards in Ireland were far lower than those in most parts of the British Isles, it is no accident that the onset of the sudden and unexpected depression was followed almost immediately by turmoil in Ireland. Irish peasants in the late 1870s were in no mood to await the long-term consequences of reforms like those which Chamberlain and other daring radicals had been advocating. They needed an immediate answer to an immediate threat of famine.

A decade on from that depression, nobody with a mind at all could say that his views had been wholly unchanged by the events and theories which had been thrown up in the late 1870s and early 1880s. What had seemed daring — almost revolutionary — in 1878, soon became commonplace among Conservatives. Ideas about "freeing the land" with which Chamberlain had excited his radical audiences in the 1870s would hardly have caused an eyebrow to be raised in the stuffiest London club by the time of the Queen's Golden Jubilee, in 1887. In Great Britain, where mineral extraction and industry were becoming increasingly important, people came to see the "land problem" not merely as an aspect of agricultural economics, but as a matter of immediate and direct importance to the townsman as well. More and more people, in more and more places, began to decide that some kind or other of land reform was essential for the treatment of their own particular economic and social problems.

Notes-1

1 Quoted in George Winder, *British Farming and Food* (see bibliog.), p. 8.
2 A. C. Humphreys-Owen to Stuart Rendel, 16 October 1881. Rendel 19,459C, fo. 109.
3 Lord Derby, "Ireland and the Land Act", *Nineteenth Century*, October 1881, p. 474.
4 See Joseph Chamberlain's speech, 19 February 1872. JC 4/1 p. 33.
5 John Bright, jr, and J. E. Thorold Rogers (ed.), *Speeches by Richard Cobden* (see bibliog.), p. 493.
6 Newspaper cutting 1 January 1874. JC 4/1 pp. 103-4.
7 Examples from J. MacAskill, *The treatment of "land" in English social and political theory 1840-1885* (see bibliog.).

2 STORMS IN THE WEST

*It is in Ireland that the crash of feudalism will
be first heard.*

Richard Cobden
Quoted as the text of Michael Davitt's book,
The Fall of Feudalism in Ireland.

The Irish land agitation of the late 1870s and early 1880s is of
immense importance to the subsequent history both of Ireland
itself and of Great Britain. The fact that the tenants of Irish
farms were much poorer than the vast majority of British people
in the 1870s is attributable to differences of history and of human
relations, and not to any remaining differences of substantive law.
In 1881, Gladstone was able to tell the House of Commons that
"the land laws of Ireland chiefly differ from the land laws of England in the very special provisions which they present to us on
behalf of the tenant."[1]

How, then, did the recent history and the prevailing social conditions in Ireland differ from those of the rest of the United
Kingdom?

The appalling potato famine of 1845-7 and its scarcely less
terrible aftermath, lay well within the memory of many people,
and within the living tradition of all. The number of deaths resulting from starvation, and from diseases exacerbated by starvation,
may lie anywhere between half a million and a million and a half,
out of a total population not much in excess of eight millions.
Enormous numbers of people emigrated, and many perished on
the emigrant ships. As if this horror were not enough, the survi-
vors who remained in Ireland were evicted wholesale from their
wretched hovels. In the three years 1849, 1850 and 1851,
over 50,000 families were evicted; and even if we deduct the
13,000 or so who were readmitted, the total in terms of human
misery was enormous.[2] The decline in population in Ireland was
almost universal. Between 1841 and 1851, all but two Irish
counties lost more than a tenth of their population. In every
county in the whole Province of Connaught, and in several within
Leinster and even Ulster, there was an overall decline of more than

21

a quarter. To see the situation in perspective, there were only three counties in Great Britain — one each in England, Scotland and Wales — which showed any perceptible decline, and in most cases there was a very marked increase.

The depopulation and the evictions were much exacerbated by the Encumbered Estates (Ireland) Act of 1849, which is a striking example of how similar measures may produce totally different effects in different places. The Irish Act followed one of similar content which had been passed for England in the previous year, to which we have already referred. Both Acts sought to remove obsolete legal restrictions on land transfer. This might have been expected to benefit landlords and tenants alike, by ensuring that incompetent or impoverished landlords could sell their estates to men with ability and capital to improve them. Such, indeed, appears to have been the general effect in England; but in Ireland old landowning families transferred land to newcomers (often of Irish peasant stock themselves), who evicted peasants on a massive scale in order to use the land for grazing, and who really did rack-rent those tenants whom they suffered to remain.[3]

The trouble, though, was not merely the behaviour of these crude and avaricious newcomers. Even the "old" landowners of Ireland, who still ruled in most of the country, stood in a very different relationship to their tenants from that which prevailed in most of England or the south of Scotland. The landlords usually belonged to the Church of Ireland, a body which was in communion with the Church of England; the peasants were mostly Catholics. In the more remote districts, the peasants spoke a different language. To an increasing extent, the landlords were absentees. A landlord in England usually took pride and interest in the well-being of his people. Many landlords in Ireland took little interest in their tenants' welfare, and made few or no improvements. In both countries most farms were held on annual tenancies. In England, a tenant was seldom evicted so long as he paid his rent, and so it usually did not matter that the landlord was legally entitled to retake the land after any year; in Ireland, however, it was widely believed that landlords would often evict arbitrarily;[4] and in such conditions the tenant was naturally disinclined to plan for more than the yearly needs of himself and his family.

A landlord who retook land was legally entitled to take over any improvements, even if they had been made by the tenant, without giving any compensation. To what extent landlords exercised their legal rights to the full in this matter is very difficult to decide; but, as a Royal Commission commented in 1881: "Even a single case, very likely misapprehended, in which a landlord of previously good reputation in this respect, is thought to have acted unfairly by a tenant, may largely affect the condition and good feeling of an entire neighbourhood."[5]

The real harm which this state of affairs did to the Irish tenantry was not so much that they suffered individual expropriation by avaricious landlords, but that the fear of such expropriation discouraged them from making improvements. Irish farms were frequently more or less derelict, and bore every sign of extreme poverty. The situation was made even worse because — although nominally the rent was fixed — the sum actually payable by the tenant tended to be a matter of negotiation. As a contemporary noted, the Irish tenants' "apparent poverty was the staff upon which they relied in lieu of payment of their rent; and to preserve this appearance it was necessary that they should avoid such things as a sufficient stock, or a good breed of cattle, improved agricultural implements, or any outlay on their farms, whether for ornament or utility. Their object was, with the least possible expense, to raise a scanty crop, which would prove that they were unable to pay the rent."[6]

There was a further important difference between the structure of the agricultural classes in Ireland and in England. "Farmer" in England usually meant a substantial tenant who employed workers who were not members of his own family but worked for wages. "Farmer" in Ireland usually meant a tenant with just about enough land for his family to till — if, indeed, so much. At one time there existed a large class of landless agricultural labourers in Ireland, but this class dropped from over 1.3 millions in 1841 to about 329,000 forty years later. It is not difficult to guess the reason. The landless labourers and the very small tenants must have been killed selectively by the famine and the accompanying diseases during the 1840s, and those who survived were more likely to emigrate in the ensuing years than were men with some sort of "stake in the land".

Of course the bleak picture which we have just drawn was by no means universal. Individual landlords would often acquire a better or worse reputation than the majority of their kind. There were also very marked variations in different parts of the country. The most famous of these deviations from the general pattern was in the North.

Ulster was a good deal more prosperous than most of the country. The cultivation has been set at 50 per cent higher than that of the other three provinces.[7] This difference is usually considered to be due, at least in part, to "Ulster Custom" — a species of Tenant-Right — by which a tenant could ensure that the value of the improvements which he made to the land should not revert to the landlord. "Ulster Custom" was not universal in Ulster, nor confined to Ulster, and its details varied considerably from place to place. It recognised a sort of "dual ownership" between landlord and tenant by which a tenant who vacated his land could sell his interest to his successor. The value of that interest corresponded roughly with the value of the improvements introduced by the tenant or his predecessor in title. Furthermore, it was very unusual to disturb a tenant so long as he paid his rent. The landlord benefited from the custom because he could deduct any rent arrears from the lump sum which the outgoing tenant derived from his successor; while the tenant had a saleable interest at the end of his tenancy, as well as the advantages of the improvements while the tenancy lasted.[8]

This attribution of Ulster's relative prosperity to Tenant-Right has been severely criticised by at least one modern commentator,[9] and some people have even argued for the view that it was positively detrimental to Ulster agriculture. What influences future human actions, however, is not what happened but what people think happened, and there can be little doubt that most Irish peasants believed "Ulster Custom" to be a boon in the places where it existed.

In the decade before our principal period of study begins, Parliament began to deal with certain aspects of the Irish land problem. The Irish Church Act of 1869 is usually noted for its ecclesiastical provisions, but one of its most remarkable features was the disposal of land held by the Church of Ireland. About 1,000 leaseholds were enfranchised, and 6,000 tenancies were sold to the tenants themselves. They were required to provide a quarter of the purchase money, and repay the remainder over a period of years. This provided the first practical example of the use of legislation in order to convert traditional landlord-ownership into peasant-proprietorship, and was to form an important prece-

24

dent. The second measure — the Irish Land Act of 1870 — is a striking instance of a piece of legislation which contemporaries agreed in regarding as very radical — and which undoubtedly exerted a great influence upon subsequent attitudes — yet whose direct effect on the problems which it sought to solve was comparatively small. Like the Irish Church Act, it facilitated some sales of tenures, although the number was only a little over 800.[10] The most famous sections of the 1870 Act are those which are attributed to the work of John Bright. The "Bright clauses" sought to apply throughout Ireland something comparable with "Ulster Custom". "Ulster Custom", however, depended for its effect on the prevalence of good landlord-tenant relations, and it was exceedingly difficult to translate into legislation. Furthermore, the House of Lords had greatly reduced the scope of the Government's original proposals, and there was neither adequate control over future rent increases, nor security of tenure.[11] The Royal Commission which reported eleven years later on the workings of the 1870 Act, observed that: ". . . In nearly all cases of dispute between tenant and landlord, what the aggrieved tenant wants is, not to be compensated for the loss of his farm, but to be allowed to continue in its occupancy at a fair rent. This, as the law now stands, he cannot have; and in order to raise a question before the Court, he is forced to begin by a surrender of the only thing for which he really cares. The Plaintiff in a land claim, if he fails to prove his case, is turned out without the compensation that he claimed; but if he proves it he is turned out all the same."[12]

Yet the general wave of relative prosperity which marked the third quarter of the nineteenth century extended over Ireland just as it extended over Great Britain. The Registrar-General's report on Irish agriculture in 1875 indicated that "the decrease in the number of emigrants . . . was very considerable and the general comfort and prosperity of the people is definitely on the increase."

In the same year, Lord Hartington (until recently Chief Secretary for Ireland, but currently in opposition) noted the decline in agrarian crime — commenting that "the condition of Ireland has in this, as in other respects, enormously improved within the last thirty or forty years."[13]

This encouraging account was written just before the agricultural depression. In 1876, the value of the Irish potato crop, the staple food of the people, was £12.5 millions; in 1879, that crop was worth just over a quarter as much.[14]

25

The *Irish Times*, the country's leading Conservative newspaper, declared in the same year that "the small tenants of Ireland and a good proportion of the large ones too, have been barely able to extract from the soil the means of subsistence for their families. Their strenuously accumulated hoards have gone in rent. . . . There is absolutely only one way of relieving the strained situation. . . . The owners of the soil must consent to bear a portion of the losses entailed by causes over which legislation and the individual conduct of the tenantry were alike powerless to exercise any appreciable influence."[15]

A year and a half later, General Gordon (whose famous service in China must have familiarised him with poverty of the grossest kind) wrote to *The Times* that ". . . from all accounts, and by my own observations . . . the state of our fellow-countrymen in the parts I have named is worse than that of any people in the world, let alone Europe."[16]

Some landlords heeded the appeals for rent remission; others did not. As in the 1840s, natural disaster resulted in failure to pay rent, and evictions followed. The number of families evicted year by year had not exceeded a thousand since 1865; but the thousand mark was passed in 1879, the two thousand mark in 1880 and the five thousand mark in 1882.[17] In the desperate "Land War" which accompanied these evictions, landlords and their agents in many parts of the country went in fear of their lives, and rural crime — sometimes murder — became more and more common. The mean annual number of "agrarian outrages" — as these offences were collectively known — was 220 from 1873-8; in 1879 it stood at 860.[18] In the autumn of 1880, Joseph Chamberlain, who was by no means an unsympathetic observer of the condition of the Irish peasants, was writing that "there is no doubt that in some parts of Ireland a regular Reign of Terror has commenced. Ordinary law is entirely in abeyance."[19]

The turmoil of the Land War was not new in Ireland. Both in Ireland itself and among the Irish émigrés in America there existed, and had existed for many decades, innumerable organs of protest and revolt: everything from local and informal peasant conspiracies to national and international movements, with an almost limitless range of objectives, public or clandestine, political or social. The details of the movements which operated in the first three-quarters of the nineteenth century are quite outside our present study; but it is important to realise that the techniques

26

actually employed during the Land War were often familiar and even traditional, and therefore did not need to be taught or learnt. It is no less important to remember that the leadership was to a large extent local rather than national, and that the organisers at the centre were frequently much embarrassed by the activities of their nominal supporters.

At the General Election of 1874, more than half the constituencies of Ireland had elected MPs who supported the Irish Nationalist Party. The main aim of that Party was to establish "Home Rule". This term, like most in politics, could be used to mean different things; but it certainly included setting up an elective Parliament in Dublin, with considerable powers over Irish affairs. The new party was led by an erstwhile Conservative barrister, Isaac Butt — a man known to have a considerable partiality for the good things of life; whose personal finances were frequently precarious, but whose political methods were impeccably constitutional.

Even before the Land War really began in Ireland, some of the MPs were finding Butt's mild and gentle leadership inadequate. The most famous of the rebels was Charles Stewart Parnell, who had been returned at a by-election in 1875. Parnell was a young landowner, and a Protestant; an aloof and inaccessible man, fired with an immense contempt for England; one of the many examples which history affords of a great national leader who was utterly alien from the people whom he led. The rebel Nationalists carried parliamentary obstruction to the very limits, determined to ensure that attention should be given to the troubles of Ireland, even if all other public business seized up in consequence. These tactics made more and more appeal to the Irish at home, and even to the parliamentarians. Isaac Butt lost control of his party at the beginning of 1879, and died shortly afterwards. His nominal successor was William Shaw — more famous as a banker than as a politician — but the real leadership was already passing to Parnell. In May 1880, Parnell secured the leadership in form as well as substance.

While the Nationalists were getting tough at Westminster, the peasants at home in Ireland were promoting an agitation which became increasingly troublesome for the Government. The most prominent figure in this agitation was Michael Davitt; as a boy, he had lost his right arm in a factory accident; as a youth he joined the Fenians — a revolutionary secret society organised

27

mainly by Irish-Americans, which caused many disturbances in the 1860s. In 1870, Davitt was sent to prison for an offence of which he was almost certainly innocent; but he was released on a ticket-of-leave seven years later. He went to the United States, and there made contact with a number of émigré Irish rebels, including Patrick Ford, editor of the *Irish World* — one of the most virulent and influential of the Irish-American periodicals. In the spring of 1878, Davitt began to persuade Parnell that the Fenians and "constitutional" Nationalists should co-operate in overt political activities. This was the famous "New Departure", which, according to its proponent, would include within its scope "a war against landlordism for a root settlement of the land question."[20]

In the course of 1879, Davitt used his considerable skill and energy to organise a very effective tenants' movement in his native County Mayo, which was widely regarded as the poorest of all the Irish counties.

Davitt was by no means narrow and insular in outlook. He exerted a substantial influence upon the affairs of Great Britain as well as those of Ireland. At first he had considered the idea of making common cause with English radicals who were associated with Charles Bradlaugh,[21] and it was only later that he decided to work for an alliance with the Parnellite group of parliamentarians. The fruit of this work was the formation, in October 1879, of a body known as the Irish National Land League — or, more commonly, as the "Land League". Parnell was made President, and Davitt the Joint Secretary. The short-term aim of the Land League was that tenants should pay as little rent as possible; the long-term aim was a radical restructuring of the whole system of land ownership in Ireland in the peasants' favour.[22] Although there was no unanimity as to what form that restructuring should take, there was general agreement that the immediate demands should be what are usually called the "Three Fs": Fair Rent, which should be fixed by some sort of tribunal; Fixity of Tenure, which meant that a tenant should be irremovable so long as he paid his rent; and Free Sale of the tenant's interest, which meant an effective and thoroughgoing application of "Ulster Custom" to the whole of Ireland: what the 1870 Act had attempted, but largely failed, to achieve. Nobody regarded the "Three Fs" as the final aims of the Irish peasantry, even though they represented a good deal more than

Butt had been urging a few years earlier.[23] They did represent, however, an immediate programme upon which land reformers and Nationalists with very different long-term objectives could unite without too great a sacrifice of principle.

The Land League and the Irish Nationalist Party were largely complementary, although for some purposes they were kept completely separate; it was prescribed, for example, that Land League funds should not be used to help Parliamentary candidates. The alliance between the two bodies may have helped to hold random acts of violence in check; it also harnessed together the agrarian revolt and the activities of the parliamentarians.

The principal source of finance is quite evident. The American Irish, many of whom were actual victims, or sons of the victims, of the Famine diaspora, had been active in providing both money and organisation for innumerable Irish rebel movements for many years. They made massive contributions to the Land League, and also to later movements for political and social revolt in Ireland. The *Irish World* was particularly effective in organising contributions; in April 1882 it was reported that the total sum collected through this source alone had exceeded $300,000.[24]

By 1880, Parnell's prestige was supreme, and yet his position was precarious. On one hand he sought to extract what favours he could for Ireland from the British Government; on the other he needed to keep the extremists, in Ireland and in America, both sufficiently well-disposed to continue supporting his movement, and patient enough not to rush into violent action which would vitiate its chances of success.

In the early spring of 1880, the Conservative Government decided to call a General Election. They accepted the view that there was a need for some kind of Irish land legislation, and one hard-pressed Ulster Conservative secured a promise from his Party leaders that they would legislate on the land question in accordance with the wishes of Ulster.[25] The General Election resulted in the return of the Liberals with a substantial majority, and the Queen, to her vast distaste, was compelled to accept Gladstone once again as her Prime Minister. The task of dealing with the Irish Land War therefore fell upon the new Government.

The Minister who was principally responsible for Irish affairs was the Chief Secretary for Ireland, W. E. Forster, who was best known as the author of the great Education Act of 1870. Forster, who was generally counted a Radical, was a political "fighter", though a man of somewhat limited vision; he was in no sense a natural oppressor. At one point he had received serious consideration as a possible Liberal leader.[26] He acquired in Ireland the nickname "Buckshot Forster", yet this unfortunate *cognomen* arose through a decision of his Department to arm the police with buckshot rather than the more lethal missiles which had hitherto been employed. Forster came much under the influence of the permanent officials of his Department working at Dublin Castle, who succeeded in persuading him that the prime task was the physical repression of unlawful activity. Almost incredibly, "during the whole of Mr Forster's occupation of the Irish Secretaryship, he never once consulted any member of the Parnellite party on any part of his Irish policy; never asked their advice or even their opinion, on any Irish affairs whatever."[27]

The first departure from the policy of the previous government occurred by accident. From 1847 onwards, Parliament had passed a series of Acts giving special powers to the Government to deal with crime and disorders in Ireland. Each of these so-called "Coercion Acts" expired automatically after a limited period, but thus far they had always been succeeded by others to a similar effect. The current measure, which had been passed by the Conservatives, was due to expire on 1 June 1880. When the time came for the Cabinet to consider its renewal, there was no time to push a Bill through Parliament.[28] The Government decided to let coercion lapse, and try the effects of conciliation. At Forster's suggestion, a Bill was introduced — the Compensation for Disturbance Bill — to stay the evictions which were proceeding apace in the Irish countryside. The Bill was moderate enough. It provided that a tenant evicted for non-payment of rent could claim compensation if he could prove that his inability to pay was caused by the last two bad harvests, and that he was willing to continue his tenancy on fair terms. It was designed to apply only to a part of Ireland, and to low-rented tenancies. Yet Forster was compelled to make concessions in the Commons; even so, twenty Liberals voted against the Bill and many more abstained; it was finally thrown out ignominiously by the Lords.

Predictably, there were more, and worse, agrarian disturbances in the latter part of 1880. Some parts of Ireland, however, were remarkably quiet; but the reason could scarcely have given much satisfaction to the administration. As the Lord Lieutenant of Ireland told the Cabinet, they were peaceful because "those who would profit by (crime) are complete masters of the situation, and . . . their temptation is therefore removed."[29]

The leaders of the Land League indicated — probably with complete sincerity — that they deplored the many acts of physical violence against men and beasts which characterised the closing months of the year. On the other hand, they gave full support to a policy of economic and social ostracism against those who fell foul of their organisation. This policy acquired its name from a certain Captain Boycott, a land agent who was an early and famous victim of the practice. Whether as a consequence of the official Land League policy of boycotting men who took the farms of evicted tenants, or through the more violent measures which many anonymous peasants continued to apply, there was a very marked decline in evictions during the last quarter of 1880.

The Government then decided to prosecute Parnell and certain other Irish leaders under the ordinary criminal law, on charges of conspiracy. Not surprisingly, the Dublin jury which had been empanelled for the trial failed to convict the accused. Thereupon, Forster brought forward proposals for renewed coercion, which were to include the suspension of Habeas Corpus. To these the Irish MPs responded by "obstructing" more furiously than ever in Parliament, and the Government found it necessary to introduce new parliamentary procedures in order to facilitate the passage of the Coercion Bill. While the excitement in Parliament was at its height, the Government returned Davitt to prison, on the rather thin pretext that his Land League activities had violated the ticket-of-leave on which he had been released.

In Ireland the Land War continued to be waged. Most of the parochial Catholic clergy, who had been rather hesitant at the beginning, gave increasing support to the work of the Land League. Some of the hierarchy opposed it, but Archbishop Croke of Cashel spoke in its defence, and thereafter was greeted with enormous enthusiasm wherever he went. In the early stages of the struggle, the Northern Protestants[30] as a whole would not support the Land League, and even the celebrated Captain Boycott was able to recruit Ulstermen to bring in his crops; but later there were signs of Orangemen coming to participate in the League's activities.[31] Several years more were to elapse before the Ulster Protestants settled into a mood of intransigent opposition to the Nationalists and all their works. In the General Election of 1885, one of the Nationalist candidates found that a voting paper in his own constituency of South Tyrone had been marked with the words "No Landlord!" against the name of his Conservative opponent, and the words "No Pope!" against his own. This he considered "a perfect picture of the mentality of the Ulster Presbyterian farmer".[32]

Shortly after the Liberals took office in 1880, Gladstone had appointed a Royal Commission to enquire into the workings of the 1870 Irish Land Act. The Chairman was the Earl of Bessborough, an Irish landlord and also the rector of an English village. Bessborough's Report appeared at the beginning of 1881, and unambiguously advocated "the reform of the Land Law of Ireland upon the basis known as 'The Three Fs' — i.e., Fixity of Tenure, Fair Rents and Free Sale."[33]

Gladstone decided that the Irish peasantry would never be satisfied until the experiment was made. The Government was far from united, but was prepared to defer to its leader. The Prime Minister made no secret of the true position, telling the House of Commons that: "With a political revolution we have ample strength to cope. . . . But a social revolution is a very different matter."[34]

In April 1881, just over a month after the Coercion Act was passed, Gladstone therefore brought forward his great conciliatory measure, the Irish Land Bill, which proposed to grant all the "Three Fs".[35]

The Government had a good deal of trouble over the Bill; but its critics failed to suggest any alternative course of action which had the slightest chance of both passing through Parliament and restoring peace to Ireland, and the Bill was duly carried in the Commons, receiving 220 votes to fourteen on the Third Reading. Most of the Conservatives abstained. The Irish were much divided, for many of the Land Leaguers had already set their sights much higher than the "Three Fs", and some enthusiasts had even decided that the "Three Fs" would prove prejudicial to the sort of long-term settlement which they desired. Accordingly, the Land League gave no clear lead, but effectively delegated the decision to the parliamentarians. The Nationalist MPs were also divided; some voted for it, but Parnell and many of his principal followers abstained.[36] In the Lords, the Conservative leader, the Marquis of Salisbury, recommended acceptance — although scarcely with good grace. Some rather drastic amendments were proposed by the Lords, but most of them were rejected by the Commons, and in August the Bill was enacted in substantially its original form.

Fixity of Tenure and Free Sale did not present serious legal difficulties, but Fair Rent certainly did. The Act did not attempt a definition of what could be considered a "fair" rent, and left the matter to the Court. These "Fair Rents" — or Judicial Rents, as they were sometimes called — were to hold for fifteen years, after which time they could be revised. Thus a tenant was virtually in the position of a leaseholder. The Act also sought to encourage Land Purchase. When landlord and tenant were both willing to conclude a sale, a Land Commission established under the Act was empowered to grant a sort of mortgage of up to three-quarters of the purchase price, while capital and interest were repayable as a 5 per cent annuity over thirty-five years.

John Morley, a future Irish Secretary himself, wrote that: "The history of the session was described as the carriage of a single measure by a single man. Few British members understood it, none mastered it. The whigs were disaffected by it, the radicals doubted it, the tories thought that property as a principle was ruined by it, the Irishmen, as the humour seized them, bade him send the bill to line trunks."[37]

One of the most telling contemporary comments on the Act was that of Lord Derby, who wrote in *Nineteenth Century*: "There is no loud boasting on the side of those who have succeeded; no outcry of resentment and despair from those who have been worsted. Perplexity and doubt, rather than confidence, seem the prevalent feelings. . . . 'We were bound to try something, and, on the whole, there seemed nothing else to try', is perhaps the most common judgment."[38]

Whether viewed from the aspect of jurisprudence or the aspect of economics, there were very serious objections to the 1881 Act; and, as we shall later see, it proved far less than the final solution which the Bessborough Commission seems to have hoped that it would be.[39] Yet it had a great and real value, even though this was not seen until many years afterwards. It also provided a breathing space — or perhaps we should say a thinking space — when men could seriously consider a more permanent solution. Michael Davitt, the most radical of the Irish leaders, concluded more than twenty years later that it was "a legislative sentence of death by slow process against Irish landlordism", and went on to describe its author as "the greatest statesman England ever produced".[40] There seems little reason for disputing either of these judgments.

Although the 1881 Act went a great deal further towards the satisfaction of the peasant demands than Isaac Butt had ever wished to go, and probably went further than Parnell himself would have gone a year or two earlier, yet the events of the Land War had implanted in the minds of the Irish leaders the notion that Gladstone and his Government were their enemies. Parnell contended at first that it would be impossible to create "Fair Rents", although he later shifted his ground to the extent of recommending the peasants to use the Land Courts which had been set up, in order to test their efficacy. Nor was there any overall amelioration of the state of public order in Ireland. In October 1881, Forster told the Cabinet that: ". . . In one or two counties, especially in Mayo, there is improvement, but in the south-west, and in many of the midland counties, there is more lawlessness and intimidation. The number of actual outrages has increased, but a more serious fact is the increase of intimidation by 'Boycotting' and threats of 'Boycotting' . . ."[41]

In Chamberlain's view, the situation had become ". . . war to the knife between a despotism created to re-establish constitutional law and a despotism not less completely elaborated to subvert law and produce anarchy as a precedent to revolutionary changes."[42]

On Forster's advice, the Government decided to use the special powers granted by the Coercion Act. Parnell and other leaders of the Land League were arrested on 13 October 1881, and lodged in Kilmainham Jail. Patrick Egan, the League's Treasurer, escaped to Paris and continued to receive large American contributions, although apparently much less money was actually available for the prosecution of the Land War than before the arrests.[43]

A few days after their arrest, the imprisoned leaders issued the famous "No-Rent Manifesto", requiring tenants to pay no rent at all, presumably until their own release. The Government promptly retaliated by proclaiming the Land League itself an illegal organisation. The Ladies' Land League carried on the work of the proscribed organisation to an extent, but Forster considered that "they mismanage their business and it is a mistake to suppose that they have taken the place of the men."[44] Nevertheless, they seem to have been a considerable nuisance to the Government, and the decision not to proceed against them was taken

34

for political rather than legal reasons.[45]

When the Land League leaders had been in detention for some months, it became possible to make some general appraisal of the condition in Ireland. The "No-Rent Manifesto" had proved a relative failure,[46] perhaps because of the general opposition of the ecclesiastical authorities. There was "no open resistance to the law"; boycotting, though still widespread, was less prevalent than previously; and the Land Act was in full operation by the spring of 1882.[47] The Act, however, did not prevent evictions in respect of past debts for rent, and 1882 was the worst year since the early 1850s. Chamberlain's view of the general position was that: "Agitation was rampant everywhere. Outrages were frequent and serious: no convictions of the criminals were obtainable, and the police did not know upon whom to lay their hands. Mr Forster's confident assurance that the police were acquainted with the disturbers of the peace and that their arrest would speedily lead to the settlement of the country had proved to be altogether illusory, and Mr Forster himself confessed that in this respect he had been disappointed and that his policy had failed. He appeared to be at his wits' end and could only suggest wholesale arrests and further coercion."[48] Parnell's well-known prophecy that "Captain Moonlight" would take over in his place was evidently being fulfilled. Even apart from obvious considerations of personal inconvenience, this situation was scarcely less pleasant for the imprisoned leaders than it was for the Government. If the "grass-roots" agitation succeeded, their own authority was in jeopardy; if it failed, the whole movement could collapse.

Eventually Forster was overridden in the Cabinet. Parnell and his associates were released from Kilmainham early in May 1882, and — to the Queen's indignation[49] — Davitt was released a few days later. Forster resigned, and was replaced by Lord Frederick Cavendish, brother of the Marquis of Hartington.

The release of the prisoners was the product of a *quid pro quo* agreement between Gladstone and Parnell — the so-called "Kilmainham Treaty". This was to the effect that the Government would drop coercion, release its civil prisoners, and pass an Arrears Act, which would relieve the tenants of liability for back rent; while Parnell would exercise control over the turbulent elements of the peasant movement, and strive to secure acceptance for the Government's policies. The agreement came under fire from two quarters. Some of the Conservatives were almost

35

hysterical at the Government for treating with the Irish leaders at all; while the more vehement Irish partisans, both in Ireland and in America, attacked it no less sharply. As Patrick Ford of the *Irish World* was one of the men seriously alienated by the Kilmainham arrangements, it is likely that the Irish tenant movement suffered a very serious financial loss as a result. Davitt, who also deplored the "Treaty", was later reconciled to Parnell, and played a large part in restoring confidence between his leader and Ford.[50]

This alliance between the Government and the Irish leaders was almost shattered a very few days after it was effected by the assassination of Lord Frederick Cavendish in Phoenix Park, Dublin, at the hands of a small group of terrorists unconnected with the Land League. This set the whole new policy of conciliation at risk for a while; but the earnest endeavours both of the Government and of the Irish leadership led to a gradual restoration of peace and order. No doubt they were much assisted by the decisions of the Land Court; the average rent reduction over the first couple of years was more than 20 per cent.[51]

As the Land League had been proscribed, it was necessary to form a new organisation which would seek to redress the peasants' grievances. This body, the Irish National League (usually known as the National League) was formed in October 1882. Parnell was rather reluctant at first to consent to its establishment, but eventually became its President.[52]

The events of 1882 did not terminate the Irish land agitation, even temporarily, but there was a real abatement of violence. Civil disturbance was closely related to the yield of the potato crop. The bad year of 1882, which had furnished only 2.4 tons per acre, was followed by three good years, with 3.8 tons or more.[53] By the spring of 1885, Lord Spencer (who had succeeded Cavendish as Chief Secretary) was reporting that the condition of Ireland had "greatly improved".[54] In these circumstances, it did seem possible that the Irish land problem might admit of a peaceful solution. Yet although the flames had for a time died down in Ireland, sparks from the blaze had already ignited a good deal of dry tinder elsewhere.

Notes-2

1 Parliamentary Debate 3S, 260, Col. 891, 7 April 1881.
2 *Return . . . of cases of evictions . . .* P.P. 1881 (c.185), lxxvii.
3 *Report into working of Landlord and Tenant (Ireland) Act 1870*
   (Bessborough Report), pp. 6-7.
4 See B. L. Solow, *The land question and the Irish economy, 1870-*
   1903, pp. 32-4, 77-8; see also Bessborough Report, pp. 3-4.
5 Bessborough Report, p. 8.
6 Rt Hon. M. Longfield, Essay on Ireland in J. W. Probyn (ed.),
   Systems of land tenure . . . (see bibliog.), p. 25.
7 Brian A. Kennedy, "Tenant Right before 1870" in *Ulster since*
   1800, T. W. Moody & J. C. Beckett (eds.), (see bibliog.), p. 41.
8 For a fuller discussion, see W. L. Burn, "Free Trade in Land: an
   aspect of the Irish question", *Trans. Royal Historical Society*,
   4s, vol. 31 (1949), pp. 61-74.
9 Solow, *op. cit.*, pp. 30-32.
10 On both Acts, see H. Shearman, "State-aided land purchase under
   the Disestablishment Act of 1869", *Irish Historical Studies*, iv
   (1944), pp. 58-80.
11 On the functions and defects of the Act, see Gladstone's memorandum to Cabinet, 9 December 1880 (CAB 37/4/81).
12 Bessborough Report, p. 7.
13 *Annual Register*, 1875, pp. 19, 230-31.
14 F. S. L. Lyons, "The economic ideas of Parnell", *Historical Studies*,
   ii (1959), pp. 60-75, at p. 63.
15 *Irish Times*, 15 July 1879, quoted in *Kerry Sentinel*, 16 July 1879.
16 *The Times*, 3 December 1880.
17 Michael Davitt, *The Fall of Feudalism in Ireland* (see bibliog.),
   p. 100.
18 W. E. Forster's memorandum to Cabinet, 10 May 1880, CAB/37/
   2/23.
19 Chamberlain to Ashton Dilke, 27 October 1880 (copy?), JC 5/26
   fo. 1.
20 Davitt, *op. cit.*, pp. 111-13.
21 Davitt to William Haley, 7 January 1880 (misdated 1879), Haley
   3,905, fos. 28-31.
22 A highly tendentious, but rather original, account of the League's
   activities is provided in Anna Parnell's unpublished *The Land*
   League: the tale of a great sham, NLI Ms. 12,144. Davitt's book
   is far more balanced and credible. For some of the imperfections
   of the Land League, see Harrington to Parnell (copy?), 12
   October 1881. Harrington 8,578.
23 See, e.g., notes headed "Connie's Case". Butt 8,705.

24 *Irish World*, 22 April 1882.
25 J. L. McCracken, "The consequences of the Land War", in *Ulster since 1800*, T. W. Moody & J. C. Beckett (eds.), (see bibliog.), p. 62.
26 See, e.g., Carvel Williams to Joseph Chamberlain, 18 January 1875. JC 5/76/10.
27 Justin MacCarthy, *Ireland since the Union* (see bibliog.), p. 245.
28 W. E. Forster's memorandum to Cabinet, 10 May 1880. CAB/37/2/25.
29 Lord Cowper's memorandum to Cabinet, 9 November 1880. CAB/37/3/31.
30 The word is here used in its modern sense to include any non-Catholic Christian. In the nineteenth century it was frequently used to mean "Church of Ireland", and thus excluded the numerous Ulster Presbyterians, who were distinguished as "Nonconformists".
31 *Annual Register*, 1881, p. 211; Henry George's dispatch to *Irish World*, 11 February 1882.
32 William O'Brien, *An olive branch in Ireland* (see bibliog.), p. 169, fn.
33 Bessborough Report, p. 19.
34 Parliamentary Debate 3S, 268, col. 391, 2 April 1881.
35 The first draft of the Bill, as Gladstone proposed it to the Cabinet, had not included Fixity of Tenure, but at the next meeting he accepted this "F" as well. JC 8/1/1, p. 17.
36 See F. S. L. Lyons, *John Dillon* (see bibliog.), pp. 48-51.
37 John (Viscount) Morley, *Life of Gladstone*, ii (see bibliog.), p. 220.
38 *Nineteenth Century*, October 1881, p. 473.
39 Bessborough Report, p. 15.
40 Davitt, *op. cit.*, pp. 317, 670.
41 W. E. Forster's memorandum to Cabinet, 9 October 1881, CAB 37/5/22.
42 Letter to Morley, 18 October 1881, quoted JC 8/1/1, p. 21.
43 W. E. Forster's memorandum, 17 April 1882, CAB 37/7/24; WEG 44,160 fo. 131.
44 Forster, *loc. cit.*
45 Lord Cowper's memorandum to Cabinet, 19 April 1882, CAB 37/7/25.
46 For a different view, see *Irish World*, e.g. 10 December 1881.
47 Forster, *loc. cit.* See also Spencer's circulation of Jenkinson's memorandum, 22 July 1882, which seemed to conclude that all disputes should be settled in four years, and possibly less. CAB 37/8/42.
48 JC 8/1/1 p. 31.

49 Sir Charles Dilke to Chamberlain (copy), 6 May 1882. Dilke 43,885, fo. 233.
50 F. Sheehy Skeffington, *Michael Davitt* (see bibliog.), p. 129.
51 Report of the Royal Commission on the Land Law (Ireland) Act 1881 (etc.), P.P. 1887 (c.4969) xxvi (Cowper Commission), p. 6.
52 T. M. Healy, *Why Ireland is not free*, p. 15.
53 B. R. Mitchell & Phyllis Deane, *Abstract of British Historical Statistics* (see bibliog.), p. 92.
54 Spencer's memorandum to Cabinet, 23 March 1885. CAB 37/14/13.

3 THE FERMENT OF IDEAS

A survey of the whole question of tenure leads to the conclusion that, wherever the land is of easy access and widely distributed among the inhabitants of the country, the soil is well cultivated and the people industrious, prosperous and contented. On the other hand, wherever the land is in the hands of a few large proprietors, cultivation is checked, and the mass of the people are idle, indigent and improvident.

"The Land Question in England"
Westminster Review, vol. 38 (1870), pp. 233-62

The first phase of the Irish "Land War" produced profound effects in Great Britain during the early and middle 1880s. These effects need to be considered at three quite separate and distinct levels: the reactions of the British rural classes; the economic and political ideas which were sparked off by the conflict on both sides of the Irish Sea; and the effect which it had upon the attitude of the governments and parties towards economic and political questions.

When Irish farmers were fighting for, and winning, the "Three Fs", it was inevitable that some sort of parallel movement should appear in other parts of the British Isles. The peculiar problems of the Scottish Highlands and Wales will be dealt with later; but the effects in England and the South of Scotland were also important. As we have already seen, the agricultural classes were very different on the two sides of St George's Channel. Irish agriculture was essentially a two-tier structure; English and lowland-Scots agriculture was usually a three-tier structure, with landlords, tenant-farmers and landless farm labourers. In certain parts, such as Cumberland, the farms usually had few or no labourers, and in some districts there was a substantial class of peasant-proprietors or "yeoman-farmers"; but, broadly, the triple division prevailed. Tenant-farmers were conscious not only that they had complaints against landlords, but also that labourers had complaints against them. Even labourers, however, were in a somewhat less depressed state than most Irish peasants, for the rise of industry meant competition for labour, and in some districts (though by no means all) labour had a considerable scarcity-value. In most places, rural customs and religion, and in all places language, were shared by the social classes. Furthermore, the landlords were generally resident among those whom they ruled. Thus the relationships between the social classes were a great deal better than they were in Ireland. Neither tenant-farmers nor labourers could closely identify their own interests with those of the Irish peasants.

The agricultural depression of the late 1870s and early 1880s was a most uncomfortable time for all the British rural classes. Large numbers of farm labourers moved to the towns, or emigrated. Evidence was given to a Royal Commission in 1881 that 700,000 members of farm workers' families had emigrated in the previous nine years. The tenant-farmers at first suffered disaster. The 1881 census revealed a 10 per cent drop in numbers of farmers and graziers over the previous decade. In a few years, however, the worst shock was over and, though agriculture never recovered its old buoyancy, the numbers remained constant for the rest of the century. The influx of foreign food which we have already discussed led to a fall in market prices, and the long-term effect of this was an enormous and permanent decline in farm rents. Thus the social predominance of the great landlords was gradually undermined. Even the mightiest of them could no longer maintain the rôle of "kings in their counties". Not long before the First World War, Lloyd George was to speak of a "great slump in Dukes"; but that slump really began in the late 1870s.

Landlords, great and small, were affected in another way, perhaps more serious for their reputations. Traditionally, the English landlord had performed many of the functions which in modern times are discharged by public authorities. A good landlord provided both the money and the initiative for local improvements: housing, farm buildings, drainage, improvements of stock and so on. He encouraged good husbandry. He provided a sort of "welfare state" for folk who fell upon hard times, and gave financial support to a variety of local activities. In so doing, he was able to draw on personal knowledge. He could distinguish betweeen the "deserving poor" and the scroungers; he knew which farmer was likely to set a capital grant to good use. As he was neither bound by past precedents nor fearful of establishing new ones — and the money he used was his own — it is likely that

41

the proportion of his income which was eventually devoted to the public good was often much higher than in the case of modern state or local authorities. When the farm rents suddenly fell, however, landlords were frequently unable or unwilling to engage in the useful activities they once performed. People who had once looked to the landlord as a guide and benefactor now came to see him as a man who took rent, but gave little or nothing in return.

As the landlords became less and less useful, and the tenants became more and more harassed by the agricultural depression, it was inevitable that some sort of pressure should be mounted for redress. Very soon after Gladstone's 1880 government was formed, the tenants were able to secure relief for one old grievance. Agricultural tenancies often reserved shooting rights to the landlord, and this produced a serious complaint that "ground game" — hares and rabbits — were fed on the tenants' crops, in order to provide sport and meat for the landlord. The Ground Game Act of 1880 gave a tenant the right to shoot these animals on his own land.[1]

The closest English parallel with the Irish tenant movement was provided by a body called the Farmers' Alliance which was strong in the early 1880s, and whose declared aims were the "Three Fs". These objects, however, hardly fitted the English situation. Improvements were usually the creation of the landlord, and it was powerfully argued that the practical effect of conceding these demands would be to convert the landlord even more into a mere receiver of rent, with no interest in improvement.[2] It was also contended that the "real object" of the Farmers' Alliance was "to give tenants large borrowing powers for speculative expenditure, chargeable on the security of the landowner. It is manifest that the Alliance are thinking chiefly of large farmers, and that the legislation they advocate would be ruinous to small proprietors.[3] Accepting these contentions, the Government was unwilling to legislate on the proposed lines, but instead considered amending the Agricultural Holdings Act of 1875.

The 1875 Act had created a legal presumption that a tenant was entitled to compensation from his landlord for the unexhausted value of certain kinds of tenant's improvements at the end of the tenancy. The vital weakness of the Act had been that landowners were empowered to contract out of its provisions — and usually did so. A Royal Commission under the Duke of

Richmond was set up a few years later to consider the agricultural depression, and unanimously recommended that a tenant should receive the statutory and inalienable right to compensation at the end of the tenancy. A bill embodying this proposal was accordingly passed, and became the Agricultural Holdings Act of 1883.

Far more important than these legislative measures, and far more significant for the future, were the ideas about land which were germinating during the same period.

In a peasant country like Ireland, where relations between the social classes were often bad, no idea was more simple and attractive than that the landlords should get off the peasants' backs, and the peasants should be converted from tenants into owners. This idea of peasant proprietorship appears again and again in the speeches of the Irish leaders. By April 1879, Parnell had already decided that "the man who cultivates that soil (should become) the owner of the soil . . . when by purchasing the interests of the landlord it might be possible for every tenant to be the owner of the farm which he at present occupies. . . ."[4]

There was, of course, room for considerable argument as to the terms on which the transfer should occur: whether it should be voluntary or compulsory; whether there should be compensation; whether and to what extent public money should be used to facilitate the process; and what — if anything — should be done to help peasants who had no land, or whose land was quite inadequate for their needs. Most of Parnell's own utterances seem to accept the idea of full compensation: the State should buy out the landlord, and the peasants should then repay the State in the form of an annuity spread over a prolonged period. Even Davitt seems to have accepted the idea of a ten-year purchase, or something like half the value of the land, as a basis for compensation.[5]

Ideas which were a good deal more radical than peasant proprietorship began to appear about the same time. Often they were quite incompatible both with peasant proprietorship and with each other; but this point does not seem always to have been appreciated at the time. When Davitt was in America in the late 1870s, he contacted the American land reformer, Henry George. George was already a well-known figure in his own country, although his doctrines had not yet been developed to their full extent. His *magnum opus, Progress and Poverty*, had not yet appeared; but George had already decided that land was fundamentally different from other forms of property, both from an economic and from a moral point of view. Land (so the argument ran) is the creation of no man, and therefore no man has a better title to a particular site than any other man. The sharpest distinction, however, must be drawn between the site and the various improvements (such as buildings, drainage or crops) which man has introduced upon that site. The site itself, and the improvements, each have a value; but these two kinds of value are fundamentally different. The value of the improvements is due to the exertions of some particular human being, and morally belongs to that person or his successor in title. The value of the site, however, has nothing to do with the exertions of the owner. George argued, with considerable persuasiveness, that the existing system of land ownership was the most demonstrable cause of human injustice and exploitation, and perhaps the principal cause. There has been a somewhat sterile discussion as to the extent to which Davitt had already developed these ideas himself before he met George;[6] but the vital fact was that the two men were thinking on similar lines. Parnell could also be quoted in support of the same view. He was reported, for example, to have said: "The land of a country, the air of a country, the water of a country, belong to no man! They were made by no man! They belong to the human race."[7]

The doctrine that "land belongs to no man" and the doctrine of peasant-proprietorship are not developments from each other; they are based on utterly different and disparate social philosophies. Peasant-proprietorship offered nothing to the urban population, or to the landless labourer of the countryside. To the very small tenants of the West of Ireland, it offered a respite from the tiny rent which could be claimed from their miserable farms, and perhaps it represented an extra security of tenure; but it could offer no prospect of advancement, or even sufficiency, in the future.[8]

In 1881, all of this was blurred. Men like Parnell and Davitt made speeches in support of the disparate themes, and neither they, nor their supporters, nor their detractors, seemed for the most part to have noticed the difference. Henry George himself visited Ireland on a reporting tour sponsored by the *Irish World*. When *Progress and Poverty* appeared in 1880, its sales were promoted by the Land League; the figure of 100,000 copies has been given for its circulation[9] — which is astonishing for a quite sober textbook of economics. A companion volume, *The Irish Land Question* (later republished as *The Land Question*), appeared in 1881, and also made heavy sales.

By 1882, when the new Irish National League was formed, the differences between the doctrines had begun to be understood. Parnell had moved firmly towards peasant-proprietorship, while Davitt had moved equally firmly towards ideas much closer to those of George. Parnell's prestige in Ireland stood absolutely supreme at the moment, and without his support the National League was practically foredoomed to failure. He finally agreed to become President only on condition that Davitt would not press his own ideas about land — at least at the inaugural meeting. As Davitt's biographer wrote, the National League "represented, both in its programme and in its constitution, the counter-revolution to the movement started by Davitt."[10] Davitt obviously intended to raise the matter later, although his devotion to the political cause of Home Rule, and the intense personal loyalty which formed so large an element in his character, prevented a clear confrontation between the two doctrines. By the time he felt himself free to expound his own ideas, the die was cast, and Ireland was set irrevocably upon a course which would lead to the Parnellite conclusion and not to his own.

In Great Britain, however, the course of events was profoundly different. As we shall later see, the idea of peasant-proprietorship was much in vogue during the 1880s, and most of the current land theories seem to have derived more or less inspiration from either the Irish Land War or the works of Henry George. Some of the movements of the time (like Stewart Headlam's Guild of St Matthew's, in Bethnal Green), had a strong religious flavour. Some, like Henry Broadhurst's Leasehold Enfranchisement Association, had rather limited objectives. The notion which gained particular currency in Britain was not peasant-proprietorship, but the idea that all land should belong to the community as a whole. This doctrine of a common and universal right to land was one which itself might develop along several different lines, and at an early date some quite distinct currents of thought began to appear — as different from each other as they all were from "peasant-proprietorship".

The first organisation which was committed to the idea of communal ownership of land was the Land Nationalisation

45

Society, which was set up in 1881, and produced many pamphlets over a long period. The leading spirit was Alfred Russel Wallace. Wallace's main claim to distinction lay in a completely different field, for he had arrived at the theory of organic evolution through natural selection independently of Charles Darwin, and it was a chance communication from Wallace which led to their famous joint paper to the Linnaean Society in 1858, and which spurred on the publication of Darwin's *Origin of Species* in the following year.

The term "land nationalisation" was not always used in the same sense, either during the 1880s or afterwards, and an immense amount of confusion has derived from the widespread failure to appreciate this fact. In its narrowest sense, land nationalisation was little more than an extension of the principle which had long been applied in practice when canals or railways needed to be built, and one which within a couple of decades became accepted by most political thinkers. In this sense, land nationalisation meant no more than that public authorities should be empowered to acquire land compulsorily, as and when it was required, for smallholdings, crofts, allotments and other public purposes, with provision of compensation for the dispossessed landowner. Some land nationalisers soon came to envisage a much broader application; that land should be compulsorily purchased by public authorities, not because they proposed an immediate new use for it, but in order gradually to extinguish private ownership of land altogether. As time went on, this notion became increasingly popular among the land nationalisers. A few of them were also disposed to argue that compensation should not be granted at all; but that doctrine never became general in the movement. In its early days, the Land Nationalisation Society actively promoted the sales of *Progress and Poverty*, even though the Society's ideas were really quite different from those of George.[11]

Another approach to the idea that land (or rather, land values) should belong to the community as a whole was developed through a body called the Land Reform Union, which was formally constituted on 5 June 1883, and changed its title a year later to the English Land Restoration League. While at first its members were not willing to commit themselves to George's doctrines *in toto*,[12] the movement soon became for practical purposes the vehicle for the propagation of "orthodox" Georgeist teachings.

Meetings were promoted which were addressed by such personalities as Michael Davitt, and the future Socialist luminary H. H. Champion. When George himself delivered a series of addresses in the British Isles in 1884, these also were organised through the Land Restoration League. It is evident that they were an enormous popular success, and exerted a massive influence upon "progressive" public opinion. One author has claimed, probably with justice, that in the early 1880s George was the most discussed man in England after Gladstone himself,[13] and the Land Restoration League was therefore a body of considerable importance. An organisation with similar aims to the English body was formed in Glasgow on 25 February 1884 under the title of the Scottish Land Restoration League, and the statement which its Committee issued shortly afterwards made quite clear what the objects of the "orthodox" Georgeists were: "We propose to effect this restoration" — that is, restoration of the land — "by the simple and obvious expedient of shifting all taxation on to the value of the land, irrespective of its use or improvement, and finally *taking all Ground Rent for public purposes*."[14]

Like its English counterpart, the Scottish League made considerable use of Davitt as a platform orator.[15]

Within a few years, the distinction between the various ideas of Socialism, peasant-proprietorship, land nationalisation and land value taxation became drawn more and more clearly by commentators. George's book on the *Irish Land Question* in 1881 drew a sharp contrast between his own opinions and the notion of peasant-proprietorship.[16] That book was certainly very widely read in Ireland,[17] and may have played some part in causing Parnell and Davitt to appreciate the nature of their differences at the inception of the National League in October 1882.

The monthly magazine, *The Christian Socialist*, which first appeared in the middle of 1883, served as a sounding-board for various kinds of land reformers and socialists, and within its pages one may trace the way in which the different movements moved apart. Wallace recognised the essential difference between his own views and those of George by 1883,[18] and the first issue of 1884 contained an article which argued that: ". . . Up to the present time the social agitation can hardly be said to have taken definite shape. Land Nationalisers and Socialists have all been classed together in the mind of the public; hence Socialists have been willing to work in hand with the 'rent confiscators'. But if, as seems likely, the agitation is about to take definite shape, probably materially assisted by Mr George's lecture tour, we warn Socialists to stand by their colours, and not to be moved by considerations of policy or anything else."[19]

This discovery was exceedingly important. Both groups came to realise that the difference between them was not merely that the immediate remedies which they proposed were different and perhaps conflicting; rather did they differ at the very root of their whole philosophy. The Georgeists sought a single reform which, they considered, would strike at the whole basis of poverty and human injustice; the Socialists, for the most part, drifted towards a "Stateist" view which required a constant and detailed intervention by the organs of government into the activities of the citizens. Some people who started from George's intellectual position were drawn towards socialism. The advocates of land nationalisation (in Wallace's sense of the term) provide an important example. The problem was further complicated by the fact that "men more often change their religion than the name of their faith", and people who had applied to themselves some particular designation were often unwilling to relinquish that label when their ideas underwent a fundamental change.

Throughout the 1880s, it was the land reformers who had most of the energy, initiative and publicity at their command. Henry George was incomparably better known to the British public than any avowed Socialist. When Karl Marx died in 1883, there must have been dozens of Englishmen who had argued about Henry George for every one who had even heard of the Prussian Socialist.

The first major political figure to propose land reforms related to the idea that land ought to belong to the community as a whole was Joseph Chamberlain, who served in Gladstone's Cabinets of 1880-5 and 1886, and was the cynosure of the most radical Liberals. We have already seen that he was preaching "freeing the land" (in the old sense of the term) as far back as 1873. Not yet forty-four when Gladstone's government of 1880 was formed, Chamberlain had already been Mayor of Birmingham, and had acquired a great reputation as chief architect of the National Liberal Federation — indeed, he was the political "machine man" *par excellence*. His mind was still exceedingly receptive of new ideas, and he gave serious attention to the views of both George and Wallace.[20] Chamberlain's eventual conclusions were different from both, but many contemporaries did not really notice this. What impressed them much more was the similarity of tone between the attacks which all three men made upon the existing land system.[21]

Many of Chamberlain's views, both on land and on other topics, were set out in a series of articles which appeared in the *Fortnightly Review* from 1883-5, and were later published as a book entitled *The Radical Programme*. Chamberlain did not commit himself to all aspects of the *Programme*,[22] and it was never in any sense an official statement of Liberal policy — indeed, it was a Liberal critic who first described it as the "Unauthorised Programme". Nevertheless, Chamberlain, as a member of the Cabinet, obviously had some *locus standi*, and his colleagues often showed visible signs of embarrassment. In the very free political atmosphere of the time, these disagreements were frequently aired in public, without either side considering it necessary to resign ministerial office, or to try to force the resignation of the other.

The interest of the *Radical Programme* does not lie so much in the actual proposals which were advanced as in the effect which it had in further exciting men's minds about the land problem, and in bringing ideas home to people whom George and Wallace were not likely to influence. The authors repeated the old radical cry against entails and strict settlements, and also the familiar proposal that succession duties should fall more heavily on landed property.[23] These reforms had long been more or less common ground to all who called themselves "radicals". Beyond that the land proposals of the *Radical Programme* look very half-baked. Although its authors had been influenced by George and Wallace, they demonstrably misunderstood the teachings of the former, and probably those of the latter as well. The authors were more conspicuously impressed by the idea of peasant-proprietorship, although they were very far from clear how a peasant-proprietary was to be created, and were willing to try out a variety of different methods. The most famous proposal of the whole *Radical Programme* was related to this question: the so-called "three acres and a cow" doctrine: "Besides the creation of smallholdings, local authorities should have compulsory powers to purchase land where necessary at a fair market price . . . for the purpose of garden and field allotments, to be let at fair rents to all labourers who might desire them, in plots up to one acre of arable and three or four acres of pasture."[24] This proved of immense political importance at the ensuing General Election. Oddly enough, Chamberlain seems to have had little personal acquaintance with conditions of agricultural workers at the time when the *Radical Programme* was being drafted, and apparently did not consult their great trade union organiser, Joseph Arch. He even discouraged fellow Radicals from seeking nomination in agricultural constituencies.[25]

The Land Question was not only producing a great ferment of ideas; it was also changing the character and outlook of all the political parties. The Liberals, however, were particularly vulnerable — partly because there was a Liberal government in office; partly because the Liberal Party was already generally regarded as the "party of change", and partly because of its profoundly mixed composition. Of all Liberals, those whose position was most uncomfortable were those landed aristocrats and their acolytes whom we designate by the very loose term "Whigs".

The Whigs had been the most important of the groups which contributed to the establishment of the Liberal Party in the middle of the century. Half or more of the 1880 Cabinet might be called Whigs. They included such formidable figures as the Marquis of Hartington (who had nearly become Prime Minister in 1880) and the Duke of Argyll. Many Whigs found the policies which were forced upon Gladstone's government by the exigencies of the Irish Land War increasingly unwelcome. Gladstone's administration of 1880 had hardly been formed when the trouble started. The ill-fated Compensation for Disturbance Bill of 1880, which was considered in the previous Chapter, proved sufficient to dislodge the Marquis of Lansdowne, a junior Minister and an Irish landlord. Intimating his intention to resign, he told Gladstone that the Bill would "produce an immense amount of mischief, while its remoter consequences extending as they will to the whole country and beyond the present time, will be most unfortunate."[26] Gladstone tried to dissuade Lansdowne, but eventually concluded that "No limitation of the Bill would satisfy him; only its withdrawal."[27]

This Gladstone would not concede, and so Lansdowne went. The Whig discomfort, however, was fairly general. One future Conservative Prime Minister, A. J. Balfour, wrote to another, Lord Salisbury: "The position of the Whigs is more amusing even than usual. Great pressure has been put on them: and they have been told that to defeat the Bill would be to break up the Government. In these trying circumstances the compromise they adopt is that of violently abusing the Bill and everybody connected with the Bill both in public and private — and of going out of the House whenever there seems a chance of practically stopping it."[28]

The Irish Land Bill of 1881 was a far more important measure, and produced a far more important secession: the Duke of Argyll, the Lord Privy Seal. Argyll was a man of impressive intellectual calibre, and the most effective of all the defenders of traditional landlordism. He baulked particularly at the "free sale" clauses, even though he had been a member of the administration which made concessions in that direction in the much less compelling circumstances of 1870. Free sale, in the Duke's view, would "destroy all the virtue of ownership — and render impossible the only operations which have hitherto produced improvement among the cottier tenantry of the West."[29]

Although the Whigs did not like the government's actions, it would be wrong to think that they necessarily advocated some alternative course of behaviour. Even Lansdowne and Argyll did not suggest that the government should resist the demands for those proposals which they disliked; still less did they analyse what the likely consequences of such resistance would have been. Yet there was no doubt that many Whigs were profoundly disturbed and politically disaffected by what was being done. The fact that their disaffection was hard to set down in logical terms did not mean that it was any less deep. Whig landlords came to feel more and more affinity with Conservative landlords; less and less affinity with other Liberals — especially those members of the rank-and-file who were receiving with glee and enthusiasm the disparate doctrines of Chamberlain, George and Wallace.

Although the Irish land problem had a divisive effect upon the Liberals, it also produced another effect which contemporaries do not seem to have observed so keenly. A large measure of agreement began to appear between the leaderships of the three Parties. Once the 1881 Land Act had been passed, nobody would dare suggest repealing it; while by about 1883 or 1884, most politicians agreed that the solution of the Irish land problem should come by developing a peasant-proprietary under some kind of land purchase system. Most tenants evidently wished to own their land; landlords were finding Irish land a wasting asset. There was every prospect that a country whose people had a stake in its land would

51

be a good deal less prone to crime and civil disturbance than one populated by an aggrieved and desperate peasantry.

The 1881 Land Act did much less than had been hoped in fostering peasant proprietorship. By the beginning of 1887, only 731 tenants were purchasing their holdings under its provisions.[30] Drafts of other possible measures to promote land purchase by Irish tenants came under active and sympathetic discussion in the Liberal Cabinet;[31] and in March 1885 Lord Spencer was able to write that: "There is every reason to believe that the Conservatives would accept and support such a measure, and Mr Parnell is on good authority said to be himself desirous of a settlement."[32]

Soon after this was written, Parnell decided for tactical reasons to bring down the government. He was helped in this object by the abstention of many disaffected Liberals on a Budget division. The administration was defeated, and in June 1885 Lord Salisbury (who had now "emerged" as the overall Conservative leader) formed his first government. The so-called "Third Reform Act" of 1884 had greatly increased the electorate, but the new registers were not yet ready. Accordingly, an agreement was made between the Front Benches to the effect that the Liberals would not harass the new government unduly, while Salisbury would go to the country as soon as it was possible to face the wider electorate.

The Conservative administration carried — with Liberal support — the Irish Land Purchase Act which is associated with the name of Lord Ashbourne, the new Lord Chancellor of Ireland. The Act differed from the earlier Land Purchase measures in that the peasant was not required to put down any part of the purchase price. The repayment period was forty-nine years, and by returning a four per cent annuity he could repay the principal and pay a reasonable commercial interest at a total cost to himself which was not more than his original rent. A sum of £5 millions was set aside to assist land purchase. Lord Ashbourne himself freely admitted that this measure was essentially an experiment. Whether that particular experiment worked or not, however, there could be little doubt that future governments, Liberal or Conservative, would continue to legislate in the same general direction, and that the political issues involved would probably be questions of detail and administration rather than matters of principle.

The Ashbourne Act was the one important piece of legislation which the minority Conservative government set upon the statute book before they went to the country at the end of 1885. This was the first election at which the bulk of the rural labourers had the vote, and their views would be likely to prove decisive in many places. The election had another remarkable feature, for Parnell issued clear instructions to the Irish voters in British constituencies to support the Conservatives. Presumably he considered that a measure of Home Rule, and further land purchase legislation on the lines of the Ashbourne Act could be elicited from Salisbury. Davitt, however, saw very clearly the logic of Parnell's new associations: "Parnell and his crowd are going in for a new form of toryism. They fear the democracy. Priests, parsons, Parnellites and peers appear to be on the one platform now, and the programme is: keep the democracy out of Westminster."[33]

The results of the election were no less remarkable than the circumstances in which it had been held. The Liberal representation almost exactly balanced the Conservatives and 86 Nationalists combined. The Liberals retained a majority of seats in all three parts of Great Britain; but while these were overwhelming both in Scotland and in Wales — well over 85 per cent — yet in England the overall preponderance was slight. The English towns — hitherto Liberal — showed a small Conservative majority; while the traditionally Conservative English counties returned mainly Liberals. Not long before the election, there had been considerable signs of a Liberal resurgence in Ulster. This proved illusory, and the whole Liberal representation in Ireland was wiped out.

By common consent, one of the factors which had contributed to the striking Liberal success in the British rural areas was the appeal which radical land policies possessed for the newly-enfranchised agricultural labourers — and particularly the appeal of Chamberlain's demand for "three acres and a cow". What the Liberals lacked was — in Labouchère's words — "an urban cow". A few people saw how ideas of radical land reform could be translated into urban terms; most did not. The Liberals (as we shall see) eventually acquired their urban cow, which lactated very freely indeed; while the rural cow, grazing on her three acres, was a good deal less productive.

The Cabinet decided "after much discussion", not to resign, but to meet the new Parliament.[34] On the other hand, they had no intention of preserving the alliance with the Irish Party. As Salisbury told the Queen, the Government "have nothing in common"[35] with the Parnellites. After considerable argument, the Cabinet even decided to introduce legislation aimed to curb the National League.[36]

While the brief and disreputable flirtation between the Conservatives and the Irish was being broken, some moves hardly less remarkable were taking place in the Liberal Party. On 18 December 1885, it was reported in the Press that Gladstone had "definitely adopted the policy of Home Rule for Ireland". This was certainly a recent and startling conversion.[37]

Contemporaries saw the Home Rule issue as very closley linked to the land question. Irish land was no longer a matter which was of direct concern only to Irish peasants and Irish landlords. The various pieces of land purchase legislation had given the British electorate a powerful interest in security for the money which had been advanced. Nor was this the only financial interest. The *Freeman's Journal*, which was generally regarded as the most authoritative Nationalist newspaper, stated (perhaps with exaggeration), that "more than half the land — two thirds we believe — is out of the hands of the landlords, and is the property of London usurers and money-lenders."[38]

As *The Times* asked (in a slightly different context), if an Irish Parliament later repudiated its obligations, "how is it to be coerced, except by war?"[39] Even if the current Irish leaders were fully determined to carry out existing arrangements, there was no certainty that these leaders would not later be thrust aside.

The Times in particular played on these fears in no uncertain manner, and emphasised the central importance of land in the Home Rule question: "Whatever else may be doubtful, this at least is certain, that the leading Irish idea at the present time is to transfer the land from the landlords to the tenants. Hence the concession of an Irish Parliament would unmistakably mean the concurrence of this country in an act of general spoliation."[40] This fear of "general spoliation", whether realistic or not, must have acted powerfully on the minds of the more Whiggish Liberals. Nationalist Irishmen had long been conscious of the existence of such fears. Two and a half years earlier, John Redmond — a Catholic landowner, and the future leader of the Nationalist Party — had written that "no system of Home Rule would succeed in Ireland unless (the land) question were first settled."[41]

Davitt wrote scathingly of "apprehensions . . . about 'confiscation', 'separation' and the other hobgoblin fears conjured up by *The Times* and the alarmists in general", but he also was conscious that it was necessary, as a preliminary to Home Rule, "to work at once to get the *land* question out of the way."[42]

When the new Parliament met in January 1886, J. W. Barclay moved an Opposition amendment to the Address, which sought to extend the principle of the Irish Land Act to England. Ten Liberals, including three very important ex-Ministers — Lord Hartington, Sir Henry James and George Goschen — voted with the Government. On the following day, Jesse Collings (author of the agricultural section of the *Radical Programme,* and sometimes characterised as Chamberlain's Sancho Panza) moved a further amendment, regretting that no measures were proposed benefiting the agricultural labourer. This time eighteen Liberals — again including Hartington, James and Goschen — broke ranks. The decision to impose the official Opposition Whip in favour of Collings's amendment had been Gladstone's own, and was deeply resented by some of the Whigs.[43] The Irish voted with the Liberals, the amendment was carried and the Government resigned.

On 29 January, Gladstone received the Queen's commission to form his third government. The auguries for the new administration were not good. The Premier noted that "a full half of the former ministers declined to march with me".[44] The Whigs were particularly disinclined to "march with" Gladstone. Men like the Lords Hartington, Derby, Selborne, Morley[45] and Roxburghe; Sir Henry James and George Goschen, who all still ranked as Liberals, refused to serve. Chamberlain, although apprehensive about Gladstone's Irish policy, was prepared to join the Government. Apparently Chamberlain was persuaded that his leader was "squeezable", and in any case unlikely to remain long at the head.[46] Sir Charles Dilke, whose views on land and many other topics were close to those of Chamberlain, was excluded from the Government because the scandal which eventually led to his divorce had just commenced.

Gladstone accepted the view that Home Rule must form part of an arrangement which should also include a settlement of the land problem on the basis of peasant proprietorship. Accordingly he brought forward two Bills: a Home Rule Bill and a Land Purchase Bill.

Each of these proposals entailed much trouble in the Cabinet. The Land Bill represented a vast extension of the Ashbourne

55

principle. All owners of Irish agricultural land would be allowed to sell to the State if they wished. In order to finance this, a sum originally proposed at £113 millions but later reduced to £50 millions, would be raised in three per cent stock. Tenants would receive the opportunity of purchasing their land on an annuity basis. There were also special proposals for the "Congested Districts" where holdings were too small for the tenants' needs. As security for the money, a Receiver-General would be appointed, under the British authority, and all rents and Irish revenues would be paid in the first instance to him.

The Land Purchase Bill was set on its progress through the House of Commons a few weeks after the Home Rule Bill, and it was on the question of political separation and not land that the crisis came to a head, although the land question provided important overtones to the Home Rule Bill. When the Home Rule proposals were revealed, Chamberlain resigned in dissent; and when the Bill came to its second reading in June, the Government found itself in a minority, with no fewer than ninety-three Liberals voting against it. These dissident Liberals received the designation "Liberal Unionists".[47]

The Home Rule split did not correspond with the differences in the Liberal Party upon other matters. Lord Hartington and Joseph Chamberlain had long been thought to represent the opposite poles of the Liberal leadership; yet they now emerged as the Dioscuri of Liberal Unionism. Most, but by no means all, of the Whigs moved into the Liberal Unionist camp; but so also did some of the men who stood at the other end of the Party. Jesse Collings went the same way as Chamberlain; other friends and political associates of Chamberlain, such as Dilke and Morley, remained with Gladstone. A man whose main interest was land reform could be excused for doubting, in 1886, which section of the Liberal Party was more likely to give him what he wanted.

In the General Election of 1886, which followed the Government's defeat, the issue of Irish Home Rule was completely dominant. No Party received an overall majority. The Conservatives won 125 seats more than the Gladstonians, but 85 Irish Nationalists and 78 Liberal Unionists could between them determine the Government. In the circumstances, the Irish could scarcely return to the Conservative alliance, and so it was the dissident Liberals who really had to decide.

Salisbury tried to persuade Hartington to form a government, but the great Whig decided against it, concluding that: "I am convinced that I could not obtain the support of the whole or nearly the whole of (the Liberal Unionists) for a Government the main strength of which must be Conservative. They have represented themselves to their constituencies as Liberals, and nothing will induce many of them to act with Conservatives in general opposition to Liberals."[48] So Salisbury formed the Government after all, and was not able to include Liberal Unionists within its ranks.

Although Hartington's attitude was of real importance, the remaining Whig Unionists — "mere waifs and strays from the Whig wreck", in Balfour's delightful words — were of less use to the Conservatives. Balfour's view, which seems to have been endorsed by his uncle, the Prime Minister, was that "They are much more usefully employed as nominal Liberals in (?) the Liberal tactics, than they ever could be if they called themselves Tories, and brought us nothing but their eloquence and the reputation of turn-coats."[49]

Although no one could have foreseen it at the time, the formation of Salisbury's second government in 1886 was the beginning of a period of nearly twenty years in which the Conservatives were to dominate the House of Commons, save for a short and rather discouraging Liberal interlude. The position of the Liberal Unionists was still far from clear, but several vital considerations had already emerged. A very large section of the Whigs had at last detached itself from the Liberal Party. It was a fairly safe guess that most of them would never return, and therefore that the Liberal Party would come increasingly under the influence of the radicals, among whom were to be numbered many enthusiastic land reformers of various kinds. On the other hand, the Conservative government would fall if ever a substantial majority of the Liberal Unionists should decide to return to the place from whence they came. At the beginning of 1887, a "Round Table Conference" of Liberals was held, and for a moment it seemed likely that this would result in Chamberlain's reunion with the main body of the Liberal Party. In fact Chamberlain stayed where he was; but for a long time he and his closest associates considered themselves still to be as good radicals as they had been in the brave days of 1885. Besides, it must have been obvious to many of them that they could scarcely hope to hold their places in Parliament unless they appeared to their constituents to be acting on the radical side. They were therefore compelled, both by inclination and by self-interest, to exert every pressure upon the Government to ensure that it should adopt radical land policies. Hence the unexpected result of the division of the radicals was considerably to strengthen the cause of land reform on both sides of the House.

Notes-3

1   See discussion in F. M. L. Thompson, "Land and Politics in England in the 19th Century", *Trans. Royal Historical Society*, 5s, vol. 15 (1965), at pp. 41-2.

2   G. S. Lefevre's memorandum to Cabinet, 1 February 1883. CAB 37/10/14.

3   Memorandum to Cabinet on Tenant's Compensation by T. D. Acland, 20 February 1883. CAB 37/10/23.

4   F. S. L. Lyons, "The economic ideas of Parnell", *Historical Studies*, ii (1959), at p. 64, quoting *Freeman's Journal*, 15 April 1879.

5   Joseph Biggar to John Mishelly, 7 November 1882. Ulster Record Office T1160.

6   F. Sheehy-Skeffington, *Michael Davitt* (see bibliog.), pp. 75-6.

7   *Irish World*, 3 December 1881.

8   For a discussion of Davitt's views, see T. W. Moody, "Michael Davitt and the British Labour Movement", *Trans. Royal Historical Society*, 5s (1952-3), at pp. 58-60.

9   Max Beer, *History of British Socialism*, ii (see bibliog.), pp. 242-3.

10 F. Sheehy-Skeffington, *op. cit.*, p. 130.

11 George used the term "nationalisation of the land" for his own views in *The (Irish) Land Question*, 1965 edition, p. 64, but demonstrably in a very different sense from that of the LNS. It was also used in the appeal of the Council of the Land Reform Union, quoted in *Christian Socialist*, June 1883, p. 4.

12 *Christian Socialist*, June-July 1883.

13 Elwood P. Lawrence, *Henry George in the British Isles* (see bibliog.), p. 34.

14 *Christian Socialist*, July 1884, p. 23.

15 Moody, *op. cit.*, at p. 64.

16 *The (Irish) Land Question*, p. 53.

17 Compare the use of the same analogy by George in *The (Irish) Land Question*, p. 36 and by the Rev. J. Brennan at Carlow, 20 March 1881: see *Annual Register*, 1881, p. 207.

18 *Christian Socialist*, August 1883, p. 38.

19 *Christian Socialist*, January 1884, p. 114.

20 See memorandum "Nationalisation of Land", n.d., JC 6/5/10/1.

21 Lawrence, *op. cit.*, pp. 89-106.

22 See C. H. D. Howard, "Joseph Chamberlain and the 'Unauthorised Programme' ", *English Historical Review*, 65 (1950), pp. 477-91.

23 *The Radical Programme*, p. 66.

24 *Ibid.*, p. 146. For examples of the influence of George and Wallace, see pp. 19, 67-9.

25 Michael Barker, *Gladstone and Radicalism* (see bibliog.), pp. 37-8.

26 Lansdowne to Gladstone, 2 July 1880. WEG 44,465 fos. 49-50.

27 Gladstone to Rosebery, 10 July 1880. R. 10,022 fos. 60-1.

28 A. J. Balfour to Salisbury, 9 July 1880. S.E.

29 Argyll to Gladstone, 28 March 1881. WEG 44,105 fo. 18.

30 Report of Royal Commission on the Land Law (Ireland) Act 1881 and the Purchase of Land (Ireland) Act 1885 . . . 1887 c. 5015 xxvi ("Cowper Commission"), p. 7.

31 CAB 37/12/17, 19 & 20.

32 Spencer's memorandum, 23 March 1885. CAB 37/14/13.

33 Davitt to Richard McGhee, 23 November 1885, quoted in Moody, *op. cit.*, p. 64.

34 Salisbury to Queen Victoria, 14 December 1885 (copy), S. D/87/295.

35 Salisbury to Queen Victoria, 4 December 1885 (copy), S. D/87/287.

36 Salisbury to Queen Victoria 15, 17, 24 January 1886 (copies), S. D/87/317 ff.

37 Compare letter of his son, Herbert Gladstone, to William Haley, 20 February 1883. Haley 3905 fo. 36.

38 Quoted in *The Times*, 24 December 1885.

39 *The Times*, 18 December 1885.

40 *The Times*, 30 December 1885.

41 J. E. Redmond to Marquis of Lorne, 18 June 1883. Redmond papers, 15,237 (1).

42 Davitt to Labouchère, 29 January 1886 (copy). WEG 44,494 fos. 89-90.

43 Barker, *op. cit.*, pp. 37, 44.

44 John (Viscount) Morley, *Life of Gladstone*, ii (see bibliog.), p. 398.

45 That is, Earl Morley, not John (later Viscount) Morley.

46 Chamberlain to Jesse Collings, 26 September 1885 (copy). JC 5/16 fo. 108.

47 The tern "Unionists", *simpliciter*, was sometimes used in the late 1880s to mean "Liberal Unionist". Later it was used to comprehend both Conservative and Liberal Unionists.

48 Hartington to Salisbury, 24 July 1886. S. E.; Salisbury to Queen Victoria, 31 December 1886. S. D/87 fo. 425.

49 Balfour to Salisbury, 24 July 1886. S. E.

4 OVER THE SEA TO SKYE

Without exception or interval, the mass of the Scottish High-landers have always lived a life of as great penury and privation as can be imagined or endured.

"Men, sheep and deer"
Edinburgh Review, vol. 106 (October 1857), p. 470.

Of all the places in the British Isles which might be expected to play a major part in a social revolution, the Isle of Skye, in the Hebrides, must come low on the list. Yet Skye was to witness the first stages in a great revolt which not only swept the Highlands and radically altered the character of the area, but also served to connect the Irish Land War with an urban movement which appeared first in Glasgow and moved from there to most of the great towns of Britain.

In 1880, while the Irish Land War was at its height, the people of Skye were living a very isolated life. Their numbers had long been declining at a rate of about 100 a year, and currently stood at about 16,000, of whom the majority spoke only Gaelic. They were fishermen and crofters; several contemporaries spoke with some amusement of their "amphibious" existence. The crofts on which they lived were exceedingly poor. The plots were small and barren, and the doors of the tiny hovels were often the only apertures through which light could enter, or smoke from their peat fires could leave. They were ill-fed, ill-clad, unwashed — and, not surprisingly, they were often prematurely aged.[1]

Conditions in the other Western Isles, and in parts of the adjacent mainland, were similar. In the view of one qualified contemporary: "The people of the western islands were quiet and law-abiding, very simple and easily led, fairly contented with their circumstances, knowing and caring little for the outside world, their food oatmeal (chiefly imported), home potatoes, and fish, their money chiefly from home and east coast fishing and the sale of their young cattle and few sheep."[2]

Much of this seems redolent of conditions in Ireland, but there were some important differences. There was very little tradition of revolt. Disturbances had occurred in Lewis in 1874, and a radical Inverness newspaper, *The Highlander,* was vigorous in its advocacy of land reform;[3] but the area as a whole was remarkably quiet. The Hebridean crofters were even more isolated than the Irish peasantry. In most of the Isles, including Skye, they were Presbyterians adhering to the very strict Free Church of Scotland.

In Skye, as in most of the Western Highlands, the system of "runrig" had persisted down to the turn of the eighteenth and nineteenth centuries. Arable fields were sorted periodically by lot between the crofters, while pasturage on which they grazed black cattle was held in common. Some extremely primitive features remained in the economy of Skye long after the abolition of runrig. Even in the 1880s, at least one Skye landlord extracted his dues not only in money rent, but also partly in servile labour, reminiscent of mediaeval serfdom.[4]

The next stage of the story is described by Sir William Harcourt, Home Secretary in Gladstone's 1880 government, and the member of the Cabinet who at that time was principally responsible for the affairs of Scotland: "Presently the proprietors discovered that these worthless hills could be turned into gold by converting them into large sheep farms. The proprietors became first rich, then extravagant, and finally bankrupt, and with half a dozen exceptions, the great Chiefs — the Seaforths, the Glengarrys, the Clanronalds — of the West and the small lairds have disappeared, and the land has passed into the hands of strangers. I think that, from the latitude of Ullapool to that of Oban, there is hardly a single ancient Highland proprietor extant except Kenneth Mackenzie,[5] and all the islands north of Mull have passed into new hands except for the portion of Skye still held by Macleod and Macdonald. The result of all this, of course, has been to destroy all sense of feudal attachment, and the land has been dealt with on purely commercial principles, with the sole desire to extract from it the greatest possible amount of gold. For this purpose every acre of ground was subtracted from the crofters and the townships in order to enhance the rent of the sheep farms, and when it was found that deer forests yielded a higher revenue, the sheep had to give way to deer."[6]

The events which Harcourt was considering did not belong to the remote past, but to comparatively recent times; as Gladstone reminded his Home Secretary: "In point of moral title to live upon the land, enjoyed uniformly *ab antiquo,* I scarcely know how to distinguish between the chief and his followers. It was might, and not right, which was on his side when, during the half century and more which followed the '45, he gradually found that rearing men paid him in a coin no longer current, and took to the rearing of rent instead, backed by the law, which took no cognizance of any rights but his. This was but four or five score years ago, and I cannot think that we have here a sufficient prescription against the legislature to bar it from redressing wrong . . ."[7] Gladstone was referring to the "Highland Clearances" which took place at the turn of the eighteenth and nineteenth centuries, by which many thousands of people had been evicted to make way for sheep; a process which reached its climax in the infamous Sutherland clearances of 1811-20. The legal ownership of the clan's land had mattered little when the chief accepted a quasi-parental duty to his followers; it mattered much when their relations assumed an essentially financial character, and the Courts were willing to regard the chief as the landlord.

In Skye, there had been some clearances — one writer claimed that about 3,500 people had been affected[8] — but these were confined to certain parts of the island, and most districts had no such traditions. For the greater part, the Skyemen still lived where their ancestors did; but their condition differed from that of earlier times in that they had even less land from which to obtain food.

The estates of Lord Macdonald of the Isles, whom we have already noted as one of the few surviving "old proprietors", play a large part in our story. These estates were extensive in the island, and among them were lands in the district known as the Braes, about six miles from Portree. The local hill, Ben Lee, had once been common pasturage, but early in the century it was taken from the crofters for use as a market stance and cattle pound. Nevertheless, the crofters were permitted to graze their cattle there until the middle 1860s, when Ben Lee was let, and the crofters were excluded from it.[9] By the early 1880s, we find Lord Macdonald in rather poor health, and spending most of his time in the South of France, while his visible representative on the island was his factor, Alec Macdonald. According to one report, this factor was "also factor for other absentees, so that he controls about four fifths of the island. Besides this he holds all the offices, and is pretty much everything else that gives any influence. He is bank agent, justice of the peace, solicitor, distributor of stamps, chairman or clerk of all the school boards in Skye, chairman of the parochial boards, hotel keeper, captain of the volunteers, and Parliamentary agent for the Conservatives, and to crown all, the sheriff's officer is one of his clerks."[10] Although Alec Macdonald was a controversial figure in his capacity as land agent, it is interesting to note that he was also a landlord on a smaller scale in his own right, and apparently there were no complaints at all from tenants on his own land.[11]

In 1881, some Skye fishermen landed at Kinsale, Co. Cork, and caught the highly infectious ideas of the Land League.[12] Irish Gaelic was still widely spoken in the south-west of the country; the language is sufficiently close to Scots Gaelic for communication to be possible. This may have provided a significant bond of sympathy between Goidels on the two sides of the Irish Sea. At Martinmas 1881, the crofters of the Braes refused rent, giving as the reason (or excuse) the Ben Lee episode of seventeen years earlier. A lengthy appeal from Alec Macdonald[13] produced no effect, and evictions were ordered. On 7 April 1882, a sheriff officer attempted to serve notices of eviction, but was met by a crowd, mainly of women. The officer was compelled to burn his own papers, and his assistant was ducked in the local burn. The Glasgow police authorities, without consulting the Government, ordered the despatch of fifty or sixty police to Skye. Ten days after the earlier incident, there occurred what contemporaries knew as the "Battle of the Braes". A hostile crowd — again mainly of women — assailed the police with stones. In the *mêlée* several women were injured, at least one very seriously, and William Ivory, Sheriff of Invernessshire and several other Counties, seems to have been spattered with mud. None of the police, however, sustained injuries of any gravity, and they succeeded in their main objective, which was the capture and abduction of five men who had been ringleaders of the earlier disturbances. These five crofters were returned to Portree a few days later on bail, and were met with great jubilations. Some weeks afterwards, they were brought to trial. The serious charge of deforcement (roughly the Scottish equivalent of "resisting an officer of the law in the execution of his duty") was abandoned, and on the lesser charge of assault they received small fines, which were promptly paid by a sympathiser.[14] Sheriff Ivory, who had considerable executive and discretionary powers in the Highlands, became an intensely controversial figure in the area, and remained so until his resignation four or five years later.

In the immediate aftermath of the Braes "battle" — as Lord Lovat told a Conservative cabinet some years afterwards: "agitation spread rapidly, grazing lands were seized at Glendale" — Glendale is on the opposite side of Skye — "and those who protected them assaulted. Interdicts were obtained, and disregarded. Additional police were sent. A few days later a messenger-at-arms attempted to serve summons for breach of interdict; some 2,000 people turned out and drove messenger and police out of the district. The Procurator Fiscal of Skye, having gone to Dunvegan to make investigations, was forced to retire before the mob."[15]

Eventually forces were landed from a gunboat in February 1883, and four particular crofters were ordered to surrender. They agreed to stand trial, but refused to go on the gunboat. After a good deal of official muddle, they travelled unescorted to Glasgow, where they announced their presence to the authorities and were eventually arrested. They were then conveyed to Edinburgh for trial, and sentenced to two months' imprisonment each.[16] From this incident, the recognised ringleader of the crofters, John Macpherson, acquired the *sobriquet* "the Glendale Martyr", and was much in demand at land reform meetings all over the country.

Apparently through the instigation of men from Skye,[17] activities by crofters rapidly spread into other districts. In Skye itself the rents were not paid, and there was a further deforcement at the Braes in the late summer.

How, and by whom, was this agitation being led? There was nothing in the Highlands remotely comparable with the "conspiratorial" tradition which had evolved among the Irish peasantry over centuries, and which each generation learnt from its predecessors. Nor would the crofters have had the money, or the organisation, necessary for an impressive campaign. It has been suggested that the credit — or blame — resides with a body called the Highland Land Law Reform Association which operated from Inverness; but the HLLRA categorically denied responsibility, and even declared that they had not acted illegally, or counselled illegality, at any time.[18] It is much more likely that the main organisational effort came from Ireland — at first from the Land League, later from the National League. A middle-class body, the Skye Vigilance Committee, had been formed in 1881, and administered a fund of £1,000 granted by the Land League to resist evictions in the Highlands.[19] Gladstone's Lord Advocate, J. B. Balfour, attributed "the spirit of lawlessness" in Skye to two men: John Murdoch, former proprietor of *The Highlander*, and "an Irishman named McHugh, said to be an agent of the Land League".[20] Some of the publications circulated on Skye appear to have been printed in Dublin, and Catholic influence is certainly suggested in "cartoons showing mitred ecclesiastics crushing a snake marked 'Landlordism' ".[21] At this time the crofters' most impressive advocate in Parliament was Donald Macfarlane — a man who, albeit of Scottish origin, was currently sitting for an Irish constituency. Whether through a fraternal interest in the welfare of Celts on the other side of the Irish Sea, or through a desire to embarrass the Government by creating a political "second front", the Irish were plainly doing everything they could to foster the Highland revolt.

Parliamentary pressure was mounted for a Royal Commission to investigate the crofters' grievances. The establishment of this body — the "Napier Commission" — damped down "direct action" for a considerable time, even though the spring of 1883 was a time of great privation in the Highlands, through crop and fishing failures.[22] When the Report eventually appeared, in the middle of 1884, it drew a gloomy picture of Highland conditions, and decided that the most general complaint was the small size of the holdings.[23] Another serious grievance which the Commissioners recognised was that, for technical reasons, the Agricultural Holdings Act of 1883 had proved of very little value in securing compensation for improvements (such as they were) in the crofting areas.

A few radicals maintained consistent pressure on the Government to bring forward legislative proposals. Unfortunately most MPs did not give the matter much attention, and in the course of an important debate on the subject the House was "counted out" for want of a quorum.[24] Interest was largely confined to a comparatively small number of Scottish MPs — largely, but by no means exclusively, from Highland constituencies — and some of the Irish, notably Donald Macfarlane. Some percipient observers began to point out that a baleful moral would soon be drawn if violent behaviour in Ireland produced redress, while generally lawful behaviour in Scotland did not.

Public sympathy was soon canalised into political activity. The HLLRA was reconstituted at a meeting held in London in 1883, and received the support of at least four MPs, including Joseph Chamberlain's henchman, Jesse Collings. Another very active figure in the Association was J. S. Blackie, Professor of Greek at Edinburgh University and a friend of Gladstone. The objects could be described as the "Three Fs", plus more land for the crofters.[25] In August 1884, we find them holding an enthusiastic meeting at Portree, addressed by Donald Macfarlane, and also by the Conservative MP and organiser, John Gorst — who was currently much at loggerheads with the leadership of his party. Early in September, the basis of the organisation was broadened further at a meeting in Dingwall, which attracted a great deal of public attention in the Highlands, and resolved that the various interested organisations should "unite on a common platform to make the question of land reform a test one at the next election."[26] The Association served thenceforth as the main coordinating body for political action in support of the crofters' claims.

The combined effect of the Dingwall meeting, the interest aroused by the Royal Commission, Henry George's second visit to the British Isles, and a very substantial increase in some rent demands, produced a further spate of "direct action" among the crofters towards the end of 1884. This time again Skye was the centre, and public attention was drawn to the village of Kilmuir, a mile or so south of Dunvegan, on the estates of a certain Major Fraser. The police were not able to control the situation as they had been a couple of years earlier; at the end of October a contingent from Inverness was driven back violently.[27] A few days later, notices of eviction were threatened, and for some time large crowds with cudgels appeared in the ports of Uig and Portree, determined to resist. The situation was so menacing that the Lord Advocate instructed the Procurator-Fiscal of Skye that no arrests were to be made in connection with the recent deforcement.[28] Eventually a landing was effected at Uig by a force of twenty police, and a number of marines which one authority sets at no fewer than 250, supported by a gunboat and a steamer. A second gunboat was soon brought to control the Skye disturbances. The landing was timed carefully, so that the Sabbatarian crofters would be at church, and unable to interfere. On the following day, a similar show of force was made at Staffin, another disaffected part of the island. Apparently the crofters, in spite of their intense dislike for the police, held the marines in high regard. A promise of redress for grievances seems to have been received, and within a few days the Skye agitation had died down. Yet more than half a year elapsed before it was considered safe to withdraw the two gunboats from the island.[29]

On this occasion, Skye was not alone. There was a deforcement case on the large island of Lewis which was sufficiently serious for a contingent of eighty marines and a gunboat to be sent to Valtos to arrest the ringleaders.[30] Crofters on the peninsula known as Black Isle, on the Moray Firth, declared "that they (would) insist on their ancestral rights and pay only the original value of the land, and that if concessions (were) not immediately granted they (would) unite with other associations to bring their views to an execution."[31] Land on the island of Tiree, which was included in the County, and belonged to the Duke of Argyll, was seized by crofters for allotments.[32] The Duke was well-known for the trenchant and persuasive logic with which he defended landlordism; yet even the Whiggish *Scotsman* somewhat tarnished his image by revealing the appalling conditions which prevailed on Tiree. The situation in North Uist was sufficiently serious to require the personal attention and presence of Sheriff Ivory,[33] and there were many other cases of rent strikes and physical seizure of land throughout the Isles.[34]

It gradually became obvious that something would have to be done to allay the crofters' grievances. A very representative body of Highland proprietors met at Inverness in the middle of January 1885, and decided to offer the crofters more land, long leases and proper compensation for improvements.[35] Nevertheless, Harcourt correctly recognised that there would soon be strong pressure for legislation — adding that: "What we do in this matter will be the 'letting out of the waters' and . . . it must be in the end the prelude to the opening of a new land question which will not be confined to the West Highlands."[36]

Meanwhile, trouble in the Isles continued — there was another deforcement case at Glendale, for example. In spite of considerable administrative and technical difficulties,[37] the Government decided to bring in a Crofters' Bill, to implement some of the Napier Commission proposals. The Bill was introduced in May; but in the following month the Liberals fell, and Lord Salisbury formed a minority Conservative administration.

When at last a General Election was held, just before the end of the year, special excitement and interest surrounded the constituencies of the "crofting areas" in the North-west Highlands.[38] In county constituencies everywhere the effect of enfranchising rural workers was to set a large and politically unknown quantity on the register; nowhere was this more important than in the crofting areas. It was inevitable that these crofters should notice that their Irish counterparts had already secured a great deal of success through the Land Act of 1881 and the Land Purchase Act of 1885, and seemed poised to gain a great deal more. Why should Scotsmen be denied what Irishmen had been able to win?

At that time, the political parties had very little formal organisation in the North of Scotland. Many of the candidates in that area who were described as "Liberal" or "Conservative" do not seem to have been adopted by any recognised local body, or to have received endorsement from the national leaders or organisation of the parties. Scotland was overwhelmingly Liberal, and a large proportion of the Highland proprietors still ranked as Liberals — although they were not always much of a recommendation for their Party.[39] The candidates who challenged them are occasionally described under some designation like "Radical" or "Independent Crofter", but the use of these labels does not seem to have caused either friends or foes to consider them disentitled to the alternative appellation "Liberal". There were fourteen cases in Scotland where "Radicals" of one kind or another challenged the more traditional type of Liberal candidate, and contests of this kind were particularly common in the Highlands. Only one of the six "crofting" constituencies did not experience a contest between rival Liberals.

In Argyll, the former Liberal MP (a son of the Duke) was not standing again, and there were two possible Liberal candidates. The local Liberals selected Donald Macfarlane,[40] who had been such a prominent defender of the crofters in the old Parliament. Both Liberals went to the poll, but Macfarlane won a comfortable majority over an Independent Conservative, and the second Liberal fared very badly. In Caithnessshire, the former MP, Sir Tollemache Sinclair, had come under considerable criticism long before as a "Tory at heart".[41] He withdrew in 1885, but his son, Clarence Sinclair, defended the seat. Against him the crofters' movement set forth one of their leading figures, Dr G. B. Clark. Although he was a man of very "advanced" views indeed, Clark's campaign does not appear to have extended far beyond a demand for the "Three Fs".[42] At least one of Clarence Sinclair's meetings concluded amid utter uproar, and the return of Dr Clark seems to have taken nobody by surprise. In his speech on election, Clark commented — probably with justice — that ". . . he was specially indebted to Sir Tollemache Sinclair, to whose efforts he believed he chiefly owed his large majority."[43]

In Ross & Cromarty, the land reformers achieved what was perhaps their most spectacular triumph. The "orthodox" Liberal defender was R. C. Munro-Ferguson of Novar, a young landowner who had only been returned in the previous year at a by-election under the old franchise. Novar must have startled some of his Whiggish supporters by giving general assent to Chamberlain's *Radical Programme*.[44] A certain Dr Macdonald was set against him as a "crofters' " candidate. The Conservatives did not contest the seat, and Novar's return was confidently predicted. In fact he was defeated by a majority of five to three.[45]

Before the 1885 election, the only Conservative seat in the area had been Invernessshire, and the MP was retiring. As in Ross & Cromarty, there was a crofters' candidate — C. Fraser Mackintosh — who opposed an "orthodox" Liberal, Sir Kenneth Mackenzie. Again the intervention of the "crofter" was doubly effective. Mackenzie was driven to adopt a platform which, on land questions, was "a little in advance of most of the Liberal Party";[46] while these concessions were not able to prevent Mackintosh capturing the seat, and pushing Mackenzie into third place.

In the most northerly constituency of all, Orkney & Zetland, the pattern was rather different, for the defending Liberal MP, Leonard Lyell, did not encounter opposition from advanced land reformers, and was comfortably returned in a straight fight with a Conservative. It has been claimed, however,[47] that Lyell should properly be included among the "crofter" group himself. A similar claim has also been made for MacDonald Cameron who sat for Wick Burghs.

Only from Sutherlandshire could the traditional Highland Whigs derive any satisfaction at all, and even there it must have been somewhat qualified. The defending MP was the Marquis of Stafford, heir to the Duke of Sutherland. Stafford, like those other Whigs who faced opposition from "crofters' " candidates, was forced to make great protestations in the radical direction, and practically supported the "Three Fs".[48] He alone was able to hold his seat.

The overall result from the crofting constituencies could leave nobody in doubt as to the popular will on the question of land reform. Nor could there be much doubt that the *Northern Ensign* correctly described the general political situation in the area when it speculated: "Landlords may desert the Liberal ranks. Of late a good many have done so, and no doubt there are more to follow."[49] While the main defection of the English Whigs from Liberalism took place after the Home Rule split of 1886, the movement was already marked in the Highlands before the end of 1885, and before Home Rule had become a serious political issue.

When the Liberals returned to office at the beginning of 1886, many people favoured a Scottish equivalent of the Irish Land Act of 1881. This treatment, however, was less appropriate to the situation in the Hebrides than to that in Ireland. In December 1884, Donald Cameron of Lochiel told Harcourt that: "The Irish Land Act . . . has not proved a success among the very small tenants in the west, whose condition most nearly resembles the Skye or Lewis crofter. I mean, it has not made them any richer, save by the few shillings taken off their small rents . . . Even if this were not so, the abuse in Ireland which brought about legislation . . . was the fact that almost all improvements on Irish estates were the work of the tenant, and were frequently, on a change of tenancy, taken possession of by the landlords. In the Highlands, on the contrary, there are no improvements worth the name, except in the very rarest instances. As may be seen in the evidence before the Royal Commission, custom, which in Ireland dealt with improvements worth hundreds of pounds, in Lewis or Sutherland deals with the doors and windows of the miserable crofter's cabin — a species of tenant-right which may be calculated in pence, not even in shillings, but which is jealously maintained by the tenant and scrupulously respected by the proprietor."[50] From the testimony of this particular Highland proprietor (incidentally, a Conservative MP at the time), it is evident that most Irish peasants were prosperous by comparison with the Scottish crofters.

The Government's remedial Bill was brought forward in February 1886 by G. O. Trevelyan, who held the relatively new office of Secretary of State for Scotland. It proposed two of the "Irish Fs" — Fair Rent and Fixity of Tenure — for the low-rented crofters, but did not include Free Sale of the tenant-right. Some provision was also made for crofters to acquire land compulsorily in order to enlarge their holdings. The body which would administer the measure was known, rather confusingly, as the Crofters' Commission. The area to which this legislation would apply was limited to "crofting parishes" of Argyll, Inverness-shire and the more northerly counties. The "crofting parishes" concerned in fact comprised 151 out of the 163 civil parishes in the seven counties; most of the exceptions were in the south of Argyll. Attempts were made to extend the area further, but were resisted by the Government. On the other hand, the scope of the Bill was extended in certain other features — notably in connection with compulsory powers to acquire land to increase the size of holdings and grazing areas.[51] Nevertheless, it obviously failed to give even moderate satisfaction to the Crofters' MPs. Their attitude ranged from that of Dr Macdonald who considered that it was "simply tinkering with the question" to that of Macfarlane, who thought it would actually make the crofters' position worse.[52] On the Third Reading, it was formally opposed by some at least of the Crofters' MPs, who obtained considerable support.[53] The passage of the Bill through the Lords was easy, as the Conservatives did not oppose it, and it received Royal assent in June.

As we shall see later, the Highland "Land War" was by no means over; but the obscure peasants of the Western Isles had already attracted an enormous amount of attention in the great towns of Scotland. It is very easy today to underestimate the depth and the extent of this concern. When one peruses the Scottish newspapers of the time, however, it becomes more clear. On several separate occasions, from 1882 until the end of the decade, the Hebridean disturbances provided one of the main items of news almost every day for months at a stretch. Many thousands of residents in the Scottish towns were Highlanders either by birth or by recent extraction, and found it exceedingly easy to identify their sympathies with kinsmen and friends who still lived in those parts.

Signs of great interest appeared right at the start. In 1882, no fewer than 45,000 signatures were obtained in Glasgow for a petition on the subject of the crofters' grievances, and this may have played a large part in securing the establishment of the Crofters' Commission.[54] This general concern with the crofters and their interests persisted for a very long time; nearly nine years later, Chamberlain told Balfour that "the condition of the crofters interests very deeply many voters in the Scottish constituencies, especially in the West".[55]

Very soon, aggrieved workers in Glasgow began to see that the problems of the Hebrides were not unconnected with their own troubles. In November 1884, Shaw Maxwell (later an important figure in the ILP) carried with a large majority a resolution which he submitted to the Glasgow Liberal "Six Hundred" "to petition Parliament forthwith for immediate fiscal reform, and the reimposition of the 4s. tax upon all ground values on the basis of current rental".[56]

The influence of George's ideas is obvious; but even more striking was Shaw Maxwell's reported speech, which presaged the direction which the land agitation would take: "There seems to be an opinion, he said, that land reform was a matter for people in agricultural districts, and that the cities were only indirectly interested in the question. In his opinion the question of land reform was eminently a city question, and he was satisfied that its final settlement would be determined by the people of the great towns".[57]

The same point was taken by Joseph Chamberlain in the following year in at least three speeches to English audiences. When rural labourers were driven from the land, he argued, they were huddled together in urban slums "until anything like decent and healthful dwellings becomes impossible".[58] The root of urban poverty was to be sought in the land problem.

At the General Election of 1885, the various ideas which had been implanted by Henry George, underlined by the Highland land agitation, and developed in a different direction by Joseph Chamberlain[59] exerted a massive influence not only in the Highlands but throughout the Northern Kingdom. In four or five constituencies of the Clyde area, candidates whose main plank was land reform stood in opposition to the recognised Liberals. All of them fared disastrously — and they must be regarded not so much as precursors of a great movement but as rather embarrassing enthusiasts for a movement which was already well established, and whose main activities took place within the Liberal Party and not in opposition to it. Nevertheless, the fact that they appeared at all is an indication of the depths of feeling which the land question was stirring. It has been claimed, probably correctly, that until 1885 or even 1886 the principal concern of Scottish radicals had been the disestablishment of the Church of Scotland;[60] but from the middle 1880s land reform became more and more dominant as a matter of public interest. The people who rioted at the Braes in the spring of 1882 could have had no idea whatever of the influence which they would exert within four years.

72

1 For a general picture of life in Skye, see *Glasgow Herald*, 20 April 1882; *Scotsman*, 21, 25 April 1882. For a somewhat different view, see Malcolm McNeill's report to Lord Lothian, October 1886. Lothian papers SRO GD/40/16/32 fo. 21 ff. ("McNeill's Report"). On the historical background, see J. P. Day, *Public Administration in the Highlands of Scotland* (see bibliog.).

2 Lord Lovat's letter to the Lord Advocate, circulated to Cabinet, 8 October 1885. CAB 37/16/54 ("Lord Lovat's letter").

3 James Hunter, "The politics of highland land reform 1873-1895", *Scottish Historical Review*, 53 (1974), at pp. 47-8.

4 *Scotsman*, 22 April 1882.

5 Sir Kenneth Mackenzie, Bart., Liberal candidate for Inverness-shire in 1880 and 1885.

6 Harcourt to Gladstone, 17 January 1885; circulated to Cabinet, 29 January 1885. CAB 37/14/7. For examples of clearances of sheep (and shepherds) in favour of deer, see SRO papers AF/50/9/5.

7 Gladstone to Harcourt, 19 January 1885, also circulated in CAB 37/14/7.

8 Alexander Mackenzie, *The Isle of Skye 1882-3* (see bibliog.), p. xli.

9 J. B. Balfour (Lord Advocate), 24 April 1882. Parliamentary Debate 3S, 268, col. 1246; *Glasgow Herald*, 20 April 1882, etc.; *Scotsman*, 20 April 1882.

10 *Irish World*, 20 May 1882.

11 James Cameron, *Old and New Highlands and Islands* (see bibliog.), p. 51.

12 Lord Lovat's letter; McNeill's Report. Lothian papers GD/40/16/32 fo. 21 ff.

13 Printed *in extenso*, *Inverness Courier*, 15 April 1882.

14 See *Scotsman* 19, 20, 21 April 1882; *Glasgow Herald*, 18, 19, 20, 21 April 1882; *Inverness Courier*, 18, 22 April 1882; *The Times*, 12 May 1882; *Justice*, 13 December 1884; J. B. Balfour, Parliamentary Debate 3S, 268, col. 1246. An extensive account is given by Alexander Mackenzie, *History of the Highland Clearances* (see bibliog.), pp. 427-33, quoted at length in H. J. Hanham, "The problem of Highland discontent 1880-1885", *Trans. Royal Historical Society*, 5S, vol. 19 (1969), pp. 21-65. See also J. G. Kellas, "The Crofter's War 1882-1888", *History Today*, xii, pp. 281-8.

15 Lord Lovat's letter. An interdict is the Scottish equivalent of an injunction.

16 Cameron, *op. cit.*, pp. 53-4.

17 McNeill's Report.

18 *Inverness Courier*, 25 April 1882; Dougald Cowen to J. S. Blackie, 4 February 1886. Blackie 2636 fo. 150. See, however, Hunter, *op. cit.*, pp. 50ff., for more detailed information about later activities of the HLLRA.

19 Kellas, *op. cit.*

20 J. B. Balfour to Gladstone, 7 September 1882. WEG 44,476 fo. 244; McNeill's Report. Murdoch's newspaper, *The Highlander*, ceased publication in 1881. A manuscript autobiography of Murdoch, which unfortunately only covers the period up to 1880, exists at the Mitchell Library, Glasgow.

21 McNeill's Report.

22 Sir William Harcourt, 21 April 1883. Parliamentary Debates 3S, 278, col. 56; Robert Rainy to Blackie, 21 March 1883, on Assynt. Blackie 2635, fos. 39-40.

23 *Report into conditions of crofters and cottars* . . . P.P. 1884 xxxii, p. 7.

24 24 June 1884.

25 *The Times*, 30 May 1883.

26 *Inverness Courier*, 4 September 1884.

27 *Glasgow Herald*, 1 November 1884; see also Harcourt's statement of 30 November 1884. Parliamentary Debates 3S. 293, col. 539.

28 *Glasgow Herald*, 6 December 1884.

29 *Annual Register* 1884 (chron.), pp. 40, 42, 43, 49; *Glasgow Herald, Scotsman, North British Daily Mail*, November and December 1884 (many references); Lord Lovat's letter.

30 *Annual Register*, 1884 (chron.), p. 53. *Glasgow Herald*, 11 December 1884.

31 *Glasgow Herald*, 5 November 1884.

32 *Scotsman*, 5 November 1884; *Justice*, 1 November, 27 December 1884.

33 *Glasgow Herald*, 2 December 1884.

34 See police reports, especially for South Uist. Ivory papers, SRO GD/1/36/2.

35 *Scotsman*, 15 January 1885.

36 Harcourt to Gladstone, 17 January 1885, circulated to Cabinet, 29 January 1885. CAB 37/14/7.

37 See R. C. Munro Ferguson (Novar) to Rosebery, 9 March 1885. R. 10,017 fos. 1-4.

38 Here understood to mean Argyllshire, Invernessshire and all places north thereof— eight constituencies in all, two of them Burghs.

39 C. Innes to J. S. Blackie, 26 July 1883. Blackie 2635, fo. 31-2.
40 *Glasgow Herald*, 12 November 1885.
41 *Northern Ensign*, 13 April 1882.
42 *Northern Ensign*, 16 December 1885.
43 *Scotsman*, 11 December 1885.
44 *Rossshire Journal*, 13 November 1885.
45 Compare, for example, *Rossshire Journal*, 20 November and 4 December 1885. Novar himself was less sanguine. Argyll to Gladstone, 4 December 1884. WEG 44,105 fo. 238.
46 Mackenzie to Blackie, 8 August 1885. Blackie 2636 fos. 71-2.
47 *North British Daily Mail*, 9 July 1886.
48 *Scotsman*, 4, 18 November 1885.
49 *Northern Ensign*, 23 December 1885.
50 Lochiel to Harcourt, 20 December 1884. Circulated to Cabinet, 29 January 1885. CAB 37/14/7.
51 Crowley, *op. cit.*, pp. 119-20; Kellas, *op. cit.*, p. 285.
52 Macdonald, 8 March 1886. Parliamentary Debates 3S, 303, col. 195; Macfarlane, 10 March 1886. *Ibid.* 305, col. 679.
53 The Third Reading was carried by 219:52. Hansard does not publish the Division list, but Cameron, *op. cit.*, p. 71, claims that all Crofters' MPs voted in the minority.
54 Cameron, *op. cit.*, p. 41.
55 Memorandum on smallholdings, marked "A. J. Balfour", January 1891. JC 5/5 fo. 47.
56 *Glasgow Herald*, 20 November 1884.
57 *Ibid.*
58 Michael Barker, *Gladstone and Radicalism* (see bibliog.), p. 38.
59 Compare J. L. Garvin, *Life of Joseph Chamberlain*, ii, p. 66.
60 Donald C. Savage, "Scottish Problems", *Scottish Historical Review*, 40 (1961), pp. 118-35.

5 THE GOIDELIC REVOLT

What fools the Irish landlords are!

A. J. Balfour to Marquis of Salisbury
2 November 1889, Salisbury papers.

Although the Hebridean land agitation caused many people to examine the urban aspects of the land problem, yet for several years the urban reformers exerted little influence upon the main course of events. The seed had been planted, but it was still germinating underground. In the rural parts of the British Isles, by contrast, interest in the land problem was acute, and it exerted a great effect on the policies of the Conservative Government which Lord Salisbury headed.

Ireland was still much the centre of attention, but the political alignments there were still very far from clear. On the one hand, it was possible that the Union with Great Britain might be disrupted, either through changes at Westminster, or through a social revolution in Ireland. On the other hand, a powerful Unionist movement had appeared in Ulster, and had received enthusiastic support from most Protestants in all social classes. There was still something to be said for the view that Irish Nationalism was really the dream of middle-class romantics; that the peasant Nationalism which had seemed so terrible during the Land War period had no deep roots even among the Catholics, and would soon abate if drastic action were taken to deal with the land question. A government which was prepared to deal with that problem with courage and imagination might perhaps succeed in "killing Home Rule with kindness".

Unfortunately for the Government, economic depression returned to the rural areas of the United Kingdom in about 1886. This new depression was quite different in character from the one which they had experienced seven years earlier. Crops were not ruined, and yields on the whole remained quite high,[1] but prices fell heavily as food began to flood in from abroad. As the margin of comfort was much less in Ireland than in most of the United Kingdom, it was again in Ireland that the signs of discontent first became evident. Tenants who relied on marketing a large part of their produce to pay rent were in great difficulties. There was another spate of evictions — even Lord Salisbury, writing to the Queen, described them as "harsh".[2] Between 1884 and the autumn of 1886 8,000 families suffered that fate.

Parnell introduced a Tenants' Relief Bill in the early autumn of 1886. This Bill sought to stay evictions, to revise "fair rents" in the light of current prices, and to admit leaseholds to the benefits of the 1881 Act. The Government feared that these ideas would undermine the loyalty of Protestant tenants in the North who had been supporting the Union. Nevertheless, the Ministers were conscious of even bigger dangers, and a memorandum was circulated to the Cabinet, arguing that "Evictions could not be suspended without at the same time suspending all the other remedies for the recovery of rent, and it is almost certain that any legislation in this direction would be followed by an entire cessation of payment of rent in Ireland".[3] Eventually the Government decided to oppose the Bill on all counts, and it was defeated. The Liberal Unionists were deeply split on the Bill. Thirty-one, including Hartington, voted with the Government, while the remainder, including Chamberlain, purposely abstained.[4]

The influence both of Parnell and of the National League in land matters was very much one of restraint, and this fact had not been lost upon the Government.[5] Nevertheless, the Government also recognised the very precarious nature of the whole situation: "If the National League should depart from its present policy of conciliating and keeping in touch with British Radicalism, its organisation is so complete and powerful that it would be very dangerous; while on the other hand if this policy is continued, the Secret Societies, especially the I(rish) R(epublican) B(rotherhood) in which considerable activity now prevails, may at any moment break into action."[6]

In fact the challenge to the Government came from a rather different quarter. On 23 October 1886, three well-known Irish politicians, T. C. Harrington, John Dillon and William O'Brien, launched what became known as the "Plan of Campaign". Their scheme was that the tenants on an estate should send a deputation to their landlord and ask for rent reductions. If this request were refused, the tenants should pay no rent at all, but should contribute what seemed to them a reasonable rent into a campaign fund, which could be used to resist the inevitable attempts at eviction.

In spite of the large drop in agricultural prices, the existence of "judicial rents" which had been fixed comparatively recently set the "campaigners" at something of a moral disadvantage. Yet the judicial rents which the sub-commissioners fixed during 1886 were markedly lower than those which they had established in earlier years, and tenants whose rents had been prescribed during the more prosperous years inevitably developed a sense of grievance.[7] Lord Salisbury oversimplified the position, but he appealed to a strong and widespread English attitude, when he castigated the Plan of Campaign as "fraud" and "swindling".[8] Parnell also strongly disapproved of the Plan, and urged Davitt not to support it — arguing that it would antagonise British voters and thus prejudice Home Rule.[9]

The Government was far from certain how to tackle the Plan. There may even have been some initial doubts whether it was actually unlawful[10] but they eventually decided to arrest and prosecute O'Brien and Dillon. Predictably, the jury disagreed, and the prisoners were discharged.

Yet again, the familiar amalgam of coercion and conciliation was applied. A Land Bill was introduced by the Government, designed to halt the evictions. In its original form, the Bill was also intended to allay, so far as possible, the fears of the Irish landlords;[11] but the Liberal Unionists issued an ultimatum to the Government[12] and compelled them to bring forward a much stronger measure. The Liberal Unionists were by no means free agents in the matter. Not only were they of very mixed origins and composition but their more radical members were all too conscious that many of their own voters were far from happy about the estrangement from Gladstone, and were being constantly stirred to revolt by the Liberal organisers. Having made concessions to the Liberal Unionists — Salisbury regarded them as "the price we have to pay for the Union, and it is a heavy one" — the Ministers suddenly found themselves fighting a war on two fronts. Salisbury had by no means complete control over the House of Lords, and some compromise between the two Houses was necessary before the measure could be passed.[13] When the Bill eventually became law, it provided that judicial rents could be revised when the recent price fall had affected the peasants' ability to pay. It also brought 100,000 leaseholders within the ambit of provisions similar to those of the 1881 Act.

The 1887 Land Act was accompanied by a Crimes Act which

gave extraordinary powers to the Irish executive. Passage of the Crimes Act caused considerable discomfort to a section of the Government's Liberal Unionist allies, four of whom were driven back to the ranks of the Gladstonians.[14] The Irish peasant agitation continued, and the new powers granted by the Act were soon used. On 19 August 1887, the Government "proclaimed" the National League as a dangerous organisation, and proceeded a month later to suppress some of its branches.[15]

Coercion, however, brought its own difficulties, both in Ireland and in England. Five of the Liberal Unionists, including Chamberlain himself, went so far as to vote in favour of Gladstone's motion condemning the Government's decision to "proclaim" the National League.[16] Not long after the "proclamation" a crowd of 8,000 gathered for a demonstration at Mitchelstown, Co. Cork. A Government reporter who arrived late sought to push his way, with police escort, through the assembly. John Morley described the *dénouement*: "What followed is a matter of conflicting testimony. One side alleges that a furious throng rushed after the police, attacked the barracks and half murdered a constable outside, and that the constables inside, in order to save their comrade and to beat off the assailing force, opened fire from an upstairs window. The other side declare that no crowd followed the retreating police at all, that the assault on the barracks was a myth, and that the police fired without orders from any responsible officer, in mere blind panic and confusion. One old man was shot dead, two others were mortally wounded and died within a week."[17] Whatever actually happened, three new martyrs were certainly made. Gladstone's injunction, "Remember Mitchelstown!", delivered not long after, became a great watchword with the Irish and with the Liberals.

The Plan soon came under attack from another quarter, and one where it was much more vulnerable. In its early stages, it had received widespread support from the Catholic clergy, including many of the hierarchy. In the autumn of 1887, a body of Catholics, including the Duke of Norfolk, met the Pope, and seem to have exerted an influence upon him. In April 1888, he formally condemned the Plan of Campaign, and, indeed, the practice of "boycotting" as well. Although Dillon had declared earlier that Irish Catholics would "no more take their political guidance from the Pope than from the Sultan of Turkey", and many local tenants' organisations in Ireland indignantly repudiated the Papal authority on such matters, yet the Plan of Campaign certainly declined sharply, and in 1888 its receipts were well under a third of what they had been two years earlier.[18]

In October 1890, Dillon and O'Brien fled the country to avoid arrest. This, in the view of one distinguished modern scholar, "marks the end of the Plan as a vital, purposeful movement".[19] It did not die at once, however, and seventeen disputes were still outstanding in 1893. The Plan was operated on 116 estates in all, and the total sum which it received was set at £234,000.[20] Nor was the Plan wholly confined to Ireland, for it was also set into action by tenants on the Ellore estate in Aberdeenshire.[21] On some particular Irish estates — such as the Smith-Barry estates in Co. Tipperary — there were long and complicated struggles, involving large numbers of people, and attracting immense public interest over a prolonged period. So far as its defined objectives were concerned, the Plan of Campaign was only a very qualified success; but it was an extremely effective means of keeping the Irish land agitation alive, and probably exerted a substantial indirect effect upon political attitudes.

The Government was disturbed no less by the militancy of some landlords than by the militancy of the tenants. The most recalcitrant of these Irish landlords was the Marquis of Clanricarde — "Lord Clan Rack-Rent" — absentee owner of nearly a hundred square miles of Ireland. His estates in Co. Galway were divided into two sections. The one at Woodford was notorious for agrarian crime, and was indeed the first place where the Plan of Campaign had been set in operation. The other, at Portumna, however, was exempt from crime down to the autumn of 1888, largely through the influence of Bishop Healy, who was also the local parish priest. Some of the Portumna tenants had obtained much greater reductions than others under the 1881 Act, and in 1886 the aggrieved tenants decided to adopt the Plan of Campaign. The Bishop, however, persuaded them to abandon it — promising to use his influence upon Lord Clanricarde to obtain a fair concession. Clanricarde did not reply to the petition — described by the Chief Secretary for Ireland, Arthur Balfour, as "most respectful" — which had been sent by the tenants and signed by the Bishop. Instead, Clanricarde made a counter-offer which was practically worthless. Balfour told the Cabinet: "The Clanricarde property has already cost the country about £9,000, and is costing it at this moment £100 a month for protection. These sums will probably be doubled, and it is, in my opinion, intolerable that a man like Clanricarde should be permitted to endanger the Union by his selfish stupidity. The terms of arrangement suggested by the Bishop are certainly not in excess of those which are commonly granted by good landlords throughout Ireland . . . The Bishop has defeated the Plan of Campaign and has preserved the peace of the district, solely by his personal influence . . . if, through the rejection of his terms his influence is shattered, as it most undoubtedly will be, a state of affairs will arise ruinous to the landlord, ruinous to the tenantry, and most dangerous to the whole cause of the Union."[22]

Eventually Balfour and the Prime Minister went so far as to see Clanricarde personally in order to attempt to obtain some concession, but they were completely unsuccessful.[23] Balfour thereupon refused protection to the bailiffs who sought to enforce ejectment decrees on the Portumna estates. He even contemplated new legislation whereby the estates of a peculiarly obstructive landlord might be administered, in his own interest, by public authorities.[24] Apparently nothing came of these endeavours, and the Clanricarde properties provided a constant vexation to successive British governments until they were acquired by the Congested Districts Board in 1915.

Nor was Lord Clanricarde the only Irish landlord who excited Balfour's ire. The Chief Secretary gave the Cabinet his own answer to the familiar argument that the Irish landlords functioned as a sort of English garrison in a hostile country: "I do not dissent from the premises, but I draw from them an opposite conclusion. The landlords are no doubt like a garrison, but like a garrison in a hostile country which they are unable to hold, which they cannot conquer themselves nor help us to conquer, and who are constantly hampering our movements by the necessity we are under of not abandoning them to our enemies. I may add that they are a garrison totally without discipline, wholly ignorant of elements of strategy, and who are much more successful in embarrassing their friends than in beating their foes."[25]

If this was the impression which Irish landlords made upon a man who was by class, race, religion and politics their natural friend, it is not difficult to gauge how they must have looked to their enemies.

In the teeth of these difficulties (or perhaps because of them) the Government went ahead with its policy of fostering peasant-proprietorship in Ireland. As we have seen, the 1870 and 1881 Act had had only very qualified successes in this particular direction. The Act of 1885, however, was far more effective. A Royal Commission which reported in February 1887, showed that almost half of the £5 millions allocated had already been requested, and over 5,000 applications had been received.[26] By 1888, 14,000 purchase agreements had been concluded, and nearly half of them related to holdings with an annual value below £30. Half of the agreements, it is true, concerned land in Ulster; but even in stricken Connaught there were more than 1,500. The instalments had been paid remarkably — one might almost say incredibly — well. Of a total sum of £90,000 which had been due, only a little over £1,000 was outstanding, and there was reason to think that this sum would soon be met. Indeed, the success was in one sense an embarrassment, for agreements had been concluded to a value of nearly £6 millions,[27] while the sum authorised under the Ashbourne Act was only £5 millions.

Encouraged by this success, and pressed strongly by the Liberal Unionists,[28] the Government procured the passage of another Land Purchase Act in 1888 which doubled the sum available, and this loan was speedily taken up. Again success made further legislation necessary, and Balfour contemplated a measure which would be more far-reaching than its predecessors. Not to put too fine a point on it, the Government was still acutely conscious that the preservation of the Union would turn largely upon its capacity to allay the grievances of Irish tenants. Even the Protestant areas of what men were pleased to call "loyal Ulster" continued to provide signs that they might not be immovable in their support for the Union. While the Land Bill of 1887 was wending its way through Parliament, the Liberal Unionists had needed to remind the Government that "unless considerable alterations were made in the Land Bill, Ulster itself would very probably be lost to the Unionist cause".[29] A powerful body, the Ulster Tenants' Defence Association, demanded that landlords should be compelled to sell farms at their tenants' demand.[30]

This question of possible compulsion upon recalcitrant land-owners was the thorniest of all those raised by the Government's policy of promoting peasant-proprietorship. Unlike the English or lowland-Scots tenant farmer, who was willing to move from farm to farm, the Irish peasant usually exhibited an immense attachment to some particular piece of land. What he demanded was not simply the freehold of any farm with the required acreage and soil, but the freehold of the particular farm which he and his ancestors had tilled for generations. Hence he sought compulsion upon some specific landlord to sell the property, not merely that an economic climate should be created in which landlords as a whole would be disposed to sell.

From the landlords' point of view, land ownership could have had few attractions in the prevailing state of Ireland. It might not even yield rent for much longer. As one modern commentator has observed: "If the administration waited too long before acting, the chances were that the Irish landlords would be lucky to escape with the clothes on their backs."[31]

It was a fair guess that wise, kindly and progressive landlords would be likely to sell voluntarily, while those who would refuse would be obstinate and obstructive men of the Clanricarde type, whose characters were not even softened by enlightened self-interest. Neither Balfour nor Salisbury seems to have been opposed to compulsion as a principle; nevertheless, Balfour decided that "however desirable compulsion may be, it will very likely be impossible to get Parliament, public opinion, or the Irish land-lords to think so".[32] Lord Salisbury, after recording "a tremendous scream" from one of his supporters at the prospect of compulsion, endorsed the view that it "would have broken up the Cabinet, the Party and the Union".[33] Corresponding — or perhaps even deeper — splits appeared between the Chamberlain and Harting-ton wings of the Liberal Unionists.[34] An Irish Land Purchase Bill of some kind was essential; but it was exceedingly difficult to frame one which would not split the Government and its sup-porters along every imaginable line of cleavage.

The Bill which Balfour eventually proposed, in March 1890, firmly excluded compulsion. As with the Ashbourne Act, no initial payment was required from the tenant, and the annuity instal-ments were four per cent. The cost of purchase, however, would be defrayed by Treasury stock created *ad hoc* — rather as Glad-stone had proposed in 1886.

The initial reaction of the Nationalists was hostile, for they argued that only a small proportion of tenants would benefit, and it would be difficult to raise credit for any schemes which might later be devised to assist the remainder. In the later stages of the Bill, however, the Irish were disposed to accept it. By that time they were in no position either to impede the passage of the Bill or to improve its contents, for their Party had been shattered by the disputes which attended Parnell's divorce. The Bill took an exceptionally long time to pass through Parliament, and eventually became law in August 1891. Parnell was within a few weeks of his death, and nearly a decade would elapse before his Party was again able to speak with something like a united voice.

The Balfour Act of 1891 was not only concerned with land purchase. It also began to deal with the special problem of these densely-populated rural areas which were known as the "Congested Districts". This problem had deep roots, and it deserves a digression.

During the early part of the Land War, the peasants who attracted most attention were those whose problems could be met, at least in part, by the "Three Fs". The gravamen of the complaint of those peasants was that they were over-rented; that their improvements were liable to be arrogated by landlords; and that the risk of arbitrary eviction hung over their heads. Such people would (in theory) be completely satisfied if they could become proprietors instead of tenants, secure in their holdings and without the obligation to pay rent. Yet there also existed in Ireland considerable numbers of peasants whose problems were of a completely different kind. Their holdings were so tiny that it would have made little difference if rent had been abolished altogether. Their improvements were of negligible value; and even eviction could hardly make their lot much worse. In about 1890, William O'Brien went to live in one of the worst of these Congested Districts, in Co. Mayo. He later described the situation thus: ". . . While the overcrowded villagers . . . lived on patches of heather hills or morasses in which the periodical failure of crops was a necessity of nature, these scenes of wretchedness were surrounded by wide-ranging pastures from which the villagers or their fathers had been evicted in the clearances following the Great Famine of 1847 . . . The peculiar conditions of the western problem were then as little known over three-fourths of Ireland, or even by five-sixths of the Irish Party, as the geography of mid-Africa."[35]

"Congested Districts" extended over a large part of the West of Ireland, and their origin was not always the same. Sometimes, as in the cases which O'Brien observed, they had been brought into existence by mass-extirpation of peasants after the Famine.

84

Others were quite different. An important official in the Local Government Board for Ireland described the situation on another estate, also in Co. Mayo. The landlord there, Lord Dillon, did not evict wholesale, or even discourage the peasants from subdividing their holdings if they wished. As a result: "The people married early, bred in swarms, and squatted down upon their bits of reclaimed bogs in the winter, migrating to England in the summer to earn money enough to pay their rent, and keep them alive till the spring came round again . . . The population has increased since the famine years, though in Ireland the total population has enormously decreased. The rent roll was greatly increased, of course; how much it would be hard to say, but it is popularly believed that it was raised from £5,000 a year to £25,000. It was not contended, however, that individual rents were too high and both Lord Dillon and Strickland" — Lord Dillon's agent — "were liked by the people and the rents were fairly paid, the people saying that whereas Lords Lucan and Sligo cleared off thousands and made large grass farms of the holdings . . . Lord Dillon was a kind man and not an exterminator. As long as good wages could be earned in England and the people were left to themselves all went well and evictions on the property were, I believe, almost unknown." The inauguration of the Plan of Campaign, however, coincided with a time when earnings were fifteen to twenty per cent lower than usual, and "the agitators . . . told the people that they were being defrauded as the land could not pay the rent, making no mention of course of the fact that if the people were living rent free the land could not support them for six months of the year." By the middle of 1887, when this account was written: "The tenants, flushed with the success of last year's fight, now say that the terms dictated by the plan of campaign are too high, and that next year they will take the matter into their own hands and go in for a larger reduction than last time."[36]

This account shows obvious bias. It might be contended, for example, that a species of kindness by which a man multiplied his rent-roll fivefold and bought a long period of peace from his tenants as well was something less than sublime altruism; yet nevertheless the description throws some interesting light on the problem of the origin of the Congested Districts. It also gives an interesting illustration of the mechanism by which disaffection could easily grow in areas which had previously been contented. Finally, it serves to remind us that seasonal work in Great Britain was often very important to the economy of Ireland, as many peasants were not "full-timers". Whether we regard O'Brien's explanation of the Congested Districts or that of the Local Government Board official as the one more generally applicable, it is evident that land purchase would be no solution to the peasants' problems in places where the land was not sufficient to support the people.

Balfour's 1891 Act did not solve the problem, but it did make a serious attempt to face it. The Act set up a Congested Districts Board, with considerable powers to provide technical instruction in fisheries and other industries, and also to purchase land, to amalgamate and improve holdings, and to resettle tenants thereon.[37] Here at least an important beginning had been made.

In the West of Scotland, events were in some ways closely parallel to those of Ireland, but in other respects they were markedly different. The "Crofters' Party" was not united over the Home Rule question in 1886. Three of the four MPs supported Gladstone, while Fraser Mackintosh of Inverness-shire went the other way. At the ensuing General Election, Mackintosh was returned unopposed as a Liberal Unionist. The "Crofters" captured Sutherland, but lost Argyll. For all practical purposes, they merged thenceforth into the main body of Gladstonian Liberalism. Fraser Mackintosh came under heavy fire from his sometime supporters, and it is likely that his return was due largely to the practical difficulty of finding a rival candidate in a hurry[38] — but the presence of one undoubted Highland land reformer on the Unionist side was of considerable importance to Chamberlain. At the beginning of 1887, the last serious attempt at a *rapprochement* between Gladstonian and Unionist Liberals — the "round table conference" — collapsed in failure, and Chamberlain was evidently anxious to give tangible proof of his continued radicalism. He shortly set out on a tour of Scotland, "to fight in a Radical style for his old friends the crofters and to inspirit Liberal Unionism".[39] This visit was followed by the preparation of a draft Crofters' Relief Bill, which was widely circulated, but went no further.

Meanwhile, the Hebridean land agitation continued. The Crofters' Act gave little immediate assistance, and the general effects of the renewed agricultural depression were very similar to those in Ireland. The economic difficulties of Ireland led to the Plan of Campaign in 1886; the same year saw the outbreak of a further spate of disturbances in the Western Isles. The little island of Tiree had a population of 2,700, and a total rent-roll of £6,000. The agitation there was so severe that a large contingent of police was incapable of coping with the trouble, and the authorities needed to send a hundred marines, each of them equipped with a hundred rounds of ammunition.[40] Skye was again the principal centre. This time the trouble was not the failure of crofters to pay rent, or to observe notices of eviction. The local Parochial Boards (which were effectively dominated by the landlords of the district) were under a statutory duty to collect money for the upkeep of the poor. These Boards failed to perform the obligation which the law had set upon them.[41] By the end of March 1886: ". . . The total amount of arrears of poor and educational rate in Skye was £5,200. Of that sum, £3,600 was owed by the landlords, £1,000 was owed by tacksmen and farmers paying more than £30 rent, and under £600 was due by crofters. And not alone were the lairds the chief defaulters, but leading men among them — magistrates, commissioners of supply, deputy lieutenants, and so forth, were reported openly and publicly to have declared that they would not pay their poor-rates until they themselves received their rents."

In Ivory's view, the rent arrears stood at about £20,000 by late April.[42] Thus was the Government confronted with open and flagrant defiance of the law, not only by peasants but by the wealthy classes on Skye as well. The behaviour of both groups was understandable but no Government could possibly allow it to continue.

A. J. Balfour, who was briefly Secretary of State for Scotland, countenanced sending a gunboat and fifty marines to Skye, to co-operate with fifty police who would be serving writs for rents and rates.[43] He was by no means prepared to give a *carte blanche* to Ivory; when he heard that Alec Macdonald had "taken upon himself to apply for writs only in the case of the crofters and small tenants, leaving the defaulting landlords and tacksmen to be proceeded against, if proceeded against at all, by some less summary process". Balfour told Ivory that unless this was reversed immediately, the whole expedition would be withdrawn. Macdonald complied; the rates, and a good many of the rents, were soon paid.[44] Balfour was particularly pleased with the initial result, but advised Ivory that difficulties were likely to arise when stock had to be distrained and sold to pay the rents which were still outstanding.[45] In fact, the trouble was not over at all. At Bornaskitaig, in the far north of the island, it proved impossible to serve writs without military assistance, and there were arrests at Herbista,[46] near Dunvegan.

For a time, attention swung to the Assynt district in the west of Sutherlandshire, where in May 1887 another serious deforcement occurred; women seized and burnt summonses which were being conveyed by the Sheriff Officer.[47] There were several separate, but evidently related, disturbances in the area, and troubles in the township of Clashmore and at other parts of Assynt continued until the end of the year. Hugh Kerr, one of the Clashmore ringleaders, became something of a hero through his remarkable skill at avoiding arrest[48] — although he was eventually caught and imprisoned.

At the turn of 1887-8, conditions in the Isles were appalling, as bad harvests brought a serious threat of starvation. In February 1888, for example, the Crofters' Commission revealed that in parts of the Isle of Lewis "on all sides . . . we observed evidence of the deepest poverty and dejection; everywhere the potato crop is nearly consumed . . . within the next two months, as far as we have been able to discover, the bulk of the population in Lochs and elsewhere will be brought face to face with the necessity of killing their cattle and sheep to sustain life, while those who have no stock must either approach the parochial board or starve."[49]

The main disturbances which inevitably accompanied these privations took place in the chain of the Outer Hebrides which is collectively known as Long Island. As in 1882 and 1884, the Scottish Press gave major coverage to these events and the English newspapers also gave them frequent attention. The first major target of the crofters was a great "deer forest" — a reserved shooting area — of 80,000 acres in the Isle of Lewis, known as New Park Forest. The creation of such an area, devoted to what men were pleased to call "sport", had involved the destruction of seventeen villages.[50] In November 1887, 2,000 Highlanders, headed by pipers, and equipped with rifles, tents and baggage, decamped on New Park Forest with the avowed object of exterminating the deer, so that the land might be returned to productive use. This disturbance was sufficiently serious for a contingent of police to be sent with a support of marines and soldiers. The peasants quite speedily destroyed about a third of the 600 deer, and Lord Lothian — who by this time had succeeded Balfour as Secretary of State for Scotland — told a delegation soon afterwards that he "was not one of those who thought that people who had recently broken the law there had broken it for any very bad motive at all."[51] Nevertheless, a prosecution was inaugurated against the ringleaders. They were eventually acquitted through a defect in the indictment under which they had been charged.[52]

Although the "Park Raid" — as the incident became known — was the most spectacular attack on "sporting" land, it seems to have been by no means the only one. Lord Lothian was informed that the technique of the crofters was "to destroy the grouse eggs (which they have done already so effectively in one part of the Lews that the bag has fallen from 600 brace per annum to under 100): to kill and frighten off the deer from the forests and to make a wholesale destruction of spawning salmon and trout in the rivers."[53]

Sheep farms were only marginally less offensive to land-hungry crofters than were deer forests. According to the same informant, the crofters' technique with them was "to destroy the fences, disturb the stock, and so alarm the tenants, their servants and families, that they will soon be inclined to throw in their leases rather than endure a state of matters which will soon become intolerable". The most famous raid on a sheep farm was at Aignish, near Stornoway, where hundreds of Highlanders drove the offending beasts off the land.[54] Again it was found necessary to use marines and soldiers to quell the disturbances, and this time the Riot Act was read. The main culprits were less fortunate than the "Park Raiders"; they were sentenced to terms of imprisonment.[55] At Barvas, on the west side of the island, there was a serious conflict when police sought to intercept crofters who were destroying fences on sheep farms which, they alleged, had been unjustly taken from them some years earlier.[56]

There were also troubles elsewhere in the Isles. Harris and South Uist were in a state of much agitation. These were islands where there existed a substantial class of cottars — that is, peasants who technically had no land at all, but who were in practice allowed to "squat" on the crofters' holdings. The strategy of the land reformers — at least in South Uist — was to induce crofters to eject the cottars, and then urge the cottars in their turn to take possession of the demesne farm. Apparently the peasants again claimed a right of pasturage; and at one moment the township of Stoneybridge on this little island was described as "the cradle of the crofters' agitation in the Western Islands".[57] It is evident that unlawful acts of one kind or another were by this time endemic in the Scottish islands, and that the authorities had little power to cope with the situation, save by the use of gunboats, marines and soldiers.[58] The employment of military forces against crofters was by the late 1880s such a common phenomenon that it hardly excited any special comment.

The state of affairs which we have already observed in Sutherland shows that the trouble was by no means confined to the islands. There was also much unrest in the Coigach districts of the Rossshire mainland. By January 1888, *The Times* was fearing a general rising in the Highlands.[59]

In fact, the general rising did not occur. Instead, there was a gradual decline in unlawful activities within the Highland area from the spring of 1888 onwards. "Gradual", indeed, is the operative word. In the late autumn of that year, a sheriff's officer who visited Glendale in Skye with summonses for payment of rent was pelted with stones and clods of earth, and had some difficulty in escaping from the enraged crofters.[60] There was at least one deforcement case, and several instances of fencebreaking, in Lewis in 1889.[61] As late as the spring of 1891, land was seized at the farm of Orinsay in Lewis, and Lord Lothian took the matter sufficiently seriously to order that a gunboat or troopship should be held in readiness in case it was required.[62]

To what may we attribute the slow pacification of the Highlands? There is no single cause. At the crudest level, the forces of "law and order" became more effective when the tactical and psychological errors of the early days were understood and remedied. The authorities, for example, realised that the crofters regarded the police as no more than agents of the landlords, but respected the Queen's uniform. At the beginning of 1888, Lord Lothian was advised to keep a force of three or four gunboats and about 300 marines in the area.[63] It is not clear whether he followed this advice or not, but it would seem likely that he did.

More important, however, were the positive measures which were taken. Although Lord Lothian was told by a delegation from the Outer Isles "that the Crofters' Act of 1886 had not been of the slightest benefit to the crofters",[64] this was an exaggeration. The "security of tenure" clauses must have prevented any exacerbation of the problem by further evictions to create deer forests and sheep farms. The Crofters' Commission reduced rents and cancelled arrears on a large scale; by the end of the decade, rent reductions averaged 30 per cent, and arrears for well over 60 per cent of the money owed had been cancelled. In some places, the figures were far higher than these; at one township in Lewis, rents were reduced by 53 per cent, and 91 per cent of the arrears were cancelled.[65] A Royal Commission which reported in 1892 disclosed substantial improvements in the crofters' condition.

Yet the root cause of the trouble was peculiarly intractable. Lord Lothian told the Cabinet of the conclusions which the Royal Commission of 1884 had reached, and the Commissioners set up under the 1886 Act had later confirmed: "According to the view of the people themselves, 57 acres per head are necessary for the maintenance of a family in comfort, whereas, with the exception of Bracedale, there is no parish in Skye or the Long Island where the proportion of acreage to population comes near this figure, while the average number of acres per head over these islands is only 19.43 acres."[66]

He later made the same point more forcefully: "If the Land League doctrine of 'migration' at the expense of the State were carried into effect, and the whole of the land now under sheep or deer were distributed among people now possessed of little or no land, each family would have a croft worth little more than £4, or not more than one fifth or one sixth of what is absolutely necessary to afford a chance of decent maintenance."[67]

Although there is some argument for the contrary view, it is difficult to dissent from Lord Lothian's substantive judgment. The deer forests and sheep walks made the problem far worse than it need have been, and served as a great irritation to people who were desperately short of land, but they were not at the root of the problem. It was generally agreed that the population of the islands must be greatly reduced by emigration. Both public and private schemes of emigration were devised, and the people came to accept the inevitability of this unhappy solution.

Other measures were taken. The opening of railways, such as the lines to Mallaig and Kyle, was a considerable boon. Some Highland landowners made substantial grants of land, in the spirit of their resolutions in 1885. In 1892, an Act with similar aims to Balfour's Irish Act of the previous year was passed for the crofting parts of Scotland. County Councils in the "Crofting Counties" were empowered to purchase land by voluntary agreement with landlords, and then to sell or lease it to crofters. The Act had some effect in dealing with congestion, but it was far less successful in its parallel aim of encouraging peasant proprietorship. The only place where the opportunity was taken up was at Glendale in Skye, and there it seems to have been a failure.[68] An Act of 1897 set up a Scottish Congested Districts Board, with power to administer an annual grant of £35,000 for a variety of purposes, including roads, fishing, the provision of land for crofts, and migration to other parts of Scotland.

By the time that the Crofters' Commission came to issue its final report, in 1913, the improvement seemed, at first sight, truly startling: "Any one acquainted with the housing conditions in the rural districts of the West Coast and islands twenty-five to thirty years ago, and who revisited those districts today, could scarcely realise the improvement that has taken place . . . The black hovels in which too many of the people lived are now passing away, and have been replaced by smart, tidy cottages which would do credit to any part of the country."

Yet it would be wrong to imagine that the country had been made economically viable on a redistribution or wiser use of its own resources, or even through the injection of public money as capital. The Commission added that: "The crofter sends his sons and daughters to the large cities of the south and to the colonies, and if they prosper they are mindful of, and dutiful to, their parents at home. They are the source from which the money now invested in stone and lime comes." One can hardly conclude that a really healthy economy had been created in the Highlands when their apparent prosperity depended on the sense of filial duty felt by younger people who lived many miles away.

This, then, was the strange result of the Highland agitation. The places where the exciting disturbances of the 1880s took place slid again into the backwaters of history; much happier than before, but no more significant to the main course of events. Yet people in other places were stirred to their depths by these happenings, and the rest of the country would not forget the consequences of those stirrings.

Notes-5

1 Thus, the Irish potato yield had been only 1.3 tons per acre in 1879, but it was never less than 3.1 tons per acre in the period 1883-8. Mitchell & Deane, *op. cit.*, p. 92.

2 Salisbury to Queen Victoria, 13 June 1887 (copy). S. D/87 p. 516.

3 Memorandum (? author) to Cabinet, 14 August 1886. CAB 37/14/40.

4 Peter Davis, "The Liberal Unionist Party and Irish Policy 1886-1892", *Historical Journal*, xviii (1975), at p. 87.

5 Sir Michael Hicks-Beach's memorandum to Cabinet, 4 October 1886. CAB 37/18/46.

6 *Ibid.*

7 Rents fixed by subcommissioners had been reduced by 20.5 per cent in the year ending 22 August 1882, but by lesser sums each year down to 1885, when the reduction was 18.1 per cent. In 1886, however, the reduction was 24.1 per cent. Reductions fixed by courts declined from 22 per cent to 19.6 per cent in 1882-5, but in 1886 were 22.5 per cent. Cowper Report, p. 6.

8 *Freeman's Journal*, 8 December 1886.

9 Michael Davitt, *The Fall of Feudalism in Ireland* (see bibliog.), pp. 516-19. See also F. S. L. Lyons, "John Dillon and the Plan of Campaign 1886-1890", *Irish Historical Studies*, 14 (1964-5), pp. 313-47.

10 See speech of John Pinkerton MP, *Freeman's Journal*, 23 December 1886.

11 Salisbury to Queen Victoria, 13 June 1887 (copy). S. D/87 p. 516.

12 Salisbury to Queen Victoria, 13 July 1887 (copy). S. D/87 p. 524. Chamberlain to A. J. Balfour, 30 March 1887 (copy). JC 5/5 fo. 42.

13 Salisbury to Queen Victoria, 9 August 1887 (copy). S. D/87 p. 533.

14 Peter Davis, *op. cit.*, at p. 89.

15 Balfour to Salisbury, 21 September 1887. S. E.

16 Peter Davis, *op. cit.*, at p. 92.

17 John (Viscount) Morley, *Life of Gladstone*, ii (see bibliog.), p. 466.

18 A. J. Balfour's memorandum to Cabinet, 20 February 1889. CAB 37/23/5.

19 F. S. L. Lyons, "John Dillon and the Plan of Campaign 1886-1890", *supra*.

20 A. J. Balfour's memorandum to Cabinet, 20 February 1889. CAB 37/23/5; F. S. L. Lyons, *John Dillon* (see bibliog.), pp. 109, 345.

21 *The Times*, 31 December 1887.

22 A. J. Balfour's memorandum to Cabinet, 7 November 1888. CAB 37/22/33.

23 A. J. Balfour's memorandum to Cabinet, 30 January 1889. CAB 37/23/3.

24 CAB 37/22/33; CAB 37/23/3.

25 A. J. Balfour's memorandum to Cabinet, May 1889. CAB 37/25/31.

26 Cowper Report, p. 7.

27 *Annual Register* 1888, p. 206-7.

28 Peter Davis, *op. cit.*, at p. 98.

29 J. L. Garvin, *Life of Joseph Chamberlain*, ii (see bibliog.), p. 307.

30 Patrick Buckland, *Irish Unionism 2: Ulster Unionism and the Origins of Northern Ireland 1886-1922* (see bibliog.), pp. 23-4.

31 L. P. Curtis, jr, *Coercion and Conciliation in Ireland 1880-1892* (see bibliog)., p. 345.

32 A. J. Balfour's memorandum to Cabinet "Suggestions towards a scheme for land purchase in Ireland", May 1889. CAB 37/25/31.

33 Salisbury to Balfour, 1 November 1889. AJB 49,689 fos. 79-80.

34 Peter Davis, *op. cit.*, at p. 100.

35 William O'Brien, *An Olive Branch in Ireland* (see bibliog.), p. xxii.

36 H. A. Robinson (Irish Local Government Board) to his father, 28 June 1887 (copy). Balfour papers, B.M. 49,688, fos. 141-43.

37 A. J. Balfour's explanatory memorandum to Cabinet, 8 February 1890. CAB 37/26/8.

38 James Hunter, "The politics of highland land reform 1873-1895", *Scottish Historical Review*, 53 (1974), at p. 58.

39 J. L. Gavin, *Life of Joseph Chamberlain* ii (see bibliog.), p. 307.

40 *North British Daily Mail*, 26, 27 July, 1 September 1886, etc.

41 *The Skye Expedition of 1886: its constitutional and legal aspects*, speech by Charles Cameron MP at City Hall, Glasgow, 10 November 1886, printed as a pamphlet by NLF of Scotland. Copy, with notes in ink by William Ivory, sent to A. J. Balfour, 30 January 1887. Ivory GD/1/36/4.

42 Report by Sheriff to Commissioners of Supply in Inverness-shire, 27 April 1886. Ivory GD/1/36/12/1. Ivory gives a slightly different figure from Cameron for the rate arrears.

43 Ivory to I. G. Hamilton, 3 September 1886 (copy). Balfour 49,800 fos. 129-30.

44 Balfour/Ivory correspondence, 3-31 October 1886. Balfour 49,800 fos. 132-39, 160-63.

45 Balfour to Salisbury, 19 (or 17?) October 1886. S. E.

46 Kellas, *op. cit.*, p. 286.

47 Correspondence on Lothian. GD/40/16/4, fo. 5 ff.

48 *The Times*, 16 February 1888.

49 *The Times*, 13 December 1887.
50 *The Times*, 9 January 1888, etc.
51 *Ibid.*
52 *The Times*, 19 January 1888.
53 R.W.C.P. memorandum for Lord Lothian, 30 January 1888. Lothian GD/40/16/12, fos. 62-9 ("R.W.C.P. Memorandum").
54 *The Times, Glasgow Herald*, 10 January 1888.
55 *The Times*, 4 February 1888.
56 *The Times*, 13 January 1888; *Glasgow Herald*, 18 January 1888.
57 *The Times*, 13 December 1887.
58 On conditions in the Long Island, see letters and enclosures from Ivory, printed for Cabinet, 8 February 1888. CAB 1/1 no. 13B.
59 *The Times*, 31 December 1887, 11 January 1888.
60 *The Times*, 28 November 1888.
61 *Annual Register*, 1889, p. 263.
62 Documents in Lothian papers. GD/40/16/51, fos. 4-20.
63 R.W.C.P. Memorandum.
64 *The Times*, 13 December 1887.
65 *The Times*, 21 December 1888.
66 Memorandum to Cabinet, 10 May 1887. CAB 37/19 no. 29. For a similar view among active land reformers, see John Mackie to J. S. Blackie, 24 November 1883. Blackie 2635, fo. 105-6.
67 Memorandum of 26 July 1888. CAB 37/22 no. 23.
68 D. A. Crowley, *op. cit.*, p. 123, fn.

Moreover the profit of the earth is for all: the king himself is served by the field.

Ecclesiastes v, 9

It was predictable that the revolt in Ireland and the Hebrides should evoke some sort of answering movement in South Britain, particularly among the Celts of Wales. A remarkable agitation did indeed arise; but the Welsh land movement was very different in its objectives from that of Ireland and the Hebrides. There was some protest in England as well, but not very much. Neither in England nor in Wales was any substantial measure of unlawful activity directed against landlords.

As in the Hebrides and Ireland, both language and religion played a substantial part in the land movement of Wales. Rather more than a quarter of the people living in the Principality spoke only Welsh. The religion of the people was overwhelmingly Nonconformist — "over nine tenths of the rustic population", in the view of *The Times*.[1] The conversion of Wales to Nonconformism had taken place within the nineteenth century. The Wesleyans had made no attempt to preach in Welsh before 1800.[2] In the view of one nineteenth century Welsh Nonconformist, the conversion occurred "not by force of abstract reasoning against the Establishments or in favour of the principles of Dissent, but simply because they were compelled to look beyond the pale of the Endowed Church for the means of spiritual instruction which were denied them within its pale".[3]

The main upsurge of Welsh Nonconformism had thus taken place well within the memory of the older people. Welsh Nonconformists were divided into a bewildering variety of sects, but most of these had two features in common. Their services were conducted in the vernacular, which in many parts was Welsh; and their preachers were largely unpaid laymen. Thus there were many men, sprung from the Welsh peasantry, who had acquired experience both in speaking and in organising. The landowning classes of Wales, on the other hand, were predominantly Anglican in religion and English in speech. The Welsh countryman acquired a large contempt for the Church of England, which had contributed little to the evangelisation of his country and which maintained an expensive establishment of salaried divines who addressed half-empty churches. By contrast, the little Bethels and Zions of the various Nonconformist denominations had been built through the people's faith, and were filled with large and enthusiastic congregations.

The land system in Wales was markedly different from that which prevailed in most of England. In 1887, only 10.2 per cent of the cultivated land in Wales was held by freeholders, against 15.5 per cent in England; furthermore, the proportion of Welsh land which belonged to large estates was also greater. In 1872, for example, 55 per cent of the modern Gwynedd was owned by thirty-seven families. Yet this feature was already changing rapidly in the late nineteenth century; the Royal Commission on Welsh land in 1896 reported that most freeholders had achieved that position in the preceding quarter of a century.[4] The typical Welsh farm was worked by a family, with few or no hired labourers. About half of those labourers who were employed actually lived in the farm house,[5] and Welsh farm labourers commonly had a few acres of their own to cultivate. Thus there was a much greater community of feeling between farmers and labourers than in England, and they were far more likely to make common cause against the landlords, or the Anglican Church. English farmers in most parts and at most times tended to be Conservative; Welsh farmers by the late nineteenth century were usually Liberals, and radical Liberals at that.

In the immediate aftermath of the General Election of 1868, there had been widespread evictions of farmers who voted against their landlords' wishes. These prompted a Royal Commission of enquiry, and played a large part in bringing about the Secret Ballot in 1872. The agricultural depression produced its own inevitable tensions. Wales, with a largely pastoral agriculture, was not at first hit so badly as the arable areas, but towards the end of 1883 the depression became much more serious, and persisted for most of the remainder of the century.[6] The Agricultural Holdings Act of 1883 was of very little value to the small Welsh tenants, who could afford few improvements, and were much less disposed to move from holding to holding than were the English farmers.[7]

In February 1884, contact was made between Michael Davitt

and a group of Welsh land reformers, including the Rev. Evan (Pan) Jones, editor of the monthly *Cwrs y Byd,* to discuss forming a Welsh land movement, parallel with those which had already appeared in Ireland and Scotland.[8] There were no immediate and spectacular results; although at the 1885 General Election land seems to have been a major issue in Wales, especially in the north of the country.[9] Chamberlain, however, may well have alarmed Liberals of the older type as much as he enthused the young radicals.[10] Down to the end of 1885 the Welsh land movement seems to have been impeccably "constitutional", operating through the ordinary political channels, and there was no agitation remotely comparable with the disturbances which had been endemic for years in Ireland, and had recently occurred in the Hebrides.

As in Ireland and the Hebrides, 1886 was a year of considerable turbulence in Wales. Right at the beginning of the year, the Welsh land question suddenly took a completely new twist — or rather, two new twists almost simultaneously. In the middle of January, *The Times* reported: "In Caernarvonshire the farmers have met and formed a local land league. At Holywell in Flintshire the farmers are still more determined; not merely do they meet in increasing numbers every Friday, but they are establishing branches of their League in adjoining districts. In one Merionethshire district the farmers have refused to pay their 'high rents' and insist on abatement. In Carmarthenshire the farmers are preparing to form a League, and at Aberystwyth a 'Welsh political union' is to be established, and 'political union' and 'land league' are here convertible terms. Steps will, I am informed, be taken to extend the ramifications of this union into Cardiganshire and Merionethshire, and to come to an understanding with the other Leagues formed in other parts of the Principality. Last, but not least, comes the intelligence from the Rev. Michael Jones that Mr Michael Davitt is coming to Wales next month to gather up the scattered fragments of organisation and establish the Welsh Land League."[11] The association of Davitt with Michael Daniel Jones was important. Jones had been the leading figure in the establishment of Welsh settlements in Patagonia in the 1860s — a venture which was apparently achieved on a most democratic financial basis[12] and he was very much the hero of an older generation of land reformers. Davitt had acquired from his work in Ireland an immense reputation as a stormy petrel — a "dangerous man" for all social and political establishments in the Kingdom.

Davitt addressed at least two meetings in Wales that February. The first was in Flint, where he spoke along with Dr G. B. Clark (who had recently been returned as "Crofters'" MP for Caithness); the second in Blaenau Festiniog, along with Michael Jones. This meeting is memorable as the first noted public appearance of a young Criccieth solicitor, David Lloyd George, who delivered himself of the opinion that: "Working men acting separately, were only as particles of sand to resist the power of the landlord; but let workmen combine, firmly express their opinion, and then no opposition, however powerful, would be able to stand before them. When a Land League was started for Wales he hoped they would all join it"[13]

Another young Welsh Liberal who was also in friendly contact with Davitt at this time was Tom Ellis, who was soon to become MP for Merioneth, and eventually Liberal Chief Whip.[14]

Some of the local "land leagues" refused to have anything to do with an organisation associated with Davitt;[15] but in any case, before the proposed Welsh Land League could be formed, it had already been overtaken by events. What altered the situation was not so much any political upheaval associated with Irish Home Rule (for Wales and the Welsh MPs were overwhelmingly Gladstonian) — but the inception of the Welsh "Tithe War".

Tithes were compulsory payments to the established Anglican Church. They had long been a ground of general complaint in Wales, but they had hardly formed an acute problem. They were paid by the occupier in the form of a money rentcharge. The burden of tithes varied greatly from place to place; but one Welsh valuer contended that the incidence was usually between one fourth and one fortieth of the rent.[16] Although this sum was relatively small, it was particularly resented, especially at a time when farmers were in real fear of bankruptcy.

The agitation began more or less by accident. Just before the audit of January 1886, a deputation of farmers waited upon the Rector of Llandrynog, Denbighshire (Clwyd), and asked for a reduction in tithes. The Rector referred them to his agents. Apparently the Rector had a quite honest lapse of memory, and when the farmers came to pay their tithes, the agent said that they had had no instructions on the subject. The farmers promptly refused to pay any tithes at all, and from that moment forth the movement spread rapidly.[17] The only remedy available to the clergy was to distrain the stock of the defaulting farmers — a procedure which began in August at Llanarmon. Auctioneers attempting to sell distrained stock were met with "howls of execration"; but the farmers' losses were more than met by public subscriptions. Early in September, an Anti-Tithe League was established at Ruthin.[18] The League was designed for the whole of North Wales, although for a considerable time the main activities took place in and near the Vale of Clwyd. The main inspiration of the movement appears to have come from Thomas Gee — Nonconformist minister, publisher, journalist and an avowed advocate of the "Three Fs".[19]

In the following year, 1887, the situation became far worse. At Llangwm, in Flintshire, there were considerable disturbances in May; while at Mochdre, in the same county, there was a riot on 27 June which led to the reading of the Riot Act, and a conflict in which fifty civilians and thirty-four policemen were injured. In its Annual Report, the Anti-Tithe League's successor disclosed that "about 300 farmers who were members have had their stock distrained upon, and many actual sales have taken place, but all the losses which have been suffered and all the costs which have been incurred have been paid in full, including the costs of our solicitors for attending sales etc. for the protection of our members".

Another very serious disturbance occurred in May 1888 at Llanefydd, Denbighshire, where the police seem to have lost their heads and attacked a miscellaneous crowd. Before the year was out, the agitation had extended into Caernarvonshire, and again distraint sales were held — this time in Llannor parish, at the instance of the vicar of Pwllheli. The farmers were by no means lacking in humour; at one place the distraining party was confronted with an effigy of a drunken cleric, with the Welsh inscription "This is what we do with the tithes"; at another with the effigy of a surpliced clergyman wearing shooting boots. The farmers were also quite rough; the auctioneer was pushed into the water at one village and pelted with clods of earth at another.[20]

In 1889 the agitation spread into South Wales, and there were disturbances in Pembrokeshire and Cardiganshire, some of which, at least, seem to have been exacerbated by police incompetence.[21] They continued for a long time; the Welsh Land Commission, reporting in 1896, indicated that forced sales and conflicts with the police were still going on in parts of Cardiganshire,

100

notably at Pembryn.[22]

At an early stage, the Anti-Tithe League was linked with the incipient "Land League" movement. In the autumn of 1887, the Anti-Tithe League was reconstituted as the "Welsh Land, Commercial and Labour League", which not only agitated against tithes, but also demanded "fair rents, fixity of tenure, full compensation for improvements, land courts (or a system of arbitration), limitation of mining royalties, abolition of state loans to landowners, but the grant of such loans for the purchase of land by occupying tenants and labourers, the abolition of all game laws and the throwing open of rivers to all fishermen".[23] This seems very much like the aims of the land movements in Ireland and the Hebrides, and suggests that land reformers of the familiar kind were gaining control of the Welsh anti-tithe movement.

The land reformers also promoted their campaign within the Liberal Party. In October 1887, the Liberal Federations which had recently been set up for North and South Wales were both committed to a programme which meant virtually the application of the "Three Fs" to Wales.[24]

The leading figures in the tithe agitation, and in the general land movement, made determined attempts to capture the whole Liberal organisation in Wales. Liberals of the older kind felt they were caught in a cleft stick. Stuart Rendel, who had won Montgomeryshire from the Conservatives in 1880, received a letter from a like-minded friend, who wrote gloomily that: ". . . The movement will go on and if we drop it the control will pass into other hands. If they are successful we are eclipsed; if they fail they will do so by encouraging violence and personal bullying of individual parsons. That will be a disaster to the party of which we shall not escape the blame."[25]

While the anti-tithe movement was developing in Wales, a movement against tithes also made its appearance in England. The objectives, however, were different. In the view of John Lloyd, member of the London County Council and Chairman of the Tithe Question Association: "The Welsh have their grievance, and the English corn-growing counties have theirs, the one religious and the other pecuniary, and, if just, both should be redeemed when the law is amended . . ."[26]

The Welsh were very anxious to emphasise that they did not object to paying tithes, but to the use for which tithes were employed. Nonconformist farmers were quite happy that the money should be collected, provided that it was used for "secular and national" purposes, and not for the support of the Anglican Church.[27]

In spite of the fundamental difference of objective between the Welsh tithe agitation and the much weaker tithe agitation in England, the Government did not apply different treatment to the two countries. They sought to stop the tithe agitation without making any concessions of substance which would undermine either the revenues or the establishment of the Church in the Principality.

The first attempt to deal with the situation by legislation was a miserable failure. Lord Salisbury himself confessed to the Queen "that . . . the Bill has come to an end by no means creditable to Your Majesty's advisers. It was a complication of blunders".[28]

Another Bill, however, was brought forward in 1890, and carried in the next year. The Bill provided that tithes should be payable not by the occupier but by the owner of land. This made it very difficult for the Welsh Nonconformists to continue their campaign. Direct payment of tithe served as a constant reminder to the tenant-farmer that he was contributing to the upkeep of a Church which he certainly considered alien, and perhaps heretical. Perceiving that the Bill's passage would vitiate their object, the Welsh MPs resisted it strenuously — but unsuccessfully. East Anglian farmers, who were often far more heavily tithed than the Welshmen, sought to limit the incidence of tithes to half the annual value of the land instead of two-thirds, as proposed in the Bill; but they also were defeated. The Bill passed into law substantially in the form which the Government had proposed. The great majority of farmers thenceforth paid their tithes as if they were part of the rent — no doubt with grumbles, but without effective resistance; and the trouble largely subsided.

The Welsh land agitation died down, but was not forgotten. Opposition to the Anglican Church remained strong, and even bitter, right down to its final disestablishment in the Principality in 1920. Welsh opinion could easily be roused on political questions which seemed connected with land, and in the various "land campaigns" which were launched during the twentieth century, Wales evinced special enthusiasm. In one vital respect, however, the effect of the Welsh land movement extended far beyond the Principality, for it gave immense impetus to the career of David Lloyd George, whose first recorded office was as Secretary of the

South Caernarvonshire Anti-Tithe League in 1887.[29] Lloyd George has been accused — sometimes justly — of the most incredible political gyrations; but the antipathy to landlordism which he acquired as a very young man in Wales remained constant throughout his career, and was to exert a most massive effect on the whole course of politics.

The various Celtic land movements of the late 1880s produced only a faint echo in England and the South of Scotland. Although there was a short period of heavy unemployment, real wages rose steadily and rapidly from 1884 to 1890.[30] This affected not only the industrial workers but the farm workers as well, for it meant that there was alternative employment available in the towns, and therefore wages in the countryside were bound to rise as well. People were not under extreme pressures, and there is little or nothing comparable with the semi-revolutionary activities of the Celtic peasants. Unlike some of the measures applied to the "Celtic fringe", the English land legislation of the period was not extracted from a reluctant Government by external pressure, but represented a free application by the Government of policies which its own members desired to set into operation.

In the first half of the decade, the peasant-proprietorship movement had inevitably attracted interest among farm labourers and over-rented tenant farmers. We have already seen how this influenced Chamberlain's *Radical Programme,* and the election results of 1885. In the latter part of the decade the same idea persisted in the form of a movement in favour of allotments and smallholdings. Balfour, with his remarkably acute mind, recognised that the questions of allotments and smallholdings were in fact "entirely unrelated. A Smallholdings Bill aims at creating a Peasant Proprietary; an Allotments Bill aims at improving the position of the agricultural labourer *while leaving him in the position of an agricultural labourer.*"[31] This distinction, however, was not generally appreciated for a long time, and the movements for allotments and smallholdings were in practice very closely associated.

Allotments for agricultural labourers were no new thing.[32] In the brief Conservative administration of 1885-6, Balfour suggested further allotment provisions, although some of his recommendations were firmly vetoed by his uncle.[33] When the Conservatives returned to office in the middle of 1886, they were under great and effective pressure from the Liberal Unionists, who were much influenced by the ideas of Chamberlain and Jesse Collings.

Collings was more than the close associate of Joseph Chamberlain; he symbolised the type of man whom the Conservatives would need to attract and hold if they were to remain in office. The son of farm workers, he had achieved a successful career in business before turning to politics. He was the author of the "three acres" doctrine in the *Radical Programme*, and it was on his resolution that Salisbury's first government had been defeated at the beginning of 1886. Collings was the founder of the Rural Labourers' League, which he took over with him into the Liberal Unionist camp at the time of the Liberal schism. It was he, and the League which he founded, who were the most active proponents of the idea that allotments and smallholdings should be made available for agricultural labourers.

In 1887, the new Government gave practical evidence of support for Collings's doctrines by passing an Allotments Act. This empowered local authorities to purchase land for allotments, principally for farm labourers, and proved a major landmark in the development of the allotments system. Balfour — a good deal less tender towards recalcitrant landowners than the Prime Minister — even secured provisions for compulsory acquisition of land; but in fact this power was very seldom used. An amending Act was carried three years later, which allowed an appeal to the County Court when sanitary authorities had failed to exercise their compulsory powers.

The smallholdings question also attracted the attention of the Government, and there, too, the hand of the Liberal Unionists may be seen. In 1888, Jesse Collings introduced a Private Member's Bill which sought to empower local authorities to acquire land for smallholdings between one and forty acres in extent. Collings proposed that a quarter of the value should be paid by the smallholder on entry, while the remainder should constitute a permanent mortgage. The avowed object was to assist men who had already proved themselves sufficiently successful to amass a substantial sum of money, or, alternatively, to be regarded by others as creditworthy — and deliberately to exclude men who sought smallholdings as an escape from a career of failure. Collings's Bill proceeded to its Second Reading, but the debate was adjourned and not resumed.

Yet this did not indicate disinterest or opposition on the part of the Government. In fact, some profound change seems to have entered Conservative thinking on smallholdings in the short period since they were last in office. At the beginning of 1886, Henry Chaplin, one of the most authoritative Conservative spokesmen on agricultural matters, had argued forcefully against peasant proprietorship — which, in his contention, had signally failed in other European countries where it had been tried.[34] Perhaps under the persuasion of an altered Parliamentary situation, the Conservatives were no longer intransigent, and after Collings's Bill they showed sufficient interest to set up a Select Committee to examine the question, with Chamberlain as Chairman. When this Committee reported in 1890, it proposed that County Councils should receive powers to purchase land for smallholdings, and to borrow money from public funds up to £5 millions in the first instance. The land should be let in smallholdings not exceeding ten acres in extent, the purchasers providing at least one-fifth of the money as a lump sum.[35] Collings introduced another Smallholdings Bill to implement the Select Committee's recommendations. It received a Second Reading in March 1891, but was not proceeded with further.

A Government Bill on the subject was produced later in the same year. As on the allotments question, the Government was much vexed whether or not to introduce compulsion; but here they gave a different answer. The argument for compulsion was a good deal weaker in the case of smallholdings than that of allotments. An allotment must be near a man's existing home; while a man who is proposing to become a smallholder will usually need to move house in any case. A single landowner could effectively block allotments for a whole village, while he could scarcely exert much effect on the progress of the smallholdings movement. Chamberlain tried nevertheless to force the Government to apply compulsion;[36] but on this occasion his pressure was resisted.

When the Government brought forward its Bill in 1891, Chaplin, now President of the Board of Agriculture, had undergone a complete change of opinion. The object which he now avowed was "to recreate the class of yeomen". In its new form, the Bill proposed to empower the County Councils to purchase land and to dispose of it in smallholdings of up to fifty acres in extent. One quarter of the money would be paid at once by the incoming smallholder, a quarter would remain as a perpetual rentcharge, while the remainder would be paid in instalments or by terminable annuities. This Bill became law; but it was a great deal less effective than the Allotments Act of 1887 had been. Other small-holding legislation was introduced by the Liberals in the twentieth century; but none of these measures produced an effect comparable with the Irish Land Purchase Acts in establishing a widespread peasant-proprietorship. One is left with the persistent feeling that the idea of smallholdings, although strongly held by some intellectual thinkers and politicians, and initially popular among the more ambitious farm workers, had not struck very deep roots among the proposed beneficiaries.

Thus politicians of various kinds were willing to pass legislation which, to a degree, might benefit the farm labourers. There was very little sign, however, that the rural workers in England would take effective collective action to advance their own interests, as their Celtic brethren had done. Even their Trade Union activities were not conspicuously successful. The more enterprising among them were inclined to "vote with their feet", and betake themselves and their families to the towns or the colonies.

An interesting attempt was made by outside enthusiasts to stir up the English farm workers. In the course of 1890-1, the English Land Restoration League tried to convert agricultural labourers to the doctrines of Henry George, through the operation of its "red vans". A series of village meetings was held in Suffolk, and later in many other parts of the country. The League's report for 1891 describes the procedure: "The van arrives at each village early in the forenoon and is stationed in some prominent position. A notice of the meeting is exhibited — the meeting being also advertised by placards in advance — and some large pictures representing the workings of landlordism are shown. A thorough distribution of suitable leaflets is made in the village. The meetings are held in the open air at 7.30 and are attended by from 100 to 300 labourers. . . . The lecturers report that the labourers everywhere welcome the van with enthusiasm and so far there has been an almost complete absence of opposition."[37]

The Land Nationalisation Society began a very similar line of activity on a smaller scale, using "yellow vans", which began to tour in March 1891.[38] The two movements had noticeably different ideas, but seem to have avoided conflict — save in the pages of their respective publications — and to a considerable extent they even co-operated actively.[39]

After a time, the coloured vans encountered a measure of opposition. Often difficulties were placed in the way of people who tried to hold meetings, and once or twice there was some trouble with roughs. The landlord interest was galvanised to engage in counter-propaganda through a body sonorously entitled the Liberty and Property Defence League. It is doubtful, however, whether any of these kinds of opposition really contributed substantially to the eventual decline of the rural campaign. The "red van" accounts of the Land Restoration League balanced at about £900 a year in the middle 1890s, but this was the zenith. It appears that the venture was dependent on a few substantial contributions, and when the Treasurer, William Saunders, MP, died in 1895, the "red van" work declined rapidly. In the course of 1901-2, the remaining "red vans" were disposed of,[40] and these activities ceased. The "yellow vans" appear to have been discontinued at about the same time.

The dismal results secured by the coloured vans may be attributed to two main causes. In the first place, the campaign turned on a few enthusiasts, and never received the active support of major politicians. The Liberal leaders, in particular, were far too busily employed in the congenial task of obstructing each other's work to do anything so useful. Branches of local Land and Labour Leagues were indeed established;[41] yet it is difficult to see how they could hope to be effective without either a high-powered central organisation, or else some immediate and tangible objective. No doubt, many farm labourers were impressed by the arguments they had heard; but what were they to do about it? If a limited number of constituencies had been worked, and strong Parliamentary candidates had been advanced (as the crofters had done in the 1880s), there was at least the possibility of establishing a substantial pressure group in the House of Commons; but, as it was, the effort was largely wasted.

Although the rural land movements in different parts of the United Kingdom showed immense variations during the period 1886-1892, certain common features may be seen in all of them. In the middle 1880s, illegal and violent activities were widespread in the Celtic areas, and could easily have become general throughout the country as a whole. Gradually, these disturbances were

107

contained: partly by ameliorative legislation; partly by force; occasionally through wise concessions by the landowning classes; but to a much greater extent through the gradual adjustments which all classes made to the changed conditions of world markets. By 1892, violence was the exception rather than the rule. There was no fear of a revolutionary situation, or of public disorder on a scale too large for the organs of government to contain with ease.

By common consent of serious politicians in all Parties, much remained to be done, both through legislation and through administration. It was generally agreed that tenants of agricultural land should have substantial security of occupation, at least so long as they did their job properly; and many people were prepared to go further, and urge that the tenant should be enabled to acquire the fee simple of his holding if he so desired. It was also universally held that farm labourers and other landless men should have a real opportunity to acquire some land as a smallholding, or at least as an allotment. The special problem which was presented by those areas where the land was inadequate for the people's needs had been raised and understood. There was every reason for believing that future governments of whatever composition would try various expedients to reduce the remaining grounds of complaint among the rural populations; although it was unlikely that they would pursue any of the really drastic remedies which the various enthusiasts continued to propose.

Thus the rural land problem was no longer likely to produce acute and violent crises — at least so long as relative prosperity persisted. Land reformers were beginning to take the advice of Shaw Maxwell, and to see the land problem as one whose principal implications were for the urban areas.

Notes-6

1 *The Times*, 16 January 1886.
2 Thomas Rees, *History of Protestant Nonconformity in Wales* (see bibliog.), p. 448.
3 Henry Richard, *Letters on the social and political condition in the principality of Wales* (see bibliog.), p. 2.
4 John Davies, "The end of the great estates and the rise of free-

hold farming in Wales", *Welsh History Review*, 7 (1974), at pp. 187-88.

5   For a general description of conditions in Wales, see *Land in Wales and Monmouthshire*, Reports Commissioners 1896 (20) vol. xxiv ("Welsh Land Commission"), *passim*.

6   *Ibid*., p. 173.

7   Compare J. W. Willis Bund, *Law of compensation for unexhausted agricultural improvements.* . . . (2nd edition) (see bibliog.), p. 15.

8   T. W. Moody, "Michael Davitt and the British Labour Movement 1882-1906", *Trans. Royal Historical Society*, 5s (1952), 3, pp. 53-76, at p. 62.

9   Welsh Land Commission, p. 173.

10 S. Rendel to A. C. Humphreys-Owen, 4 February 1885. Rendel 19,461 C, fo. 248.

11 *The Times*, 16 January 1886.

12 Jones to Thomas Gee, 21 April 1866. Gee 8303D, fo. 129.

13 At Blaenau, 12 February 1886; report in *Cambrian News*. LG (B) A/6/2/1. The meetings are reported (but not Lloyd George's speech) in *The Times*, 12, 13 February 1886.

14 Davitt to Ellis, 1 March 1886. D. R. Daniel, fo. 63.

15 Notably in the Vale of Conway and Montgomeryshire. *The Times*, 13, 16 February 1886.

16 D. P. Davies to T. E. Ellis, 28 April 1888. Ellis, fo. 227.

17 *The Times*, 16 September 1886.

18 *The Times*, 23, 27 August, 1, 7, 8 September 1886.

19 Humphreys-Owen to Rendel, 28 November 1886. Rendel 19,461C, fo. 312.

20 *Glasgow Herald*, 17 December 1888; *The Times*, 17 December 1888.

21 G. A. Godfrey to Rendel, 7, 14 May, 2 June 1889. Rendel 19,450C, fos. 198-200.

22 Welsh Land Commission, p. 175.

23 *Ibid*., p. 174.

24 *Ibid*.

25 A. C. Humphreys-Owen to Rendel, 24 November 1889. Rendel 19,463C, fo. 511.

26 Lloyd to Rendel, 5 April 1891. Rendel 19,453C, fo. 411.

27 See, for example, *Annual Register*, 1890, p. 253.

28 Salisbury to Queen Victoria, 15 August 1889 (copy). S. D/87, p. 703. An amendment to the Bill was accepted by the Government. The Opposition then contended that this fundamentally altered the character of the Bill. The Speaker upheld their contention and the Bill was withdrawn.

29 Lloyd George to T. E. Ellis, 19 May 1887. Ellis, fo. 679.

30   Mitchell & Deane, *op. cit.*, p. 344, give the average UK real wages, allowing for unemployment (1850=100) as: 1884:138; 1885:140; 1886:142; 1887:149; 1888:155; 1889:161; 1890:169.

31   Memorandum, 29 December 1891. AJB 49,689, fos. 170-87.

32   See discussion on history of allotments, Balfour memorandum, 12 January 1886. Balfour 49,688, fos. 82-7. Chaplin memorandum to Cabinet, 14 January 1886. CAB 37/17/11.

33   Balfour Memorandum, 12 January 1886, *supra*.

34   *Annual Register* 1886, p. 27.

35   See Chaplin's memorandum, 28 November 1890. CAB 37/28/58.

36   Memorandum entitled "Smallholdings", January 1891. JC 5/5, fo. 47.

37   English Land Restoration League, Eighth Annual Report, 1891, p. 12.

38   Land Nationalisation Society Report for year ending 31 March 1891.

39   See, for example, *Single Tax*, July 1894. Later, however, the two movements were much less inclined to co-operate. *Ibid*, April 1899.

40   English Land Restoration League report, 1902 (Nineteenth Annual Report).

41   *Single Tax*, August 1894.

7 FIN DE SIECLE

Those who make private property of the gift of God (land) pretend in vain to be innocent, for in thus retaining the subsistence of the poor they are the murderers of those who die every day for want of it.

St Gregory the Great
Quoted in *Single Tax*, January 1896

Although the late 1880s were marked by a gradual decline in the rural land agitation, the same period also witnessed a great upsurge of interest in the land problem as a matter of urban concern. Two processes were operating simultaneously; on the one hand, moderate political thinkers were becoming interested in land reform, without necessarily receiving much prompting from the extremists; on the other hand some of the extreme land reformers were coming to realise that they could rephrase their arguments in a way which would be attractive to the moderates.

Both the peasant rebels and the intellectual land reformers paid increasing attention to "mainstream" Liberal opinion. Thus, in 1888, the Skye Land League recommended that its branches should affiliate to the Scottish Liberal Association. A year later, the Scottish Liberals recorded — with no apparent signs of distress — that forty-eight of the sixty members of the Liberal committee in Caithness-shire were also members of the local Land Law Reform Association.[1] A proportion of the militants fought a rearguard action against close association with the main body of Liberalism; but after failing to capture the Highland Land League in 1893 they lapsed into insignificance.[2]

The followers of Henry George soon perceived an easy way of presenting their case to a much wider body of people. They came to realise that the reforms which they desired could be brought about by the simple, and by no means terrifying, expedient of an annual tax on the site value of land. With State expenditure below £100 millions a year — as it remained throughout practically all of the nineteenth century — a 100 per cent tax on the annual value of land would not merely produce all the revenue which was required, but would leave a very handsome surplus as well, which could be devoted to measures of social improvement. Thus all other taxes could vanish, and a "single tax" on land values would suffice in their place.[3] The more enthusiastic followers of George came, in the late 1880s, to describe themselves as "Single Taxers". By this term they sought to emphasise that they did not wish to add to the number of taxes, but to employ one tax in place of many. A sharp and complete distinction was made between site values, which they proposed eventually to collect *in toto*, and improvement values, which they would leave quite untouched. If the "Single Tax" was introduced gradually, any errors of assessment which were made in the initial stages of the operation could be adjusted without serious damage or injustice.

Although this term "single taxing" was a very convenient slogan for expressing the aims of the extreme land reformers, it also had the practical disadvantage that it might appear crankish to moderate people who suspected all panaceas. The reformers discovered that they could appeal to men of that kind by simply urging the "taxation of land values". In the early 1880s, the terms "single tax" and "land value tax" had not been used widely, if at all;[4] from 1888 onwards, they appear constantly. This is a striking example of the way in which, without any alteration in the actual proposals made, a movement may suddenly broaden its appeal by devising suitable slogans.

Liberals for their part soon came to realise that the taxation of land values was an attractive banner beneath which to march. They began to feel their way in that direction, rather cautiously at first, and commencing in Scotland. A Conference of the Scottish Liberal Association held in Edinburgh in February 1887, gave its unanimous support to "a reform of the existing land laws" — which, as A. L. Brown, MP for Hawick, explained, meant that "they wanted to deal with those exorbitant ground rents and to put a stop to the way that property in stone and lime was being confiscated in towns under our present leasehold system" — and also that "our laws should secure for every man what he honestly made — and prevent any man from taking what another made."[5]

During the late 1880s and early 1890s, a general system of representative local government was set up throughout the United Kingdom, and public interest in local affairs was greater than it had been for many years, or has ever been since. People were disposed to expect a great deal from the operation of local government. The whole edifice was also so new that quite drastic improvements could be proposed without rousing opposition from people who were normally inclined to resist change of any kind. The land taxers sought to apply their own policies to the special needs of local government. They were not slow to see that rates for local government purposes were already assessed on the value of real property, and that it was only necessary to urge that rates should be assessed on the site value alone and not on the total value of the hereditament. Thus another exceedingly useful slogan emerged: "Site Value Rating", which simply meant land value taxation applied to the special needs of local government.

This idea caught on in many places. A new London evening newspaper, The Star, was an instant success when it appeared in January 1888, and soon had a larger circulation than any other evening newspaper in the country. The Star gave very early support to the doctrine of a "single tax" for national purposes.[6] At the beginning of 1889, the first elections for the new London County Council were held, and The Star declared that: "Taxation of Ground Rents or Values is one of the most popular cries in the election of County Councillors. . . ."[7] Allowance must be made for The Star's own enthusiasm; but there can be no doubt that site value rating had already become a major question in London. The LCC elections of 1889 were highly encouraging. Definite parties had not yet "emerged" in LCC politics; but those candidates whom The Star and other radicals favoured were able to secure a substantial majority, even though London was strongly Conservative for parliamentary purposes.

Predictably, Glasgow was another place where progress was recorded. In February 1890, the Glasgow municipal council set up a Committee to examine the question of site value rating. The report was favourable to the proposal, but it was remitted for reconsideration. Another report to the same effect followed; in June 1891 this was rejected only by the casting vote of the Lord Provost. As we shall later see, the Glasgow City Council eventually became an enthusiastic convert. Glasgow in fact became very much the centre of the land taxing movement, and remained so well into the twentieth century. Henry George made another visit to Britain in 1890, and a new organisation, the Scottish League for the Taxation of Land Values, was set up to promote his ideas. In June 1894 the first issue of a monthly organ, The Single Tax, appeared in Glasgow.[8]

113

The idea of urban land reform in general, and the rating or taxation of land values in particular, became a matter of general interest to Liberals all over the country. In December 1889, the National Liberal Federation Council, meeting at Manchester, carried a resolution embodying no fewer than five distinct kinds of land reform: the time-honoured policy of "freeing the land" from obsolete legal encumbrances; the application of "tenant-right" to compensation for improvements; leasehold enfranchisement; compulsory powers for local authorities to acquire land for allotments and smallholdings; and — most radical of all — the doctrine of land value taxation, set out in terms which Henry George himself could scarcely have criticised.[9]

Two years later, in 1891, the NLF set itself the task of expounding a compendious programme for the forthcoming General Election — the famous "Newcastle Programme". The ideas of land reform which had been promulgated at Manchester were repeated,[10] among a very wide range of reforms in other fields. On the same evening, Gladstone delivered a speech which formally commended a large part of the "Newcastle Programme" — so much, indeed, that The Times scolded him for being "mere showman of the wares turned out by the caucus". Not all of the land proposals were mentioned by Gladstone, and the taxation of land values is a very significant omission; but the public tended, not unreasonably, to consider that he had given at least a nihil obstat to the whole Programme. In fact he had done nothing of the kind. A year or so earlier, he had said some very scathing things about Henry George;[11] but by this time most of the Liberal enthusiasts were keen land reformers who sought to claim Gladstone as one of themselves, while the Conservatives were only too anxious to show that he was tarred with the brush of George's "revolutionary" doctrines. While such proposals were being ventilated in the Liberals' own organisations, the Opposition parliamentarians also sought to raise them in one form or other in the House of Commons. R. B. Haldane, who was by no means a single taxer, brought forward a Bill in the spring of 1890, and another two years later, which were designed to give local authorities power to collect a measure of land value increments. The particular concern which Londoners had shown for the taxation of ground rents in 1889 prompted other Liberals to propose Bills designed for the capital alone. Predictably, none of these Liberal proposals proceeded to enactment — indeed, not all Liberals

114

were happy about them — but they were evident signs of public interest.[12]

The Conservative Parliament of 1886 nearly ran its full legal course and the next election took place in 1892. A glance through the election addresses of the Liberal candidates who stood at the General Election of 1892 shows that a considerable number of them (although by no means all) were taking their cue from the "Newcastle programme", and were treating this as a more or less authoritative statement of Liberal policy — as one candidate called it, "the Newcastle programme of the Liberal Party".[13] Liberal candidates everywhere, but especially in London, made frequent reference to the taxation of ground rents and mining royalties, and at least one of them called for "the nationalisation of the land".[14] Keir Hardie, who was returned at the election for West Ham South as the first independent "Labour" MP (or "Labour, Radical and Home Rule", as he described himself), laid his main emphasis on land reform. An interesting example of the changing use of words is provided by Hardie's declaration that he favoured "nationalising the land by taxing land values" — a statement which both land nationalisers and land value taxers would have considered to be a contradiction in terms a few years later.

The General Election of 1892 gave no very clear verdict. The Liberals, with 273 seats, almost exactly balanced the Conservatives with 269, and a working majority could be obtained only by linking the eighty-one highly fissile Irish Nationalists to the Liberals; while the forty-six Liberal Unionists were by this time more or less completely bound to the Conservatives. In August 1892, Gladstone, well advanced in his eighty-third year, formed his fourth and last administration.

None of the radical land reformers was in a commanding position through his own personality, although H. H. Fowler (who had seconded the land resolution at Newcastle) was sufficiently important to be given a seat in the Cabinet. Yet the land reformers had made immense strides since the Liberals were last in office, and theirs was one of the principal questions which Liberals wished to tackle, once the Home Rule issue had been resolved.

The parliamentary situation was exceedingly unsatisfactory for all parties throughout the lifetime of the 1892 Parliament. The Liberals not only lacked an overall majority, but it was common knowledge that they were deeply divided on both personal and political questions. The Irish Party was even more profoundly split. The Liberal Unionists suffered from the traditional affliction of the mule: they were without pride of ancestry or hope of posterity. The Conservatives had an enormous majority in the Lords, which made it possible for them to harass the Government out of existence, or force it to go to the country, at almost any moment; yet it was not in the Opposition's interest to bring down the administration in circumstances where an appeal to the people would be likely to go in the Liberals' favour. To avoid this risk, they were bound to accept legislation which they disliked and could have blocked had they chosen. Tentative bargains were made from time to time between the Front Benches, which enabled Liberal measures to pass, although often in a form which gave no satisfaction to either side of the House.[15]

Early in 1894, Gladstone resigned the premiership, and was succeeded by the Foreign Secretary, Lord Rosebery; while Gladstone's Chancellor of the Exchequer, Sir William Harcourt, remained in office. Harcourt was under considerable pressure from radicals in the House of Commons to introduce measures bearing on land reform. Early in 1894, for example, the Chancellor received a Memorial from many Radical MPs, urging him to equalise the death duties payable on realty and personalty; for, up to that time, landed property had been assessed at a lower rate than personal possessions. Sir William complied with the request in his Budget that year. The Prime Minister disliked both the proposal and its author, but the Chancellor was able to pilot the necessary measure through Parliament without too much difficulty.

The campaign for land reform did not abate. Not long after the Budget, ninety-four MPs signed another Memorial to the Chancellor, this time urging that municipalities should be authorised to collect their rates on the basis of site values.[16] Lord Rosebery himself apparently gave support to the idea — declaring that the principle was "becoming universally established". He also counselled patience — adding that: "While you make converts like that you need not be afraid if for a session or even two these large principles do not have immediate effect."[17] Long before the two sessions had passed, Rosebery's government was out of office, and its successor had no intention of setting the proposals into legislation.

In the middle of 1895, the Liberals resigned, and Salisbury

formed another Conservative administration. On this occasion, however, the Liberal Unionist leaders were actually incorporated in the administration; yet they were still sometimes disposed to exert independent pressure upon the Conservatives.

The change of government made a General Election necessary. With Gladstone no longer the leader, and Rosebery and Harcourt more or less publicly at loggerheads, the local organs of the Liberal Party had a large measure of autonomy, and causes like land taxing, which were popular among the rank-and-file, featured prominently among the various programmes advanced by the candidates. The Scottish enthusiasts were able — apparently without challenge — to make the astonishing claim that: "Every Liberal candidate in Scotland was pledged to the taxation of land values. Many of them made it the fighting question. In Glasgow seven Liberals, four Labour men and even one Unionist declared for this great reform."[18] The overall results of the election were bad for Liberals of all kinds, and inevitably some of the prominent land reformers were among the casualties. Yet other aspects of that disastrous election were more encouraging for the land taxers. Sir William Harcourt gave public support to the taxation of ground values and mining royalties. Among the few Liberal gains were two recorded by active land-taxers in the south-west of Scotland: Robinson Souttar in Dumfriesshire, and J. G. Holbourn, a self-educated tinplate worker, in N.W. Lanarkshire.

The new Government was now safely established. In general, it had little interest in urban land reform, but much more interest in rural land policies. The urban reformers were in no position to compel action; their main aim was to cultivate public opinion so that the next Liberal administration would comply with their wishes.

The process of persuasion was conducted at various levels. Land taxing was vigorously preached among working-class organisations. Sidney and Beatrice Webb give a vivid picture of how the ideas of Henry George "completely revolutionised" the attitude of the urban workers in the middle 1890s: "Instead of the Chartist cry of 'Back to the Land', . . . the town artisan is thinking of his claim to the unearned increment of urban land values, which he now watches falling into the coffers of the great landlords."[19] The same spirit was evinced at the Cardiff meeting of the Trade Union Congress, which in 1895 urged that: "The taxation of land values and ground rents should be made a test question at the next General Election."[20]

No less striking was the ascendancy which the advocates of land value taxation were acquiring over other groups of land reformers. At a joint conference held by a number of organisations in London in May 1895 — with individuals like Dr G. B. Clark present, and bodies like the Land Nationalisation Society represented — unhesitating assent was given to a resolution in favour of land value taxation.[21]

Socialist organisations were also susceptible to the same influence. The Independent Labour Party (ILP) was founded in 1893, for socialistic objectives; but when it sought to translate these into an actual programme, the land policy of the ILP appeared in the form of a proposal that "Land values, rural and urban (should) be treated as public property"[22] — in other words, the taxation of land values, not the "socialisation" or "nationalisation" of land. So also are the doctrines of George and Wallace frequently found jumbled together in other "socialist" publications of the period, in a manner which shows that neither was fully understood[23] — but which is eloquent witness of the deep and lasting impression which land reform doctrines had exerted on the minds of the working people.

The one direction in which the land reformers had an "outside chance" of persuading the Government to inaugurate urban legislation was in connection with site value rating. Those municipal authorities where the radicals were dominant began to exert pressure, not for a uniform national system of site value rating, but for particular towns to receive authority to conduct the experiment. The campaign began even before the Liberals had left office, and it continued with growing force during the supervening period. In 1894, the London County Council appointed a committee to communicate with the Government in order to promote site value rating in the capital. Then the Glasgow Police Commissioners sought authority "to appropriate, by rating, the future unearned increment of the city to municipal purposes".[24] In 1895, it was the Dundee Council which took the initiative in summoning a convention of delegates from town and parish councils in Scotland. This convention met at the end of the year, and also decided in favour of site value rating.[25] In 1896, the dominant issue of the Glasgow City Council election was site value rating; forty-nine of the seventy-seven members of the Council which was returned were supporters. By the autumn of 1897, it was reported that: "Close upon 140 assessing bodies in England and sixty-three in Scotland have recently pronounced in favour of having powers from Parliament to tax land values for local purposes."[26]

In the years which followed, the movement continued to grow. By the early part of 1906, a petition urging that local authorities should be empowered to levy rates upon site values was sent to the Chancellor of the Exchequer with the support of no fewer than 518 local authorities.[27]

Evidence accumulated from other quarters that the idea of site value taxing, at least for local purposes, was winning support. In the middle of 1901, the Royal Commission on Local Taxation produced its final Report. This covered a wide field of local finance, but the question of urban rating attracted considerable interest. The Commission was severely split; but a substantial minority proposed that a system intermediate between the existing one and full-scale site value rating should be adopted.

This "Minority Report" — as it became known — was exceedingly mild in its proposals. The Commissioners who signed it went so far as to declare that: ". . . if proper regard be had to equitable considerations, the amount capable of being raised by a special site value rate will not be large; and that the proceeds of it, whatever the amount may be, should go in relief of local, not Imperial, taxation." Yet the Minority Report represented some sort of move in the direction which the land taxers desired; and they took particular heart from the fact that one of the signatories was the Chairman of the Commission, Lord Balfour of Burleigh, Secretary of State for Scotland in the Conservative Cabinet. The various opinions expressed by the Commissioners on this and other questions of local finance were sufficiently tentative and disparate to leave the whole question very much open to argument. None of the advocates of any point of view could reasonably claim a consensus of informed opinion in their favour.

The proposal of site value rating was taken up with increasing zest in the House of Commons. In 1902, a bill in favour was moved by C. P. Trevelyan from the Liberal benches, and was defeated by 71 votes on the second reading. A similar bill in the following year, this time moved by Dr T. Macnamara, secured a more encouraging reception; thirteen Government supporters voted with the Liberals and the Irish in favour, and the second reading was rejected by a majority of only thirteen.[28] In 1904, yet another bill actually passed its second reading in an overwhelmingly Conservative House of Commons — securing the support of no fewer than thirty-three Ministerialists.[29] In 1905, a further Trevelyan bill was carried out with a majority of ninety.[30] On these last two occasions, the Government Whips did not tell: but this fact itself is eloquent of the way in which land value rating was winning support, even in Conservative circles. A parallel Bill dealing with Scottish land values also secured a second reading; this will call for further discussion later. These Bills were not allowed to proceed to their later Parliamentary stages, but it appears that MPs who did not like the taxation of land values had become so demoralised that they were unwilling to stand up and be counted. By the early twentieth century, site value rating was scarcely an issue of controversy among Liberals, for practically all the leading figures of the Party had made public statements in favour. So had a considerable number of Liberal Unionists, even including the new Duke of Devonshire, better known under his earlier title of Marquis of Hartington.[31] It had already become quite "respectable" among Conservatives — so much so that local Councils in overwhelmingly Conservative areas like Liverpool and Croydon declared for Trevelyan's Bills.[32]

Politically and socially, the land reform movement in urban areas operated from below upwards: it was a movement of people at the "grassroots" who sought to influence politicians to legislate. Originally, the same had been true of the rural land reform movement. We have seen much of the spontaneous — often violent — action which peasants adopted in many parts of the British Isles during the 1880s. Pressure from below certainly did not cease in the 1890s; but in the last decade of the century the initiative came mainly from above, and was often met with indifference by the people whom it was intended to benefit, or whom (on a more cynical view) the Government sought to mollify in order to avoid trouble in the future.

There are two rather important exceptions — instances where pressure for rural land reform in the 1890s really did come from below. The brief Liberal administration of 1892-5 had the ill-fortune to take office during a period of agricultural depression. In 1892, there was "a harvest much under the average, except in a few favoured districts, coupled with a serious fall in the

120

value of corn, live stock and other leading agricultural products".[33] This revived interest among the tenant-farmers in the "Irish Fs", and made them also press for the abolition of distress for rent. The Government was well conscious of the existence of radical pressure-groups among its supporters, and feared in particular that a land-reforming backbencher, Francis Channing, would introduce a bill which would propose satisfaction for the farmers' demands; a bill certain to evoke strong feelings on both sides, and one which it might be equally inconvenient politically either to support or to oppose. As is very common in such circumstances, a Royal Commission was set up. The Government had considerable difficulty in finding a suitable chairman,[34] but eventually chose the Conservative Henry Chaplin — probably hoping that any legislation based on the Report of such a Commission would prove more or less non-contentious. Unfortunately Chaplin used all available methods to spin out the proceedings, presumably in the hope that the Government would fall before the Report was issued, and the initiative for legislation would devolve on the Conservatives. By the beginning of 1895 the Commission was still sitting, while two more bad years for cereals had "resulted in a real calamity. Rents — already reduced by 50 to 80 per cent — can in some districts hardly be collected at all; and in many parts of the East and South of England, farmers, owing to their necessities, have discharged large numbers of labourers during the winter months".[35]

In February 1895, some of the Liberal backbenchers, including Channing, jumped the gun of the Royal Commission, and introduced a Land Tenure Bill which sought to increase the tenants' rights to improvements, give added security of tenure and abolish the landlords' right to distraint. The Government supported the Bill, which passed its first two Readings. Before its passage could be completed, however, the Government resigned.

The second exception was a matter of even wider interest. One of the most important measures of the Liberal interlude was H. H. Fowler's Parish Council Bill, which passed through its stages in 1893-4. It brought in a number of major innovations, including the establishment of parish and district councils; and a somewhat similar measure was passed for Scotland. Certain features of the Bill had considerable bearing on land policies. On these the Government encountered difficulties, and was forced to make considerable concessions to "buy off" opposition — notably in

121

several of the clauses relating to allotments;[36] while the Conservatives managed to carry an amendment which limited the expenditure of the parish councils to the value of a threepenny rate. This looks, at first sight, like a mere point of administrative detail, but it was really very significant. The effect of the amendment was that parish councils operated on such a small budget that they became of trivial importance in local government. At the parish level, there was a real possibility that farm labourers might actively participate in local government; while considerations of time, distance and expense made it impossible for most of them to attend meetings of rural district or county authorities. The parish councils received, in name, very considerable powers to acquire land for allotments; but on a threepenny rate this power was nugatory. Thus the possibility of using parish councils as a means of securing either public ownership of land on a large scale, or the development of peasant-proprietorship, was vitiated from the start. There is no reason to doubt that the Conservatives had been sincerely converted to the idea of establishing a peasant proprietary; but they did not wish it to be brought about through the agency of local authorities which were largely controlled by farm labourers.

The Conservatives were in office from 1895 until almost the end of 1905. Their rural land legislation falls very sharply into two divisions; a few measures, which were in no sense epoch-making, which were designed for Britain; and some vastly more important legislation by which they sought to extinguish the Irish rural land problem as a live political issue.

The most important British legislation was the Agricultural Rating Act (England and Wales) of 1896. This Act had a rather extraordinary history. The Royal Commission under Henry Chaplin succeeded in spinning out its proceedings while the Liberal Government lasted and acted with peremptory haste as soon as the Conservatives returned, producing an Interim Report early in 1896. This proposed a reduction of rates on agricultural land. Contrary to the usual practice of Royal Commissions, no enquiry had been held on the subject of the Report, and no evidence had been taken from witnesses as to the likely benefits or disadvantages to various interests. Virtually, the procedure of a Royal Commission was used to introduce a new piece of Government policy.

The Government also acted with considerable alacrity, and legislation was passed in the same year to implement the proposals. Agricultural land was to pay only half the normal rates over a period originally set at six years, but which was later protracted beyond the lifetime of the Government. Opponents of the Government, who contended that the ultimate beneficiary would be the landlord and not the tenant-farmer, were able to point to a remarkable admission made by Thomas Usborne, Conservative MP for Chelmsford: "No one has denied, and he hoped no one wished to deny, that the Rating Act was in relief of the landlord and not of the tenant."[37]

The other significant piece of rural land legislation was the Agricultural Holdings Act of 1900. This simplified and cheapened the procedure for settling compensation to the tenant in respect of improvements, and it also met a long-standing subject of complaint by greatly reducing the power of a landlord to distrain for rent on his tenant's property.

To these two measures, we might perhaps add a third, although it only affected a small body of people, and them only to a marginal extent. This was the Tithe Rentcharge Act of 1899, which gave the owners of tithe rentcharges the same rating relief as the 1896 Act had given to most agricultural properties. By this Act, between 10,000 and 11,000 clergymen secured a relief which on average was not more than £5 a year.[38] The Act served as something of an irritant to nonconformist and anti-clerical opinion; it is difficult to see how anyone (including the clergymen and the Government) could have benefited enough to make the whole rather unpopular transaction worthwhile.

Not the least remarkable feature of this period of Conservative ascendancy was the absence of further legislation designed to encourage the development of smallholdings in Great Britain. The existing Acts had produced very limited results; between December 1894 and March 1902, fewer than 222 acres were acquired for the purpose. In the last couple of decades of the nineteenth century, the number of farm workers was dropping at the rate of about 1.5 per cent per year. Yet the greater the decline, the less eager the remaining farm workers became to acquire smallholdings. The dissatisfied farm worker was evidently unwilling to deepen his personal commitment to an occupation in whose future he had little faith.

Although the closing years of the nineteenth century and the first few years of the twentieth were not marked by much important

British land legislation, the Irish legislation of the same period was far more spectacular. The Liberals' Irish policy at the beginning of the 1890s had centred upon Home Rule; and presumably the settlement of the Irish land question would thereafter have devolved on the Irish Parliament which would be set up. When Gladstone's second Home Rule Bill was thrown out by the Lords in 1893, and the Ministers decided not to resign or dissolve Parliament, they were bound to inaugurate some kind of Irish land legislation. A Government bill was introduced early in 1895, by John Morley, Chief Secretary for Ireland. The most important innovation proposed was that the statutory tenancy period should be reduced from fifteen years to ten, but there were also several other modifications to the existing law. The Morley Bill passed its first two readings, but the Government resigned long before its passage was complete.

When the Unionists resumed office in the middle of the same year, the climate was favourable to a settlement. There were three main "interests" involved: the Irish landlords, the Irish peasants and the British people. As we have seen, the Irish landlords had long decided that Ireland would yield few of the spiritual delights of land ownership. The main attraction was the rent, and they had good reason to fear that this rent might one day cease to be paid. If, therefore, they could contrive to sell the land on terms which they considered reasonable, they would probably do so with considerable alacrity. The main concern of most of the peasants — now that the "Three Fs" were firmly established — was to pay as little rent as possible; and if they could also become freeholders, this, no doubt, was all to the good. The peasants living in the Congested Districts had the further interest that they wished to acquire land which would be adequate for their needs. The British people were sick of the turbulence of Ireland and the heavy expenditure involved in maintaining law and order. They were willing to assist practically any settlement which was acceptable to the Irish peasants and landlords, and did not involve more State expenditure than was necessary.

In 1895, there were other considerations which rendered it quite urgent that action should be taken. The funds which had been made available under the land purchase Acts had been taken up with alacrity; but it was by no means clear that sums which might be offered on similar terms in future would be grasped with equal avidity. The rents which had been fixed shortly after the 1881 Act would soon come up for revision, and it was obvious from current prices that the courts would make substantial further reductions. Peasants might very well decide that it was cheaper for them to pay the revised rents than to enter any new land purchase agreements which might be offered. Thus the Government was bound to consider what sums of money should be made available, and on what terms. The situation was further complicated by the fact that the Liberal Unionists were just as willing to set pressure upon the Conservatives to implement "constructive Unionism" as they had been in the 1886 Parliament.[39] Chamberlain exploited Liberal Unionist doubts to the utmost possible extent in his negotiations with the Conservatives in order to secure concessions to the ideas of his own Party; yet not all was bluff by a long way, and many Liberal Unionists in Britain as well as Ireland might well return to their original Party if the Government was not sufficiently radical in dealing with Irish land matters.

The Irish Secretary in the new Government was Gerald Balfour, brother of Arthur. In his view, the judicial rents would be revised downwards by about 20 per cent.[40] He contended that substantial modifications of current and future land purchase bargains were necessary. This opinion was not endorsed by the Treasury; but the Irish Office view prevailed, and a Bill was soon introduced by Gerald Balfour to give effect to his own Department's view, and also to reintroduce some of Morley's proposals.

The new bill did not propose a reduction of the fifteen-year period for judicial rents, but instead authorised applications to be made by either tenants or landlords at five-year intervals if price variations justified them. The main concern, however, was to devise a workable scheme of land purchase. The Government proposed to reduce the debts on existing and future agreements at the end of each of three decennial periods, and for the tenant to pay his 4 per cent towards the interest and repayment of the sum outstanding at the beginning of the decennium, and not on the total original loan. The interest would therefore be reducing, and the loan period would be extended to about seventy years. The sums paid by the purchasing tenant would remain rather less than the fixed rents on comparable properties, even though there were periodic downward revisions of rents. The Irish MPs were given to understand that the fate of the bill depended upon them;

125

if they allowed it through it would pass into law; if they obstruct-
ed it would be dropped, and other kinds of legislation would
receive priority. In fact the Irish did not obstruct, and after some
modifications which did not radically affect its character, the bill
was accepted.

The 1896 Act, like the Act of 1891, was of only limited effect
and, in particular, little was done to tackle the question of the
Congested Districts. The most important step taken in that direction under the two Acts together was the purchase of Clare Island,
and the settlement of ninety-five families.[41]

In the closing years of the century, there were new stirrings
in peasant Ireland. 1897 was a bad year for agriculture, especially
in the west, and at the beginning of 1898 a body nostalgically
called the United Irish League was founded under the leadership
of William O'Brien in the Congested Districts of Co. Mayo, as a
sort of renascent Land League. The United Irish League soon
extended its organisation throughout similar Congested Districts
in Counties Galway, Leitrim and Sligo. By the time the new body
was on its feet, however, prosperity had begun to return. This in
no way impeded the progress of the UIL, but radically altered its
character. It ceased to be concerned with the land problem as such,
but became instead the "organisation of the Nationalist Party
for political purposes".[42] By the end of the century, agrarian crime
was not much over a quarter of what it had been in 1887, yet the
problem of chronic Irish discontent had not been solved. "Constructive Unionism" had to do better than that if the Home Rule
threat was to be averted.

In 1900, Gerald Balfour was succeeded as Irish Secretary by
George Wyndham — a man who lived his rather short life to the
full, and whose contribution to a settlement of the Irish land
problem was probably greater than that of any other incumbent
of his office; yet whose career was eventually wrecked by the
intrigues of lesser men in his own Party. The situation at the
inception of Wyndham's period of office was summed up in a
document which he circulated to the Cabinet: "In spite of . . .
some forty Acts of Parliament, the land question is not pro-
gressing towards a solution. The landlords dread ruin by con-
secutive revision of judicial rents, but are powerless to improve
their property and reluctant to sell it under the existing Acts. The
tenants outside Ulster are not over eager to purchase so long as
they look to reductions of rent at the hands of an army of Sub-

126

Inspectors. . . . The Nationalist agitators advocate the reduction of fair rents to the level of purchase instalments by 'running out' farms and more lawless proceedings in order to compel the breaking up of large farms let to 'graziers'. The landlords counter these attacks on their property by multiplying appeals and keeping as much land as they can out of the Act of 1881 either by holding it themselves or letting it for eleven months to graziers. Fair rent litigation, which has already cost the taxpayer over £2 millions, not to speak of the cost to the parties concerned, must increase in acerbity with each revision and subsequent crop of appeals . . ."[43]

A year later, Wyndham developed his analysis further. Irish Land Acts which dealt with landlord-tenant relations, he argued, had invariably failed; while Acts which "abolish(ed) those relations by enabling the tenant to become an owner" had invariably succeeded. Under those Acts, "over 70,000 tenants have purchased and the State has not lost a penny".[44]

In 1902, Wyndham brought forward a new Land Purchase Bill, which had an unsatisfactory Parliamentary history, and was finally withdrawn. There followed a period of considerable violence in Ireland, in which about half the country was "proclaimed" and subjected to coercion, while eleven MPs were imprisoned.

Not long after these unpropitious events, Wyndham had to make a decision on the appointment of an Under-Secretary for Ireland — that is, the most senior permanent official in the Irish Government. The best-qualified candidate seemed to be Sir Antony MacDonnell, who was at that time serving on the India Council. MacDonnell explained his own position to Wyndham with complete frankness: "I am an Irishman, a Roman Catholic and a Liberal in politics; I have strong Irish sympathies; I do not see eye to eye with you in all matters of Irish administration . . ."[45] So far as the land was concerned, MacDonnell favoured "the solution of the land question on the basis of voluntary sale. Where sale does not operate the fixation of rents on some self-acting principle whereby local inquiries would be obviated". On these terms the appointment was made — as "the colleague rather than the subordinate of the Chief Secretary"[46] — and the two men co-operated very closely. This co-operation was to have a profound effect on the eventual solution of the Irish land problem.

Just before MacDonnell's appointment, a letter had appeared in the Irish newspapers over the signature of a certain Captain Shawe-Taylor, the younger son of a Galway squire and a man completely unknown in politics. Shawe-Taylor invited certain named landlords and certain named Nationalist politicians to a conference in Dublin. There were some important omissions, and Shawe-Taylor spoke for nobody but himself. Wyndham was at first unimpressed,[47] but eventually the Conference was held under the Chairmanship of the Earl of Dunraven, an Irish landlord of moderate views. A remarkable measure of agreement was reached, and a substantial body of proposals emerged, which recommended ways in which land purchase might be encouraged and the special problems of the Congested Districts and evicted tenants might be solved. These proposals were published at the beginning of 1903. They gained a very mixed reception indeed among the Irish leaders, but were soon followed by the Report of the official Inquiry into the functioning of the Land Purchase Acts. This confirmed Wyndham's view that the State had lost nothing by the transactions, and also showed that there had been considerable improvements in cultivation in those areas where tenants were acquiring their own land.

Thus there were some clear indications of an acceptable line of settlement, and Wyndham brought forward a new Government Bill on the subject, which was largely the work of Mac-Donnell. The Bill introduced certain important innovations in order to facilitate sales. When a landlord was willing to sell and at least three-quarters of the tenants were willing to buy, advances could be made by the State in cash, without inquiry as to the commercial wisdom of the transaction. Repayment by the tenant would be over a period of 68.5 years, through a 3.25 per cent annuity. A bonus grant of 12 per cent would be made available to bridge the gap between the figure at which the landlords would be likely to sell and the figure at which the tenants would be likely to buy. On Wyndham's calculation that the total value of the sales would be £100 millions, the landlords' bonus would be £12 millions. Treasury opposition was bought off by a bargain whereby the Irish Office agreed to reduce its ordinary annual expenditure by £250,000 — mainly on the police estimates.[48]

Just before Wyndham's proposals were submitted to Parliament, an event occurred which may have had some effect in forestalling any disposition by Conservative backbenchers or peers to tamper with the Bill. A by-election occurred in the marginal Ulster seat of North Fermanagh.[49] An Independent Unionist, Edward

Mitchell, was set forward against the official Unionist candidate. Mitchell was a tenant farmer, and concentrated on the land issue. He was prone to speak of "landlord wolves". The Nationalists did not stand, and Mitchell was elected. Evidently he had not only captured the Catholic vote practically entire, but had taken many Protestant votes as well. Here was another warning that the Unionists were not entitled to presume too much on the support of Northern Protestants.

When Wyndham's proposals came before Parliament, they were welcomed by the Irish and most of the Government supporters. The official Liberal opposition gave the measure rather lukewarm support,[50] and on the critical divisions only small minorities resisted the Bill. These included no Irish MPs from either South or North, but comprised a rather startling political amalgam — some deep-blue Conservatives who took their stand on traditional landlord principles, and some very radical Liberals who argued that it was a "gift" to landlords, or even a concession to "blackmail". Among the strongest critics of Wyndham's proposals were the land value taxers and the land nationalisers. Wallace, for example, considered that the whole idea was "unsound in principle, and entirely useless except as a temporary expedient, since it would leave the whole land of Ireland in the possession of a privileged class, and would thus disinherit all the rest of the population from their native soil".[51]

"Entirely useless" is a gross exaggeration; but there is force in the argument that the position of landless men may actually have become worse in the long run; for while they might have been able to assert their claims effectively against a small class of alien landlords under the old system, it was far more difficult for them to obtain satisfaction in any dispute where the interests of hundreds of thousands of peasant-proprietors were ranged against them. Perhaps the most powerful argument of all in favour of the Wyndham settlement in the minds of British politicians and the British public was the somewhat cynical view suggested by William O'Brien. In his opinion, the landlords' bonus "was a very modest quit-rent indeed for the £3,000,000 (the Exchequer) had heretofore to disgorge every year that came for the swollen police and judicial establishments whose real effect was to subsidise landlord oppression and to keep the wound of Irish disaffection for ever bleeding".[52] Events would later show that the quit-rent was greater than Wyndham or O'Brien anticipated, and that the wounds were not staunched.

Thus did the Bill pass safely through Parliament. The most significant feature was that it was based on an agreement derived from Irish initiative and concluded between Irishmen, which had been accepted with very little trouble by the United Kingdom legislature. Unionists and Nationalists could draw their disparate political morals from that situation.

The Government certainly had no intention of making peasant-proprietorship universal among the rural classes. Discussing the landless labourers, Wyndham himself wrote in September 1903 that: "Any concession to the sentiment of 'ownership' should be avoided. Care should be taken not to turn labourers into small owners of uneconomic holdings." The furthest he would go in the direction of land ownership for the labourers was to "extend the English Allotments Acts with modifications if any are necessary".[53]

The Wyndham Act was, for good or ill, one of the most important measures of all in the history of the Irish land problem. That problem, of course, was not completely settled; but the country had been set in a direction which has been followed to this day, through all the political upheavals.[54]

The rural land question was by no means a dead issue, either in Ireland or in Great Britain; but urban land reform was the main focus of attention. For all practical purposes, the urban land reformers were united in the view that the most urgent measure was the taxation of land values, whether for local or national purposes. The same doctrine was also preached for rural areas, but with much less effect. It is exceedingly difficult to assess just how high a priority the idea of land value taxation held in people's minds by comparison with other reforms which they also sought; but it is doubtful whether there was any other reform in the whole field of politics and economics which was positively desired by so many people. There was every reason for thinking that any government, whether Liberal or Conservative, would be driven to legislate on the subject in the near future.

Notes-7

1   SLA Minutes, 1886-1892, pp. 147, 220.

2   See discussion in James Hunter, "Politics of Highland land reform 1873-1895", *Scottish Historical Review*, 53 (1974), at pp. 63-4.

3   See argument of William Saunders, MP, 24 March 1894. Ellis, fo. 1925.

4   See discussion in Elwood P. Lawrence, *Henry George in the British Isles* (see bibliog.), p. 52.

5   Press report of SLA Conference, Edinburgh, 8 February 1887. SLA Press Cutting Book, p. 95.

6   *The Star*, 30 January 1888.

7   *Ibid.*, 8 January 1889.

8   Later known as *Land Values*; still published, now as a bi-monthly in London, under the name *Land and Liberty*. For the early history of the movement, see *Land Values*, June 1915, pp. 3-6.

9   *The Times*, 5 December 1889. Resolution moved by C. A. Fyffe (Liberal candidate for Oxford 1885) and seconded by F. A. Channing MP.

10 *The Times*, 3 October 1891.

11 Parliamentary Debates 3S 350, col. 1878.

12 Michael Barker, *Gladstone and Radicalism* (see bibliog.), pp. 141-44, 186-88.

13 G. Howell, Bethnal Green NE. All election addresses to which reference is made are in the collection of the National Liberal Club.

14 J. A. Murdoch Macdonald, Bow and Bromley.

15 For examples of these bargains, see A. J. Balfour to Salisbury, 29 December 1893 and 12 January 1894. S. E.

16 *Single Tax*, June 1894.

17 William Saunders to T. E. Ellis, 24 March 1894. Ellis, fo. 1925.

18 *Single Tax*, August 1895.

19 Sidney and Beatrice Webb, *History of Trade Unionism* (see bibliog.), p. 376.

20 *Single Tax*, October 1895.

21 *Single Tax*, June 1895.

22 Tom Mann, *The Programme of the ILP and the Unemployed* (see bibliog.), p. 8.

23 As, for example, Robert Blatchford, *Land Nationalisation* (see bibliog.), which solemnly recommends books by both authors with a comment that they "afford a clear and comprehensive view of the land question".

24 *Single Tax*, July 1894.

25 *Single Tax*, January 1896.

26 *Single Tax*, October 1897.

27 *Land Values*, March 1906; *Liberal Magazine*, 1906, pp. 64-5.

28 See analysis of the division, *Liberal Magazine*, 1903, p. 146.

29 Ministerialists supporting the Bill are listed in *Liberal Magazine*, 1904, pp. 161-62. The vote was 158:225.

30 *Liberal Magazine* 1905, pp. 237-38.

31 *Single Tax*, April 1898.

32 So also did Dublin. *Land Values*, April, July 1904.

33 Memorandum to Cabinet, 14 December 1892. CAB 37/32/45.

34 A. J. Balfour to Matthew Ridley, 14 July 1893 (copy). S. E.

35 G. Shaw-Lefevre's memorandum, 16 January 1895. CAB 37/38 No. 5.

36 A. J. Balfour to Salisbury, 29 December 1893. S. E.

37 8 February 1897.

38 For a defence of the Act, see letter of Jesse Collings in *Rural World*, 12 July 1899. JC 6/5/6 fo. 3.

39 See, for example, A. J. Balfour to Salisbury, 6 June 1895. S. E.

40 Gerald Balfour's memorandum to Cabinet, 10 March 1896. CAB 37/41/16.

41 See Morley-William O'Brien correspondence 22-23 August 1893. O'Brien 11,439 (2); 11,440 (1); Birrell to Cabinet 23 October 1908. CAB 37/95/130. The Land Commission was not able even to make full use of the powers it legally possessed until a Court decision in 1905 clarified the situation. Bryce to Campbell-Bannerman, 18, 31 December 1905. C-B 41,211, fos. 329, 330, 336.

42 Earl Cadogan's memorandum, 26 July 1901. CAB 37/57/72.

43 Cabinet memorandum (unsigned, n.d., but *circa* 1901), "The Irish Land Question and the need for Legislation". CAB 37/59/147.

44 Wyndham memorandum, "A policy for Ireland", 14 November 1902. AJB 49,804, fos. 78-95. On Ulster difficulties see Wyndham to Balfour, 14 February 1902, *ibid.*, fos. 1-2.

45 MacDonnell to Wyndham, 22 September 1902 (copy). AJB 49,804, fos. 61-2; see also Wyndham to Balfour, 13 September 1902. *Ibid.*, fo. 36.

46 Denis Gwyn, *Life of John Redmond* (see bibliog.), p. 101.

47 Wyndham to A. J. Balfour, 19 September 1902. AJB 49,804, fos. 55-8.

48 MacDonnell report to Cabinet, 17 June 1907. CAB 37/89/70.

49 See account in P. Buckland, *Irish Unionism 2: Ulster Unionism . . .* (see bibliog.), pp. 24-5.

50 See Campbell Bannerman's statement on 4 May 1903. *Liberal Magazine*, 1903, p. 306.

51 A. R. Wallace, *My Life* (see bibliog.), p. 321. Henry George jr makes the same criticism of National League policy after 1882, see *Life of Henry George* (*third period*) (see bibliog.), p. 376. Michael Davitt seems to have seen it earlier; *ibid.*, p. 346. See also criticism in *Single Tax*, March 1903.

52 O'Brien, *op. cit.*, p. xxii.

53 Memorandum, "A general sketch of Irish policy", 28 September 1903. AJB 49,804, fos. 186-94.

54 For Birrell's recognition of this fact, see his statement of November 1907. *Liberal Magazine* 1907, p. 660.

8 BATTLE IS JOINED

"I remember perfectly well going to an old friend of mine in the House of Commons before I introduced my Budget. He is, I suppose, one of the wealthiest men in the Kingdom — a man who made his money by his own brains. I said to him, 'You had better make the most of me for the next two or three days. After the Budget you and I won't be on speaking terms.' He said, 'My boy . . . you put the burden on the shoulders that can bear it; and, if you don't, I will not be on speaking terms with you.' I followed his advice, and he has consistently supported me. . . ."

David Lloyd George
Newcastle Daily Chronicle, 11 October 1909 LG (B) C/33/2/13

Lord Salisbury resigned in 1902, and was succeeded by Arthur Balfour, who for some time had been performing many of the duties usually associated with the premiership. In the following year, the first major crack appeared in the Government's front, with the inauguration of Joseph Chamberlain's "Tariff Reform" campaign, which gradually shifted from the proposal of an imperial *Zollverein* to a demand for the imposition of a unilateral system of tariffs by the United Kingdom. The Unionist Government was severely split, and most people seem to have expected an early General Election; but the administration remained in office until December 1905, when Balfour resigned and King Edward VII called on Sir Henry Campbell-Bannerman, Liberal leader in the Commons, to form a government. After some initial difficulties, Campbell-Bannerman constituted an administration which included nearly all of the leading Liberal figures, save Lord Rosebery. Parliament was dissolved a few days later, and a General Election campaign commenced, with the main pollings in January 1906.

An election fought mainly on the question of whether to preserve Free Trade or to adopt the policy of "Tariff Reform" seems a far cry from the land question, but in fact the connection was considerable. Few or none of the land reformers evinced the slightest hesitation in adopting the Liberal line on Free Trade. Henry George himself had argued powerfully that Free Trade and land reform were closely related policies,[1] and the advocates of land value taxation often described their own proposals as "True Free Trade" — as a natural and logical extension of the doctrines promulgated by Cobden, Bright and all the other heroes of the past.

The overwhelming majority of keen land reformers supported the Liberal Party, and most of those land reformers who were not Liberals were included among the supporters of the Labour Representation Committee (LRC): a body which was soon to be reconstituted as the Labour Party, but which was then operating (and continued for years to operate) as an ally of the Liberals in most matters. In some parts, notably in Glasgow, even the Conservatives appeared to tag along with the land reformers to a substantial extent.[2] Not long before the election, the land taxers knew of only two Liberal candidates in the United Kingdom who were not "sound" on their question. Rather significantly, these were men who stood at opposite ends of the Party: Harold Cox, who later achieved notoriety as one of the very few Liberal opponents of Old Age Pensions, and Leo Chiozza Money, who eventually achieved notoriety of a more personal kind, but who before that had found a home in the Labour Party.[3] As the land taxers were particularly strong in Scotland they were able to carry out a close analysis of the Scottish candidates. They found that "all the Liberals and Labourists were in favour of the taxation of land values", while more than half of the Liberal and Labour MPs were enthusiastic for the cause.[4] Campbell-Bannerman himself (who satisfied the land taxers not only in his doctrine but also in his zeal) set the tone for the campaign in a great, and oft-quoted, speech on 21 December 1905, at the Albert Hall in London: "We desire to develop our own undeveloped estate in this country — to colonise our own country — to give the farmer greater freedom and greater security; to secure a home and career for the labourers . . . We wish to make the land less of a pleasure-ground for the rich, and more of a treasure-house for the nation . . . There are fresh sources to be taxed. We may derive something from the land . . . We can strengthen the hand of the municipalities by reforming the land system and the rating system, in which I include the imposition of a rate on ground values."

The result of the election was an overwhelming majority for the Liberals over all other Parties combined; while the 29 LRC MPs and the eighty-three Irish Nationalists could be expected to give support on most issues, and brought the Government's effective majority to over 350 seats. It was not unreasonable to anticipate that some action would very soon be taken to satisfy the land reformers.

The new Government's land policy towards Ireland was very different from that which it sought to apply in Great Britain. It would hardly be too much to describe Irish land policy as bipartisan. There were some features on which a measure of disagreement existed between the leaderships of the parties; but these are of only minor importance by comparison with the common policy of extending peasant-proprietorship — where the dispute, such as it was, concerned means and not ends. The Liberals, as Home Rulers, sought to give Ireland what Ireland wanted; and this (so far as the most vociferous Irishman were concerned) was something uncommonly like a Conservative land policy. The first Chief Secretary for Ireland in the Liberal government was James Bryce, the distinguished historian — a convinced Home Ruler, and at heart a strong land-taxer; a man who in most matters stood in the Gladstonian tradition. The most important Irish land legislation which he was able to secure was the Labourers Act of 1906, which provided for compulsory acquisition of land for cottages and allotments. Bryce's appointment to the Irish Office was not really felicitous, and towards the end of 1906 he left for the much more congenial post of Ambassador to the United States. He was succeeded by Augustine Birrell, something of a literary dilettante, who remained at the post until the disasters of 1916.

The Wyndham Act had left its own legacy of problems, both in the things which it settled and in the things which it failed to settle. John Redmond, leader of the Irish Party, pointed out in 1906 that there were 15,000 fair-rent cases waiting to be heard, and over 9,000 appeals pending. Many tenants were therefore rushing to buy land under the Wyndham Act at "foolish and extortionate prices". It also became evident that the financial calculations made at the time of the Act were grossly over-sanguine; the total sum required for purchase would be in the region of £183 millions, not £100 millions, and the requisite bonus to the landlords would be far greater than the £12 millions provided for.[5]

A particularly urgent problem concerned the Irish tenants who had been evicted from their holdings prior to the 1903 Act.[6] As usual, it was civil disturbances which brought the matter to the attention of the politicians. Regularly each year, disorders occurred in the Congested Districts during March and April, when the grasslands were being relet to graziers; but normally these disturbances died down in May when the relettings were completed. In 1907, however, they actually increased in May, and continued to increase into June. In the view of MacDonnell (whose presence and influence remained, in spite of the change of government) — it was necessary to "convince the people that we are in earnest in our policy of acquiring the 'ranches' ".[7]

By that time 8,400 applications had been received from evicted tenants who sought holdings, and of these just over 1,000 had been granted. A very considerable number of the remainder were spurious, but, in Birrell's view, a number "which won't exceed 2,000", had a good case. Many of these had been excluded by the previous Government as the result of an administrative decision. Birrell, however, considered that compulsory powers of land acquisition were necessary in order to resettle these tenants, and that something like 80,000 acres would be required for the whole operation. The Government was able to pilot a bill through Parliament which gave the Estates Commissioners power to purchase land to resettle the evicted tenants, and this largely disposed of the problem.[8]

There remained the much more widespread problem of the future of the Congested Districts. In 1906, under Bryce's régime, a Commission was set up, with Lord Dudley — a Conservative and former Lord Lieutenant of Ireland — as its Chairman. The Dudley Commission reported in May 1908. It considered that holdings of an annual value below £10 were too small to be economic. In the Congested Districts, 74,500 of the 85,000 holdings were below that value. The Dudley Commission concluded that it was necessary to acquire additional land to an annual value of £450,000, and that the amount of land existing in the Congested Districts was barely sufficient for the purpose. The Commissioners considered that the land which would need to be remodelled into economic holdings would need to be kept in the hands of public authorities for something like two years in order to effect resettlement and redistribution; that the process of remodelling the holdings entailed a necessary loss in the region of 13-15 per cent; and that a very substantial increase in the grant to the Congested Districts Board would be required.[9]

The Government proposed legislation in the autumn of 1908; but the Bill was later scrapped, and introduced in another form early in the following year. The 1909 Land Bill was of general application, and was designed partly in the light of the Dudley Report. The major provisions fell into two groups: financial adjustments, and proposals relating to the Congested Districts. There would be a considerable cutting-back on the landlords' bonus in future transactions, and the annuity rates of repayment by the peasants would be slightly increased. A much larger part of Ireland would be brought within the jurisdiction of the Congested Districts Board, and the sum available for resettlement within those districts was much increased. The Bill also provided for compulsory sales. There was trouble with the Lords — who were more prepared to accept compulsion from Conservatives than from Liberals — but the Government showed considerable toughness, and the measure was eventually carried, though in a somewhat reduced state. By the time that the Bill became law there was little public interest in its provisions, outside Ireland itself, for the great storm over Lloyd George's 1909 Budget was already blowing at full force.

By contrast with its Irish land policy, the Liberal Government's land policy for Great Britain was by no means bipartisan, and parliamentary altercations of the most violent kind were inevitable. Even here, a few measures could be devised where the disagreement was not too severe. A Bill which was originally called the Agricultural Holdings Bill and later the Land Tenure Bill was introduced in 1906. It was originally a private member's bill and was later adopted by the Government. At first it seemed likely that there would be severe trouble, and many Conservatives cursed it in a way which suggested that the Lords might eventually resist it to the uttermost; but in fact it passed both Houses. Some amendments were proposed by the Lords, but did not radically affect its character. In the form in which it eventually passed, tenants received increased freedom of cultivation and added rights of compensation in respect of improvements and of damage to crops by the landlord's game. The Bill seems to have been popular among the farmers; perhaps the Conservative peers decided at the end not to offend men who could normally be numbered among their own Party's supporters.

Some members of the Government — notably Earl Carrington, President of the Board of Agriculture — were keen advocates of

138

smallholdings, and an Allotments and Smallholdings Bill had a rather easy passage through Parliament in 1907, although it ran into some trouble with certain land taxers.[10] The maximum size of allotments was increased, and their control was transferred wholly from the Rural Districts to the more democratic parish authorities. Smallholding commissioners were given power to investigate the demand for, and feasibility of, smallholdings in a locality, and then require the County Council to work out a scheme of operation; in default of which the Commissioners could execute a scheme themselves. Powers of compulsory acquisition were also granted. Although the new Act made provision only for hiring, and not for purchase, of smallholdings, the right to purchase under the Act of 1892 was not abrogated.

Far more explosive politically was the question of land value taxation. At first the land taxers were sanguine about early legislation.[11] The Government, however, did not produce a Bill for all-round land valuation as had been hoped, but only a Bill for the valuation of Scottish land. Scotland certainly felt more keenly on the subject than did England; but the attitude of John Burns, President of the Local Government Board, was also important. At first the land taxers had viewed his appointment with particular pleasure; but by the end of 1906, Trevelyan was privately declaring that Burns was "simply a Tory on the question".[12]

Even in the old Parliament, Scottish site value rating had received the sympathetic attention of the House of Commons. A Bill designed to allow Scottish local authorities to collect their rates on the basis of site values was promoted by the municipal council of Glasgow, and passed its second reading in the House of Commons in June 1905; but, like the parallel English Bill, it did not secure Parliamentary time for further progress. In the 1906 Parliament, more than four-fifths of the Scottish MPs could be regarded as supporters, and over half of the Scottish representation as enthusiastic supporters, of the "Glasgow Bill". There could be no reasonable doubt as to the general view either of the Scottish electors, or of the Scottish local authorities on whom the burden of administration would fall. As Scottish land law is markedly different from English law,[13] there was much to be said for a "pilot" scheme in Scotland.

The new Government proposed first to value the land of Scotland, and then to enact taxing legislation when valuation was complete. Their Bill for valuation was first proposed in 1906 by the new Secretary of State for Scotland, John Sinclair. It was carried with triumphant majorities in the Commons, but rejected outright by the Lords in 1907. Another Bill to the same effect was proposed in 1908. This time the Lords did not formally reject it, but passed wrecking amendments which defeated its whole purpose. For the time being, the Government was powerless to proceed further with the measure.

The Government also sought to extend the principle of smallholdings in Scotland. Behind this decision lay not only the familiar arguments in favour of smallholdings, but also a special concern about the continued emigration from Scotland, and particularly from the rural districts. A pamphlet issued by the Scottish Liberal Association, for example, argued that: "Under a favourable land system, nearly one million extra inhabitants might earn a healthy living on the land."[14] The proponents of smallholdings saw this policy virtually as an extension of the Crofters' Act of 1886 to the whole of Scotland.[15]

Two features of Sinclair's Bill were contentious. The proposal that there should be no difference of treatment between the "crofting counties" and the rest of Scotland was popular among the radicals, but was disputed by some of the more Whiggish Liberals.[16] The second issue was whether the smallholders should be tenants or whether they should be encouraged to become owners. On this matter the Government was united. There was little sympathy for the idea of applying the Irish peasant-proprietorship doctrine to Scotland. The Scottish Liberal Association, for example, unanimously carried a resolution in 1906, which urged the Government: "to resist all attempts to embody (in the Bill) any scheme of Land Purchase or the creation of any vested interests whatever, other than those which may result from the tenants' own improvements."[17] Perhaps the commonest view outside Scotland was that of Reginald McKenna, who "told a friend that he and his colleagues had accepted Sinclair's bill on being assured that it was what Scotland wanted and were perfectly indifferent to its fate."[18]

Predictably, the Sinclair Bill was carried by the Commons, but it was wrecked by the Lords. One of Campbell-Bannerman's last actions in the Cabinet, at the beginning of 1908, was to insist that it be re-presented that year to Parliament. Again, however, the Bill was ruined by the Lords. As in so many other matters, the Government could do no more than lick its wounds and plan revenge.

The difficulties with which the Liberal Government was confronted in the first three years of its existence made some serious clash between the two Houses of Parliament inevitable. An administration supported by an overwhelming majority in the Commons was again and again forced either to abandon its purpose altogether, or at least to make major concessions, at the behest of a completely unrepresentative, and frequently irresponsible, Upper House. Perhaps the Lords could be overruled on a particular issue if Parliament were dissolved and a majority in the new House of Commons upheld the Government's view; but this procedure was intolerably cumbersome for ordinary legislation.

Politically, there were serious difficulties. In 1906, the Liberals had stood on the top of the hill; and all roads from the top of a hill lead downwards. A General Election at any time thereafter would assuredly cut their majority; while a General Election fought on an issue on which most electors were disinterested would be likely to destroy it altogether, and either set a Tariff-Reforming Unionist government in office, or give the Irish that balance of power which they had exercised in 1885 and 1892, with results which were baleful both to the Liberals and to themselves.

It was the land question which lay at the root of the eventual conflict. In all conscience, the Lords had plenty of warning. In October 1906, Lloyd George told the Welsh National Liberal Council that the "next great legislative ideal" of the Government was "the emancipation of the Welsh peasant, the Welsh labourer, and the Welsh miner, from the oppression of the antiquated, sterilising and humiliating system of land tenure."[19]

In April 1907, Winston Churchill (a rising member of the Government, though not yet in the Cabinet), declared that land reform was "the most important and certainly the most fundamental part of constructive Liberal social policy". At the same meeting, Campbell-Bannerman described the proposed land valuation of Scotland as "an indispensable preliminary step" for the Government's programme.[20]

Campbell-Bannerman's health had been bad right from the formation of his ministry. Early in 1908 he fell ill, resigned, and died shortly afterwards. His successor was the Chancellor of the

Exchequer, H. H. Asquith. In Asquith's early career, there had been much evidence of great capacity, but less evidence of radicalism. Yet, like Campbell-Bannerman and Gladstone too, he became increasingly radical as his career advanced. Asquith was not the sort of man who is drawn into politics by some consuming idea; rather did his mind remain open until a decision was needed; but, once he had decided on a course he pursued it with devastating determination. Campbell-Bannerman called Asquith "the sledge-hammer" in debate; and this was largely true in other matters as well. Intellectually, he decided in favour of land-taxing at the turn of the century, though he could hardly be called an enthusiast. Once the exigencies of the situation made land reform a central issue of politics, Asquith was prepared to use all his skill to secure victory for the reformers. Not least momentous of his early decisions was the choice of Lloyd George for the Exchequer. Some have suggested that this decision was forced upon Asquith against his will; the wholly friendly correspondence of the two men at the time of the appointment — meant for no eyes but those of each other — is quite inconsistent with that view.[21] Lloyd George was already known as an ardent land reformer, an extremely skilful administrator, and a stormy petrel who had a marked propensity to infuriate all the forces of the "establishment", especially the Lords.[22]

The first Budget of the Asquith régime had been prepared by the Premier himself in his days as Chancellor, and was introduced by him into the House of Commons. That Budget proposed no new land taxes. Ardent land-taxers, indeed, were becoming more and more restive. Late in 1906, about 400 MPs had petitioned Campbell-Bannerman for the introduction of land value taxation. The United Committee for the Taxation of Land Values — formed in 1907 to co-ordinate the interested bodies — circulated over fifty million leaflets within three or four years.[23] In November 1908, a Memorial signed by 250 MPs went a good deal further than the petition of two years earlier, and urged that the taxation of land values should appear in the next Budget.

Asquith was inevitably subjected to barrages from both sides, and he circulated to the Cabinet some critical memoranda from Liberal MPs who had reservations on the subject.[24] The objections were met by the Chancellor. There was no doubt about the Liberals' general commitment; as Lloyd George pointed out: ". . . The overwhelming majority of the Party in the House are

142

pledged to the taxation of land values, and urgently press it upon the Government. There are at the outside six Members sitting on the Liberal side of the House who oppose it in principle. They have never mustered more than three in the Division lobby when the Government proposals bearing on the subject have been submitted to the House."[25]

The Government might decide what action was necessary; but if it wished to legislate, some means had to be found by which it could appease, browbeat or circumvent the Lords. If the Government decided that land should eventually be taxed, the simplest and most natural approach was first to value it, and then to tax it at a later date. This, of course, was what had been tried a year or two earlier for Scotland, with disastrous results. Thus, in Lloyd George's view: "It would be impossible to secure the passage of a separate Valuation Bill during the existence of the present Parliament owing to the opposition of the Lords, and therefore the only possible chance which the Government have of redeeming their pledges in this respect is by incorporating proposals involving land valuation in a Finance Bill. On the other hand, it must be borne in mind that proposals for valuing land which do not form part of the provision for raising revenue in the financial year for which the Budget is introduced would probably be regarded as being outside the proper limits of a Finance Bill by the Speaker of the House of Commons."[26] The general opinion at the time was that measures which could properly be included in the annual Finance Bill would be passed, however reluctantly, by the Lords. It is difficult to escape the conclusion that the Government was at this stage trying to compromise with the Upper House — to secure something in the direction of land value taxation, while avoiding an immediate confrontation.

At that particular moment, the argument for new taxation of some kind or other was overwhelming. The Government's social reform policies and its rearmament programme were both expensive. It was not, on the face of it, difficult to persuade moderate men who had no particular love for land taxation as such, that a proportion of the new burdens might fall upon land values.

Lloyd George proposed to the Cabinet two main kinds of new land taxes. First was a tax of one penny in the pound (just over 0.4 per cent) on the capital value of land. For the first two years at any rate, the tax would be levied only on mining royalties, ground rents and vacant land. Devices were proposed to avoid "double taxation", to exclude practically all householders, and to exclude agricultural land save where that land had acquired an enhanced value for potential building purposes. Very little revenue was expected from vacant land in the first year; on the other hand, a substantial revenue might be anticipated from mining royalties and ground rents.

The second kind of tax was known as the "Frankfort Tax" — as a similar tax was levied at Frankfürt, in Germany. When land which had already been valued was later sold at an enhanced price, that land would be taxed at 20 per cent on the increment. In the same way, when valued land was transferred at the death of its holder, the legatee should pay 20 per cent on any increment in value.

It was not considered that the new land taxes would bring in any very great revenue during the first year. The sum originally contemplated was £500,000, although Lloyd George later spoke of £650,000. Even the larger figure was only one-twentieth of the total increase in taxation proposed for the year. Far larger items were the increases in estate duties (£2,850,000), in income tax (£3,500,000), in liquor licences (£2,600,000) and in taxes on tobacco and spirits (£3,400,000). Yet the Chancellor had far more trouble over the land taxes than the other proposals. He later contended that "by far the most difficult fight he had was in the Cabinet, not in the country",[27] and "Loulou" Harcourt, son of Sir William, seems to have been particularly obstreperous. It was Asquith who came to the Chancellor's aid when Cabinet opposition became particularly severe.

When the Budget was announced on 29 April 1909, some changes had been made in the Chancellor's original proposals. The Undeveloped Land Duty was reduced from a penny to a halfpenny, while a new Reversion Duty of 10 per cent was proposed, which should be paid by a lessor when a lease fell in to his advantage.[28]

The Land Taxes became the great issue of discussion in Parliament and the country. The Irish fulminated against the taxes on alcohol and tobacco, and the Conservatives made a somewhat feeble attempt to incite the "beer and baccy" working man against the Government; but there could be no doubt where the main interest lay. The enthusiasm of the land-taxers on one side, and the fury of the landed interests on the other, took good care of that.

144

At first, the Opposition criticism was more or less predictable: the *Daily Telegraph*'s word "preposterous" being one of the more severe. Some of the more radical land-taxers were disappointed by the Chancellor's moderation, and by his departure from Georgeist orthodoxy. He was in the infuriating position of having the complete answer to their strictures, but being unable to use it.

At some point in 1909, the two parties' attitudes towards the land taxes underwent a profound change. The Opposition came to regard the Budget as a means for bringing down the Government; while the Liberals began to see it, not as a means of circumventing the Lords, but as a means of confronting the Lords in open battle and defeating them. These matters may be understood only in the light of the general political situation.

Although land reform was the great positive issue on which most of the active Liberals had set their hearts, the Liberals were also moved by a concern to protect Free Trade and defeat "Tariff Reform". They had a huge majority in the House of Commons and while that majority remained, Free Trade was safe. A General Election need not be held (as the law then stood) until the end of 1912. A General Election at any time involved a risk, not merely of party defeat, but that Free Trade itself would be swept away. Land Taxing, important as it was, could wait for a propitious moment; while, if Free Trade were once abandoned, the damage to the whole economy would be severe and permanent, even though the electors might soon repent of their folly and send the Liberals back again to office.

The year 1908 had been bad for trade. There was a big increase in unemployment, and a run of fearful by-election results for the Government. Eighteen Liberal seats had become vacant in the course of the year. Seven were lost to the Unionists, and two more demonstrated a really huge drop in Liberal support. The beginning of 1909 showed a substantial improvement in the unemployment figures, and also in the by-election results for the Government; but in April there was a big drop in the Liberal majority at East Edinburgh, and in May two more seats were lost — one each to the Unionists and Labour.

In this climate, the Unionists set up a body called the Budget Protest League, with the evident intention of taking the campaign into the country. The Liberals were bound to counter, and established a Budget League a few days later. There was good reason for thinking that the Opposition would try to goad the Government into holding a General Election in the shadow of the Budget; the operative question was whether the Liberals would accept the challenge.

Land taxing was certainly a popular issue. One of the best by-election results which the Government had had for a long time was recorded just before the Budget, when a strong land taxer defended a Liberal seat and received an almost undiminished majority. Even clearer evidence was provided at the by-election in High Peak, Derbyshire on 22 July — for by that time the Budget controversy was already acute. The MP, Oswald Partington, took Government office, and was obliged (as the law then stood) to defend his seat. The Liberal majority had been less than 900 in 1906, and the same Unionist candidate was still in the field. Partington fought his campaign on the Budget proposals, and won the contest. On the form of the previous year, there is not the slightest doubt that he would have been defeated.

The Finance Bill had a long and rough passage through the House of Commons. The liquor taxes were fought by the Opposition and the Irish; the land taxes, which won general support from Liberals and Labour, were opposed tooth and nail by the Conservatives. A small number of Liberals — ten or a dozen — appear in division after division against the Government. The Second Reading, in June, brought no Liberal or Labour votes in the Opposition lobby, though 33 Government supporters were absent unpaired. On the Third Reading two Liberals voted against the Government, and ten were absent unpaired. One Conservative voted on the Government side.[29] That Third Reading, however, which in most years would be reached in July, was not taken until November.

In this atmosphere of storm and crisis, Lloyd George was seen at his very best. The challenge of the Opposition was taken up. Just over a week after High Peak had polled, he spoke at a Budget League meeting in Limehouse, in East London. His speech seems mild enough to us today; but it infuriated the Opposition beyond measure, and it was evidently the Chancellor's intention that it should. We may guess that he had already decided that it was a good idea to drive the Lords into rejecting the Budget, and then go to the country on the cry of "Peers versus People". The tone of Limehouse was kept up. Even Sir Edward Grey, the Foreign Secretary, whom nobody regarded as one of the most radical members of the Government, was persuaded to make some gentle gibes about Dukes. Lloyd George's most radical (and funniest) speech was delivered at Newcastle on 9 October; this was the occasion when he revealed that "a fully-equipped Duke costs as much to keep as two Dreadnoughts; and Dukes are just as great a terror and they last longer."

While the great battle over Lloyd George's land taxes was moving towards its climax, another important and protracted contest which bore on the land question was also being fought. In February 1909, John Burns, President of the Local Government Board, introduced his Housing and Town Planning Bill. The Bill included a wide range of proposals affecting improvement schemes in working-class areas, and provisions for town planning in places where building development seemed likely. In the debates on the Bill, Burns's second-in-command, Charles Masterman, delivered himself of the observation that in urban areas housing conditions were on the whole improving, though not as fast as the Government wished; while in the countryside they were actually deteriorating.

The Government's Bill passed the Commons, but met with wrecking amendments in the Lords. The Marquis of Crewe, chief Government spokesman in the Upper House, at one point considered the differences "unbridgeable". Yet although the Lords detested many of the Government's proposals, they did not wish to incur the obloquy of taking too obstructionist a line on housing questions, lest this might harm Conservative candidates in the next General Election. Thus a compromise was eventually achieved between the two Houses. Power was given to local authorities under the resulting Act to purchase land compulsorily in connection with housing schemes, and also to acquire land by agreement, even where they had no immediate requirement of the land. A presumption of law was created in tenancy agreements to the effect that the houses concerned were, and would be kept, fit for habitation. The erection of the notorious "back-to-back" houses was at last prohibited.

On the central question of the Budget, however, the two Houses of Parliament were set on a collision course. The Finance Bill went to the Lords in November 1909, and they passed a wrecking amendment to the Second Reading with a large majority.[30] The Liberal and Labour MPs (with the help of one rebel Conservative) carried a resolution of the House of Commons which declared the Lords' rejection of the Budget to be unconstitutional. Parliament was dissolved, and a General Election began. It certainly looked very much as if the Lords had been violating the Constitution, or at least straining the Constitution to its utmost limits, in order to protect their own landed interests against taxes which nobody in the world could describe as ruinous. From the Government point of view, there could scarcely be a more favourable issue on which to face the country.

The story of what happened next is one of the most familiar in modern history, and need only be mentioned in outline. The General Election was held in January 1910,[31] and gave the Liberals and Unionists almost equal representation. The balance of power therefore went to 40 Labour and 82 Irish Nationalists (who were considerably split among themselves). Almost all of the Labour MPs knew that they depended on Liberal votes for their election, and they were hardly in a position of strength. As for the Irish, they were compelled to make the choice between on the one hand supporting a Budget which was thoroughly unpopular in their own country, and on the other setting the Conservatives in power and blighting all hopes of Home Rule. Eventually the Government proposed resolutions indicating their intention to curtail the power of the House of Lords permanently. If this could happen, at least the road was open for Home Rule, and on that understanding most (but not all) of the Nationalists supported the Budget when it was brought forward again in the new House. The Lords let it through with hardly a murmur. The Government then proposed its Parliament Bill, to give effect to the constitutional resolutions. It sought to abolish the Lords' power to block Finance Bills, and to limit their power to hold back other kinds of Bills. Suddenly, the King died, and a Constitutional Conference was set up to try to work out an inter-party compromise. After prolonged negotiations the Conference broke up, the Lords rejected the Parliament Bill, and in December 1910 there was another General Election, which resulted in almost the same configuration of Parties as in January. The official Conservative leadership in the Lords was at first truculent, but decided later to recommend abstention on their followers. After an exciting, but unsuccessful, revolt by "diehard" Conservative peers, the Parliament Bill passed the Lords.

The effect of the Budget on the Unionist opposition was in its own way almost as remarkable as its effect on the Liberals. While a "diehard" like E. G. Pretyman could contend that "the repeal of the land taxes is our trump card",[32] the Unionist leadership knew better. Joseph Chamberlain's son, Austen, told Balfour that "in London and in Yorkshire (West Riding especially) the Budget was popular and the Lords were not. The electors . . . voted against the Lords and, above all, against Landlords. In Scotland the class hatred was very bitter and the animosity against land-lords extreme. Nothing else counted very much."[33]

A few weeks later, some of the leading Unionists — including Austen Chamberlain, Wyndham, F. E. Smith and Bonar Law — discussed the question together in more detail, and circulated their conclusions to the leadership of the Party. According to Chamberlain: "They all say that in the English towns we were beaten by the land taxes of the Budget. Goulding added that he was convinced that the defeat of the Moderates in the recent London County Council election was due to the same cause and that unless we are prepared to indicate an intention of dealing with this question we have no chance of winning the towns back. . . ." All present decided that "we could have nothing to do with the taxing of ground values or with any general valua-tion scheme, and that if anything was to be done by us it must be on the lines of a reform of rating, not as in the Budget by a new national tax".

They were prepared to support a measure to enable local authorities to rate vacant plots on their letting value, and agreed to recommend proceeding on the lines of the "Minority Report" of Lord Balfour of Burleigh in 1901. Chamberlain concluded that: ". . . It was very strongly pressed upon me before I left that I should take the earliest opportunity of putting forward reform of rating on these lines as the Unionist alternative to the Government land taxes. Those present believe that if it were made clear that this was the Unionist policy it would produce an enormous effect on the boroughs. . . . It is evidently a subject of the greatest importance."[34] Lord Lansdowne, Unionist leader in the Lords, who was not present at the deliberations, seemed to endorse the conclusions.[35]

The distinction which the Unionist leaders drew between a local measure which they found tolerable and a national measure which they did not, was an important one, and it is remarkable that few or none of the land-taxers seems to have appreciated the subtlety. Austen Chamberlain stated the position with delightful candour: "It is certain that if we do nothing the Radical Party will sooner or later establish their national tax, and once established in that form any Radical Chancellor in need of money or any Socialist Chancellor in pursuit of the policy of the nationalisation of the sources of production, will find it an easy task to give a turn of the screw. . . . On the other hand if this source of revenue, such as it is, is once given to municipalities, the Treasury will never be able to put its finger in the pie again, and the Chancellor of the Exchequer will have no temptation to screw up taxes from which he derives no advantage."[36]

The Unionists also gave attention to the smallholdings question. Joseph Chamberlain's friend Jesse Collings was known to be a particularly enthusiastic exponent of the idea of smallholdings. A measure of misunderstanding existed between Collings and Balfour, which derived partly from suspicions over motives, and partly from a disagreement over the use of compulsion on reluctant landowners.[37] This controversy led Balfour to make a public statement in October 1910, which laid down a recognisable Unionist policy for agricultural land. That policy included the encouragement of owner-occupiers who were to be linked in some form of co-operative system, and receive loans from public funds through a Land Bank.

Thus when the great constitutional crisis of 1909-11 came to an end, certain general propositions could be made about the political issues which turned on land. There was no doubt whatever that interest in land questions, both rural and urban, was intense, and that it was essential for any political party to offer some quite drastic land reform. Both of the major political parties seemed to be moving in the direction of some measure of site value rating for local purposes, although neither was committed to a policy of rating exclusively on the basis of site values. Both favoured extensions in the systems of smallholdings and allotments. The Unionists wished smallholders, so far as possible, to be owners; while the Liberals wished them to be tenants of public authorities. This was, however, to a large extent a "non-problem". Neither party sought to enforce its own favoured system against the wishes of reluctant beneficiaries. The tenures offered by the Acts of 1907-8 were practically as secure as freeholds, and it is noticeable that very few smallholders seem to have had any desire to become outright owners.[38] Measures like the extension of credit facilities had received official endorsement from both great parties. If the land question in any of its aspects was again to become a central issue of political controversy, this would happen not because the politicians manufactured a question on which to fight, but because a large section of the public favoured major legislative changes which at least one of the parties was unwilling to accept. Did any such feeling exist, or would the British land problem wither away, as the Irish land problem seemed to be doing?

Notes-8

1   Notably in *Protection or Free Trade*, first published in 1886.

2   *Land Values*, February 1906, p. 167.

3   *Ibid.*, November 1905, p. 105.

4   *Ibid.*, February 1906, p. 167.

5   Birrell, 30 March 1909. Parliamentary Debates 5S, 3 col. 189.

6   For a general history of the evicted tenants, see Birrell's memorandum, 17 June 1907. CAB 37/89/69.

7   MacDonnell to Birrell, 16 June 1907, circulated to Cabinet, 17 June 1907. CAB 37/89/68.

8   See F. S. L. Lyons, *John Dillon* (see bibliog.), p. 298; see also Irish Land Commission return up to 31 March 1917. MacDonnell C471, fos. 17-22.

9   See Birrell memoranda, 23 October, 13 November 1908. CAB 37/95/130 and 151.

10 For J. C. Wedgwood's views, see *Staffordshire Sentinel*, 24 June 1907. Edwin Montagu also detested the Bill; see J. C. Wedgwood to wife, 10 November 1906, Wedgwood papers. At one point the easy passage was not anticipated. Carrington to Ripon, 2 April 1907. Ripon 43,544, fos. 125-26.

11 C. Llewellyn Davies to J. C. Wedgwood, 29 January 1906. Wedgwood papers.

12 C. P. Trevelyan to wife, 18 December 1906. C. P. Trevelyan papers ex. 21; J. C. Wedgwood to Trevelyan, 8 February 1907, *ibid.*, 7. For a milder view of Burns, see J. C. Wedgwood to Randolph Wedgwood, 14 February 1907. Wedgwood papers.

13 Scottish land-taxers themselves were not completely *ad idem* as to the best treatment of feu duties. See *Land Values*, August 1907, pp. 50-1, etc.

14 SLA leaflet (probably for one of the 1910 General Elections), n.d. HHA 23, fos. 250-51.

15 See, for example, pamphlet *Smallholdings and Land Values*, published by the United Committee for Taxation of Land Values,

April 1907. HHA 23, fos. 232-37. For a general account of the legislation, see John Brown, "Scottish and English Land Legislation 1905-11", *Scottish Historical Review*, vol. 46 (1968), pp. 72-85.

16 Munro-Ferguson memorandum, 12 January 1910. HHA 23, fos. 238-39; Sinclair to Asquith, 7 September 1908. HHA 11, fos. 178-83.

17 SLA Minute Book 1904-9, p. 334.

18 Brown, *op. cit.*, pp. 81-2.

19 *South Wales Daily News,* 12 October 1906. LG(B) B/4/2/27.

20 *Liberal Magazine,* 1907, pp. 255-58.

21 Asquith to Lloyd George, 8 April 1908. LG (NLW) 20, 462C, fo. 2285; Lloyd George to Asquith, 11 April 1908 (misdated 1907). HHA 11, fo. 77.

22 See, for example, Ripon to Campbell-Bannerman, 3 December 1906. C-B 41,207, fos. 152-53.

23 *Land Values,* June 1915, pp. 3-6.

24 Cabinet memorandum, 23 January 1909. CAB 37/97/10; HHA 22, fo. 98ff. The most adverse Liberal critic may be identified as Sir John Dickson-Poynder. One of the other two was Ernest Soares.

25 Lloyd George memorandum, 29 January 1909. CAB 37/97/16.

26 Lloyd George memorandum, 13 March 1909. CAB 37/98/44.

27 Malcolm Thomson, *David Lloyd George* (see bibliog.), p. 183.

28 For a simple summary of the new tax proposals, and how they related to expenditure, see *Liberal Magazine,* 1909, pp. 227-31.

29 The Liberal opponents were Julius Bertram and S. H. Whitbread. Of the ten absent unpaired, F. W. Chance, Sir Robert Perks and E. A. Ridsdale had been rebels on a considerable number of earlier Budget divisions. The Conservative rebel was T. H. Sloan. All but one of the Nationalists abstained. None of the five Liberal rebels defended their seats in January 1910; Sloan did, but was defeated by the "official" Conservative.

30 There were small rebel "splinters" on each side. Four Liberal peers (Lords Chichester, Northbourne, Sandwich and Temple) voted or were paired against the Bill; eight Unionists (Lords Boston, de Saumarez, Emly, James of Hereford, Monteagle, Peel, Torphichen and Rollo) in favour.

31 A few constituencies polled in early February.

32 Pretyman to Austen Chamberlain, 5 October 1910. AC 8/6/30.

33 Chamberlain to A. J. Balfour (copy), 29 January 1910. AC 8/5/1; also AJB 49,736, fos. 63-5.

34 Ms. marked "Sent to JC, AJB, Landsdowne & Wyndham", 9 March 1910. AC 8/5/14; also AJB 49,736, fos. 69-82.

35 Landsdowne to Austen Chamberlain, 16 March 1910. AC 8/5/13.

36 Chamberlain ms., 9 March 1910. AC 8/5/14.

37 See Balfour to Collings, 16 September 1910 (copy); Collings to Balfour, 22 September 1910 (copy); Austen Chamberlain to Balfour, 23 September 1910 (copy). AC 8/6/9, 13, 16.

38 Thus, in the first two years of operation of the Acts, only a little over 2 per cent of the applicants had sought to purchase their holdings. Taking an extreme case, Cambridgeshire County Council had received over 1,200 applications for smallholdings, and only one man had applied for purchase. He proved to be an undischarged bankrupt. *The Times*, 16 August 1910.

9 RADICALISM RAMPANT

"It is not that the Liberal Government want to tax land . . . The time has come when they have to find a new policy with which to get votes."

R. L. Outhwaite, MP
Quoted in *Pall Mall Gazette*, 24 October 1913

Many people regard the period between the Parliament Act of 1911 and the outbreak of war in 1914 from one of two angles: as an aftermath to the constitutional struggle; or as a curtain-raiser to the War, and to the social and political developments which occurred during the War and the supervening period. Neither of these views is a satisfactory one. It is doubtful whether anybody, in any of the parties, considered the constitutional and economic position which had been reached in 1911 to be final. Many people did not see the war coming; and those who did foresee it had, for the most part, no idea whatever of the scale of the slaughter and destruction.

The Parliament Act had provided that a Bill which passed the Commons in three successive sessions of the same Parliament should become law notwithstanding the continued opposition of the Lords. There was little doubt that any drastic and contentious land reform would be resisted by the Lords; while the current Parliament would normally be dissolved not later than 1915. It was therefore important for the various land reformers to ensure that the measures which they desired should be inaugurated at the earliest possible moment.

A Scottish Smallholders Bill, similar to the one which the Lords had wrecked twice before, was introduced. The Government — in the person of John Sinclair, who had become Lord Pentland — gave support, and this time it passed both Houses with little trouble. This measure, which is usually known as the Pentland Act, proved rather a damp squib. It came into force in April 1912. By the end of 1914, the total rent reduction and arrears cancellation together amounted to less than £10,000; while fewer than 500 smallholdings had been provided, and fewer than 300 existing holdings enlarged.

154

The principal concern of the land reformers, however, was not the promotion of smallholdings but the taxation of land values. Lloyd George's land taxes were of very little use; by far the most important ingredient of the celebrated Budget, from the land-taxers' point of view, was land valuation, on which a proper system of taxation might later be founded. The taxes as they stood, indeed, could easily prove counter-productive; for if the voters saw that nothing much happened as a result of the tremendous conflict, the whole land campaign might easily lose credibility and run into the sands. Was it possible to set a real scheme of land taxation into operation, while the public was still interested?

On 18 May 1911, several months before the Parliament Bill became law, an important delegation of backbenchers met Asquith and Lloyd George, in order to present them with a Memorial demanding speedier land valuation, and the collection of certain local and national taxes on the basis of land values. This Memorial was signed by 183 MPs, of whom eight expressed certain reservations.[1] The full list comprised most of those Liberals who were not actually members of the administration, and all the Labour MPs, except Ramsay MacDonald. Both the Prime Minister and the Chancellor gave the Memorialists a very friendly reception; but Lloyd George somewhat spoiled the effect by telling them that the valuation was expected to be complete "within five years from the date of the passing of the Budget of 1909" — that is, from 29 April 1910. It is striking to contrast the time which he considered necessary for work of this kind with that which he took for some far more difficult operations a few years later. On Lloyd George's estimate, land value taxation could not be set into operation before 1915 at the earliest. If the Government lost the next Election, or the Lords proved particularly obstreperous, the delay might be indefinite.

Needless to say, the Chancellor's information did not please the land-taxers. The Scottish Liberal Association and other Liberal bodies passed critical resolutions. Friendly remonstrances of that kind might be of some value, but they could scarcely force any-one's hand. At a time when there were so many other political issues to which attention might easily be diverted, it was exceed-ingly difficult for the land-taxers to keep public interest focused in their direction, for four more years at least. The fact that they were able to retain that interest right down to the outbreak of

155

the war is a most remarkable testimony to the inherent vitality of the movement.

Not least of their difficulties was to decide on the general strategy which they should adopt towards the Government. Lloyd George's Budget had certainly stirred the nation, and it might look factious in the extreme to turn round and attack him for failing to exhibit sufficient sense of urgency about valuation. The land-taxers had many undoubted friends in high places, of whom perhaps the most conspicuous was the Lord Advocate, Alexander Ure. Yet, as the months went by, and little or nothing was done by the Government to follow up the demands of the Memorialists, some land-taxers became restive. Josiah Wedgwood, one of the most ardent of their number, and a Liberal MP, declared openly that ". . . the valuation could be completed in a year if the Government were in earnest. . . . There are many in the Liberal Party who have had about enough of this."[2]

The *Daily Herald*, organ of the more rebellious and socialistic section of the Labour Party, took up the same theme — contending, in May 1912, that Lloyd George ". . . can tax land values, and he can tax them now, and so he can fulfil his pledges to the electorate and justify the hopes of his own followers. . . . The time for talk about land reform is over, and we are sick with the sickness of hope deferred, of (Liberals') protests and promises. They have the means to carry those promises out, for they are in power. Let them do so, or let them for ever hold their peace."[3] This was an oversimplification of the Liberals' difficulties, but it demonstrates well the feelings which were being roused.

The immediate task of the land taxers was to demonstrate the popularity of their movement in the country; to prove that it really was a vote-winner for the Government, if they cared to take it up with determination. In May 1912, a keen land-taxer, E. G. Hemmerde, stood as Liberal candidate in the NW Norfolk by-election. The constituency was agricultural and Liberal, but it was by no means safe. Hemmerde defended the seat on what he called "a campaign of robust Liberalism, on the lines of land reform". He had the exceedingly difficult task of explaining this policy to people who were unfamiliar with it, and he was triumphantly returned. A few weeks later, another Liberal land taxer, Sydney Arnold, was returned at Holmfirth, in Yorkshire — incidentally beating off a serious challenge from Labour in a strongly industrial constituency.

156

NW Norfolk and Holmfirth were followed swiftly by an even more exciting campaign at Hanley. This constituency, now part of Stoke-on-Trent, was a mixed pottery and coal mining area, bordering on Newcastle-under-Lyme, which was represented by Josiah Wedgwood. For many years the MP for Hanley was Enoch Edwards, a nominee of the Miners' Federation. Edwards had originally sat as a Liberal; but when his Trade Union seceded to the Labour Party, he dutifully followed his paymasters and contested Hanley in the Labour interest — without opposition from the Liberals.

When Edwards died in 1912, a most complex situation arose. Both the Liberal and Labour Parties claimed the seat, each contending that their own man was entitled to stand as the sole "Progressive" defender under arrangements which had been concluded in 1903.[4] No agreement was reached, and both parties advanced candidates. The Liberals put forward R. L. Outhwaite, a journalist and one of the most active and enthusiastic of the land-taxers; the Labour Party an elderly Trade Unionist of Liberal antecedents, Samuel Finney.

From the start, the Hanley by-election seemed driven by cross-currents. Many Liberals and Labour men regarded it as something of a trial of strength; and yet their leaders were anxious, for considerations of general strategy, to avoid antagonising each other too much. The Master of Elibank, Chief Liberal Whip, stoutly defended the Liberal claim to the seat, and both Asquith and Lloyd George were prevailed upon to send messages of support to Outhwaite; yet, in a sense, the Liberal leaders had one hand tied behind their backs. A further complication was the knowledge that the Unionists had a reasonable expectation of capturing Hanley on a divided "Progressive" vote.

The land taxing question swept all others aside. At one point in the campaign, three public meetings were being conducted by the land-taxers each day from 11 a.m. until midnight. The "Land Song" — "God gave the land to the people!" — was sung on innumerable occasions, and played from innumerable gramophone records. Outhwaite himself was making about ten speeches a day. Labour by no means allowed Hanley to go by default, and one night had twelve MPs supporting Finney.[5]

Outhwaite was triumphantly returned. A Parliamentary deposit did not exist in 1912; if it had done, Finney would have forfeited his, for he secured less than one-eighth of the votes cast. With such results as Norfolk, Holmfirth and Hanley behind them, the land-taxers could fairly claim that the most disparate constituencies would respond enthusiastically to a strong land-taxing challenge. In a very different way, another by-election provided an oblique justification for the land-taxers' claims. The Labour Party was so incensed by Liberal intervention at Hanley that they resolved to put forward a candidate for the vacant Liberal seat of Crewe. The Liberal candidate at Crewe was a much more orthodox, middle-of-the-road man than Outhwaite, and refused to devote his main attention to the land question. The Unionist won the seat. In several other by-elections which followed, other Liberal candidates who lacked Outhwaite's enthusiasm for the land question were also defeated.

Thus the Government leaders were put in a tight position. They were afraid that by appearing to condone the extremists they would lose support from many people who had previously helped them. To placate the "moderates", Asquith and Lloyd George were brought publicly to repudiate the assertion that they were single-taxers.[6] On the other hand, they were no less conscious that land taxing was an immensely popular policy, and they had no wish to alienate the enthusiasts. They therefore met the situation by setting up a Land Enquiry Committee. This was composed of Government supporters, among whom land-taxers were included. The formation of that Committee led to a remarkable Parliamentary incident, which gives some idea of the depth of feeling at the time. Asked by Austen Chamberlain whether the names of witnesses to the Enquiry would be published, Lloyd George replied: "Now I see what they want to get at. They want to get the names of the men who dared to give information about wages, about the conditions of labour, about management, and about game . . ."[7] The last audible word from the Chancellor was "game"; at this point, the Unionist MPs hooted and booed until he left the House.

The Unionists evidently misunderstood the whole object of the Enquiry, for the aim was not "to collect accusations against particular landlords"[8] but to provide information and recommendations which could form the basis of legislation. The Government intended that the Committee should produce separate reports on urban and rural land, and also two further reports which would deal with specifically Scottish and Welsh problems. These various studies were undertaken more or less completely in isolation from each other — although, as we shall see, they were eventually to be co-ordinated in a political campaign.

Attention was first directed to the rural question. Here the Ministers were evidently motivated both by political considerations and by a genuine concern for the agricultural labourers in particular. Earl Beauchamp, a junior member of the Cabinet, wrote to Lloyd George: ". . . It does seem to me that the important person for whom we should in the first instance do all we can is the agricultural labourer. While we need an economic revolution with regard to his wage, a moral revolution which will give his independence — i.e., an untied cottage under fair tenure — is no less necessary."[9]

On the other hand, many Liberals had doubtless noted the phenomenon which Outhwaite described after his unsuccessful candidature at Horsham in 1910: ". . . Polling day was a revelation to me. So enthusiastic had been the labourers at my village meetings that I thought I had stirred them to revolt. The last two nights the labourers did not attend, and on polling day I saw them driven to the booths by their lords and masters who polled them like Tammany bosses."[10] The farm labourers, most depressed of all the major occupational groups in Britain, were also by far the most Conservative section of the working class. It was reasonable to think that if the Government did anything really substantial to assist them, enormous numbers would move to the Liberal camp.

Although the aims of the rural Enquiry were somewhat restricted — "the prevention . . . of abuses arising out of the present system of land tenure rather than the substitution of any new system"[11] — yet several Cabinet Ministers took an active interest in its work.[12]

The proposals which emerged seemed exceedingly radical to most contemporaries. They included the establishment of minimum wages; provisions for the acquisition of land for allotments, smallholdings and housing; further compensation for the tenant-farmer in respect of disturbance; and guarantees for him against increases of rent which might arise through his own efforts and improvements. A Ministry of Lands would be set up, partly to implement these proposals, and partly to take over the existing functions of the Board of Agriculture.[13]

The rural report was·published in October 1913. The Liberals arranged to synchronise this event with the inauguration of a great

Land Campaign. This Campaign would first publicise the rural report, and then, when the other Land Enquiry proposals began to appear, would take them also within its scope. It was evidently intended that the Land Campaign should work up to a crescendo, and gradually merge into the wider political campaign which would lead on to the next General Election.

The land campaign was managed on a very substantial scale. At least eighty lecturers were appointed. Between ninety and 120 meetings were held daily. Nearly ten million items of literature were issued, and well over a quarter of a million posters produced. A somewhat wry regret was expressed by the secretary of the Central Land and Housing Council: "So far we have very little opposition from any quarter. The Campaign would go with a greater swing if we had somebody to fight".[14]

A week after the inauguration of the Campaign, Lloyd George addressed a great gathering at Swindon. He reported to the Chief Liberal Whip, Percy Illingworth: "Swindon was electric. I have rarely addressed such an enthusiastic audience. They were the picked Liberals of the West and they were as keen as mustard. The land caught on. Winston found the same thing at Manchester. His allusions to our programme were received with wild cheering."[15]

A few weeks later, Illingworth described Asquith's reception at the National Liberal Federation meeting in Leeds: "The Prime Minister's speech last night was I think the best I ever heard him make. 'Land' went like hot cakes at the delegates' meeting."[16]

The interest roused by the Land Enquiry's rural proposals was both deep and sustained. One of the many reports which Lloyd George received declared: "Speaking of the country as a whole I may say without any exception the Government's proposals are arousing unprecedented enthusiasm in the rural constituencies. In a large number of villages every elector physically capable of doing so has attended the meetings. Men walk five, six or seven miles to be present. The women are as enthusiastic as the men. The people will stand for an hour or more in drenching rain or piercing wind to hear the proposals explained. For the first time in the history of modern Liberalism farmers who do not support the Liberals are attending Liberal meetings to get information . . ."[17] The Liberals had evidently stirred the rural areas very deeply indeed, and had contrived to win massive support from farm labourers without antagonising the tenant-farmers.

160

Although the Land Enquiry produced such outstandingly successful political effects from its rural report, it experienced far more difficulty when it came to study the urban areas. The people who joined the Committee started from widely different economic standpoints, and were also subjected to a great deal of pressure in different directions from outsiders.

The representative of the land nationalisers' viewpoint on the Committee was Baron de Forest (later Count Bendern), Liberal MP for an East London constituency. His most crucial demand was that compulsory powers of land acquisition should be given to the Government "irrespective of any need for land for public services"[18] — in other words, that public money should be employed to buy out landowners, as part of a policy of gradual State acquisition of land. This view, however, was amenable to criticism from very different angles. If the landlord's title was a just one, why should his land be taken from him, save where there was some demonstrable public need for that land? Alternatively, if the landlord's title was an unjust one, why should he be compensated? Thus de Forest's view did not commend itself to the Committee. He eventually insisted on writing a Minority Report, and the Committee rather reluctantly acceded to his demand that it should be published with the main document — partly because they realised that they would not otherwise secure his promised contribution of three or four thousand pounds, and partly because they feared that he would publish damaging statements about irregularities in the Committee's work.[19] Inevitably, the land nationalisers were far from pleased with the proposals which eventually began to leak from the Committee.[20]

The keen land-taxers were also unhappy with the rumours which began to emerge about the impending urban proposals; but they were in a very difficult tactical position. The general view among them seems to have been that expressed by P. Wilson Raffan MP, one of their more balanced spokesmen: "We do not distrust (Lloyd) George, but the feeling is gaining ground that some influence must be at work to keep him silent on the Rating Question."[21] Trevelyan decided that the Chancellor was "only gradually gathering the full meaning of the change. . . . He is steadily moving in our direction. As he gets to closer grips with his subject he sees more and more."[22]

Nevertheless, some enthusiasts were more dubious. At one moment, the United Committee for the Taxation of Land Values

— an important source of propaganda — came near to a public revolt against the Government. Outhwaite wrote bitterly to Lloyd George, complaining that — in deference to him — the land-taxers had checked their propaganda at a time when by-elections "showed the workers rallying to our policy in preference to that of the Labour Party" — while "we now find that we have been swept to one side, an alternative policy to our own substituted, and that for the moment we have suffered eclipse at the hands of a Government that exists through our past activities."[23] Trevelyan reported to the Chancellor that "a large part of our best Liberals, especially where we are strongest, are remaining lukewarm about your land campaign until you are explicit about land values."[24]

Perhaps in order to allay some of these disappointments, and perhaps in order to determine the strength of the various currents of opinion before the Government had firmly committed itself, the Land Campaign spokesmen began to discuss urban land reform long before the urban report had been issued. A particularly important speech was delivered by Lloyd George at Glasgow on 4 February 1914. On the central question of site value rating, he announced that: "The Government have already, through their chief, accepted the principle of the rating of site values, and intend to give effect to it by legislation. . . . Some desire the whole burden to be transferred from the structure to the site. Others, on the other hand, object to any portion of the rates being put upon the site. As usual, I am to walk in the midst of the paths of judgement. Frankly I consider — having regard to the vested interests which have grown up — I regard the first proposition as impracticable. I regard the second proposition as pusillanimous. . . ."

The Urban Report of the Land Enquiry Committee eventually appeared in April 1914.[25] The first section dealt with urban housing questions. Noting that "over three million people, according to the 1911 census, are living under over-crowded conditions, while the great majority of the working classes dwell in long and featureless streets with no gardens or adequate playgrounds for the children", the Committee made a series of proposals for government or municipal control over existing bad housing and future developments; but the Committee itself admitted that: "They offer no single panacea with a promise that it will cure all housing evils; and on this account the recommendations, though the result of exhaustive enquiry, may fail to strike the imagination."

The second section dealt with land acquisition. Provision was made for a simplified procedure for compulsory acquisition by public authorities, and for improvements in the basis of compensation and the price-fixing machinery. The greatest concession to the land nationalisers was that: ". . . Local authorities should be given a general power to acquire land in advance either to use it themselves for public purposes as necessity arises, or to lease it to other persons."

The third section dealt with urban tenures. The Committee agreed with "immediate and universal enfranchisement" of the ancient copyhold tenures; but had much more difficulty in dealing with the far more widespread problem of leaseholds. The Committee came down against straight leasehold enfranchisement, except in a few special cases; but proposed a greater security of tenure for the leaseholder.

The fourth, and probably the most crucial, section dealt with rating reform. The Committee considered, rather in the spirit of Lloyd George's Glasgow speech, that universal site value rating would "in practice, involve considerable hardship in individual cases, and would be neither just nor politic". Instead, they proposed a rather strange compromise. There should be a penny rate on all capital site values (roughly, one-twentieth of annual values) while local authorities should have power to transfer a further proportion to site value rating if they wished. It was further recommended that "all the future expenditure of the Local Authority over and above the amount which it is expending at the time when the scheme is started, must be levied by a rate upon site values". Rather remarkably, the Committee came out against the simultaneous application of a national land value tax.

If we regard these proposals as essentially experimental, there was much to be said for the approach which the Land Enquiry Committee had taken. Power was given to those local authorities who favoured either land nationalisation or land value taxation to develop pilot schemes in those directions, and proceed far beyond the national norm. There was certainly nothing which would serve seriously to block further developments in any direction which the various bodies of land reformers and social reformers might later desire.

The urban proposals stirred far less interest than the rural report had done. At the end of May, information about public reactions was sent to the Chancellor from the Area Federation organisations of the Liberal Party, and from the Central Land and Housing Council, which was managing the campaign. This last report summed up the situation: "In the North East counties, Lancashire, Eastern Counties, Devon and Cornwall, the urban campaign has gone fairly well. Nothing like so well as the rural campaign, but still it has been fairly satisfactory. But for the rest of the country, the campaign in the boroughs has been disappointing. . . . Public attention has been so occupied with gun-running, army revolts and Parliamentary manoeuvres that it has been difficult to arouse interest on land or housing. . . ."[26]

The fundamental weakness of the urban report, from a political point of view, was its failure to rouse any of the groups of enthusiasts by an unambiguous commitment to their cause. A few years earlier, almost any move, however slight, in the direction of land reform would stir them all. By 1914, their sights were far higher, and they were in no mood for even temporary compromise.

The Government gave very close attention to the effect which the various land proposals were producing on the public. At the beginning of the whole Campaign, Lloyd George stated the position frankly enough to the Government Chief Whip: "The Tory Press have evidently received instructions from headquarters to talk Ulster to the exclusion of land. If they succeed we are 'beat', and beat by superior generalship."[27] The Government, after all, was not only engaged in a Land Campaign; it was also engaged in pushing the Home Rule Bill through Parliament in spite of a serious possibility that Ulster Protestants would resort to arms, and the military might refuse to suppress the revolt. If a referendum of the people of Britain could have been held, there is little doubt that they would have favoured the Government's line on the questions of land reform and Free Trade, and the Opposition's line on the question of Home Rule. The practical question, therefore, was whether the Government or the Opposition could stir the greater interest and excitement on its own selected issues.

The problems which confronted the Liberal Government when it spoke on land questions were bad enough; those which confronted the Conservative Opposition were even worse. The Enquiry's rural proposals might or might not be approved in Conservative circles, but they were immensely popular among the

164

people who would be most affected, and it would be political suicide in the county constituencies to condemn them. One prominent MP wrote to Bonar Law, by then Leader of the Party: "It is clear to me now that in the south of England and to some extent in the west the 'Land Campaign' *is* going down, in fact is carrying off their feet a considerable number of Conservative labourers who have voted Conservative all their lives."[28] Only atavistic and politically embarrassing figures like E. G. Pretyman could be heard to declare that the "underpayment of the agricultural labourer was grossly exaggerated".[29] As for the urban proposals, a considerable number of Unionists had come out in favour of a greater or lesser measure of site value rating themselves — ever since Lord Balfour of Burleigh's Minority Report of 1901 — and no doubt all of their leaders were immensely relieved that the Enquiry had failed to recommend a national land value tax.

The Conservative leaders were very conscious of the threat which Liberal land reform agitation posed to their ascendancy in the rural constituencies. The secretary of Jesse Collings's Rural League wrote to a Conservative peer in 1912: "I cannot understand . . . why it is the speakers of the Unionist Party are not put in a position to do more for the Party's interest than is at present the case . . . I do not hesitate to say that unless our Party leaders come out with some bold policy of Land Reform, as well as Housing Reform, in the country districts, we shall lose very heavily indeed at the next General Election . . . I feel deeply concerned at the present apathy in the Counties, and I see no hope of overcoming it unless our Leaders come out with a policy which appeals to the country people. The one topic they understand is the Land. . . ."[30]

The Earl of Malmesbury upheld these views: ". . . The Radicals (confound them!) are always much more ready with a policy than we are. All we have ever had in the past is the great Negative Policy of an 'Anti-xxx'!"[31] Those comments, it may be noted, were written before the Liberals had even won Hanley, much less commenced the Land Campaign which made such incursions in Unionist support among the farm labourers.

In the autumn of 1913, when the Land Campaign had just begun, an influential body of Unionists — including Stanley Baldwin — wrote to the new Party Leader, Bonar Law, to the same effect: ". . . An attempt simply to ignore the land problem cannot in the nature of things meet with success. . . . The ordinary Member or Candidate . . . will be compelled by the force of circumstances in the greater part of the country to give some considerable portion of his time to expounding his views on this topic. . . ."[32] Sir Arthur Steel-Maitland, Chairman of the Unionist Party Organisation, urged that a Party conference should deal with the land question; but the reaction of Lord Lansdowne was to "confess I am dismayed at the idea of introducing fresh complication into a question which is sufficiently complicated already."[33]

Pretyman was "afraid there are great differences in the Party about Land Policy".[34] Lord Edmund Talbot, Chief Whip of the Unionist Party, appointed a joint committee of various interested bodies[35] and some recommendations emerged in the early part of 1914. Inevitably, serious difficulties were encountered over the question of agricultural wages,[36] and by the outbreak of war there was still little or nothing available or in active preparation which could possibly be called an answer to the Government's proposals. The Unionists were unable either to condemn or to accept the Liberal proposals, or, *a fortiori*, to devise a policy of their own which would reconcile the competing claims of various interests within their Party.

Meanwhile, the Government prepared to implement the Land Enquiry proposals. Lloyd George's 1914 Budget statement foreshadowed a Bill to value land and improvements separately for local purposes. This proposed legislation encountered a good deal of technical difficulty,[37] but the latest plans of the Government immediately before the War were to introduce a separate Revenue Bill for that purpose in the late autumn of 1914, and to push it through Parliament in time for the Budget of 1915. The recommendation to establish a Ministry of Lands was also under active consideration, and Cabinet memoranda and proposals for a bill on the subject were being circulated in the course of 1914.[38]

Then, with dramatic suddenness, came the most unnecessary and disastrous war in the history of man. The Land Campaign, along with all other questions which were likely to evoke public controversy, was thrust aside as expeditiously as possible in the interest of "national unity". By the time that war came to an end, all the apparently fixed points of politics had shifted beyond recognition. Here, the historian of the land problem finds himself rather in the position of a critic who has attended a theatre in order to report an exciting and intricate play, and who finds himself instead recording a calamitous fire which threatens to destroy theatre, actors and audience alike.

Notes-9

1 *Land Values*, June 1911, pp. 17-18.
2 Letter in *Daily Herald*, 9 May 1912.
3 *Daily Herald*, 14 May 1912.
4 *The Times*, 4 July 1912.
5 *Westminster Gazette*, 6 July 1912; *Manchester Guardian*, 9 July 1912.
6 Asquith at Ladybank, 5 October 1912; Lloyd George (quoted by George Lambert) at Chawleigh, 7 October 1912.
7 House of Commons, 15 October 1912.
8 C. P. Trevelyan to Lloyd George (copy), 23 October 1913. CPT 15.
9 Beauchamp to Lloyd George, 15 April 1913. LG(B) C/3/5/1.
10 R. L. Outhwaite to C. P. Trevelyan, 1 February 1910. CPT 14.
11 Memorandum (not signed), 21 August 1913. CAB 37/116/56.
12 See, for example, Haldane to Lloyd George, 21 July 1913. LG(B) C/4/17/3.
13 See *Liberal Magazine*, 1913, pp. 623-38.
14 *Idem*; see also Rowntree to Lloyd George, 2 December 1913. LG(B) C/2/3/56.
15 Lloyd George to Illingworth, 24 October 1913. LG(B) C/5/4/7.
16 Illingworth to Lloyd George, 28 November 1913. LG(B) C/5/4/8.
17 G. Wallace Carter to Lloyd George, 28 May 1914. LG(B) C/2/4/22.
18 De Forest to Lloyd George, 11 August 1913. LG(B) C/2/2/36.
19 B. S. Rowntree to Lloyd George, 4 October 1913. LG(B) C/2/3/15.
20 J. St G. Heath to Lloyd George, 4 December 1913, LG(B) C/2/3/57.
21 Raffan to Trevelyan, 7 November 1913. CPT 26.
22 Trevelyan to Raffan (copy), 8 November 1913. CPT 26.
23 Outhwaite to Lloyd George, 13 November 1913. LG(B) C/10/2/32.
24 C. P. Trevelyan to Lloyd George, 6 January 1914. LG(B) C/4/12/4.
25 *Liberal Magazine*, 1914, pp. 276-84.
26 G. Wallace Carter to Lloyd George, 28 May 1914. LG(B) C/2/4/22.
27 Lloyd George to Illingworth, 24 October 1913. LG(B) C/5/4/7.
28 Charles Bathurst to Bonar Law, 4 December 1913. ABL 31/1/6.

29 At Southport, 28 January 1914.
30 J. L. Green to Lord Malmesbury, 29 June 1912. ABL 26/5/1.
31 Malmesbury to Bonar Law, 5 July 1912. ABL 26/5/9.
32 Memorandum to Bonar Law, ? October 1913, from Waldorf Astor, W. J. Ashley, Stanley Baldwin, Charles Bathurst, Henry Bentinck, John W. Hills, P. Lloyd Greame, Lord Malmesbury, Leslie Scott, Edward Strutt, Christopher Turnor, Fabian Ware, Edward Wood and Maurice Woods. ABL 30/4/12.
33 Landsdowne to Bonar Law, 26 September 1913. ABL 30/3/64.
34 Pretyman to Bonar Law, 28 October 1913. ABL 30/3/64.
35 John Baird to Bonar Law, 11 July 1913; A. E. Weighall to Bonar Law, 25 September 1913. ABL 29/6/19; 30/2/24.
36 The 4th Marquis of Salisbury to Bonar Law, 18 February 1914. ABL 31/3/33.
37 See *Liberal Magazine*, 1914, pp. 398-403; 483.
38 See Cabinet memoranda etc., January 1914; CAB 37/118/5. June 1914; CAB 37/120/71. 5 June 1914; CAB 37/120/74.

10 DIASPORA

. . . e terra quoniam sunt cuncta creata
Lucretius, *De Rerum Natura, v,* 796

. . . Out of land, indeed, all things are created.

At the outbreak of war, the leading statesmen on both sides of
the House tried to set the land question, and most other matters
not directly related to the war itself, into political cold storage.
Some backbench land-taxers argued that their long-sought reform
would provide a great source of revenue for wartime purposes;
but they were unable to persuade either Government or Parliament that it was expedient to tackle the question immediately.
Some opponents of land-taxing, like Sir Frederick Banbury, Conservative MP for the City of London, argued that land valuation
should be stopped in order that the valuation staff might be
used elsewhere. They also failed to carry their point; although
in practice the people employed on that work were largely
dispersed. At the beginning of the war, 4,760 men had been
valuing land for taxation purposes; by November 1915 (when
conscription had not yet been introduced), 2,600 had been
dismissed, and 1,000 had enlisted.[1] Some important wartime
measures related to the land question. An Act of 1915 commenced the state control of rents and mortgages of dwelling
houses. This provided a precedent on which was founded a large
bulk of postwar legislation, which has been adapted and continued
right to our own time. Early in 1917, another precedent was
established, with the introduction of minimum agricultural prices
to stimulate food production.

Yet the war proved profoundly damaging to the land-taxers'
cause. In August 1914, C. P. Trevelyan was the only more or less
"orthodox" land-taxer in the Government. He resigned in protest
against Britain's participation in the war. Among the backbench
land-taxers, J. C. Wedgwood was for a moment inclined to take
the same view; but then he had second thoughts — won a naval
DSO and later served on Smuts's staff in the army. His colleague
in the neighbouring constituency of Hanley was the no less
enthusiastic land-taxer, R. L. Outhwaite, who took a pacifist

169

attitude throughout the conflict. The most senior men of the pre-war Government, Asquith and Lloyd George, had both earned the sincere gratitude of the land reformers; but before the war came to an end they found themselves leading opposite sides of the House — for reasons which had nothing to do with the ordinary issues of domestic politics, and less to do with the conduct of the war itself than people once imagined.

Thus, almost by accident, the men who in different ways had been advancing the cause of land reform found themselves not merely dispersed, but also associated with other politicians whose aspirations were quite different from their own. By the closing stages of the war, Lloyd George was Prime Minister, and was heading a government in which Conservatives preponderated over all other groups combined. Those Liberals who sat with Lloyd George included some noted land-taxers, but also other people who in the old days had done what lay in their power to damp their party's enthusiasm for land reform. Exactly the same could be said of the Liberals who sat with Asquith. Meanwhile, men like Outhwaite and Trevelyan found themselves co-operating closely with pacifist socialists who belonged to the ILP.

As the war moved towards its end, the official organs of the Liberal and Labour Parties seem very largely to have assumed that politics would revert essentially to what they had been before the war. The Labour Party had acquired new policies; but on the familiar "land problem" both of the two Parties continued to talk the old language. The Labour Conference of January 1918 and the National Liberal Federation's Conference of September, both declared in favour of land value taxation — in terms, no doubt, which offended some purists,[2] but not in terms which differed noticeably from those which had been used before the war. What neither Party seems to have contemplated was that the circumstances in which the next election would be fought would bear no relation to those which had prevailed in the past.

The enforced national unity of wartime produced some real sympathy between social classes which had not existed before; and it would be quite wrong to regard this phenomenon too cynically. A great landowner, the Earl of Dartmouth, wrote to Wedgwood in 1916, expressing a view which was widespread among his class. National reconstruction, in Dartmouth's view, must follow the war. It would mean ". . . . sacrifices of some kind from us all, but as it is inconceivable that after all that has

170

passed we should go back to the old extremes of wealth and poverty, the old suspicion and prejudice, the continual warfare between class and class, employer and employed — it means, especially, that those who have most will have to make the largest sacrifices . . ."[3] Rather in this spirit, the Cabinet had given early consideration to the special problems of returning ex-servicemen, some of whom would certainly desire to acquire land. Lloyd George's Minister of Agriculture was a Unionist, R. E. Prothero (later Lord Ernle). Prothero's first view was that a private approach to great landowners would produce most of the land required; but he later modified this opinion, and concluded that some compulsion would be necessary.[4] The Cabinet decided, in May 1918, to set up a politically mixed committee, under the Chairmanship of the Home Secretary — another Unionist, Lord Cave. With some prodding, the Cave Committee began to prepare recommendations which — in the view of one of its Liberal members — were "fairly thoroughgoing — indeed revolutionary — when you consider who has approved them".[5]

The war ended with unexpected abruptness while the Cave Committee was still sitting. Within a day or so of the Armistice, the Government announced that a General Election would take place in the following month, December 1918, and that the Coalition would remain together to contest that election as a united body. The Labour Party declared that it would withdraw from the Government and make an independent appeal to the nation. A week or so later, the Government published the names of the candidates who would be receiving its official support. The great majority of the Unionist candidates was included, but rather less than half of the Liberals. Those Liberals who were to receive the Coalition's blessing did not include Asquith — still the official leader of the Party — nor his closest political associates.

On land questions, neither the Government parties nor those Liberals who stood outside could make any very definite pronouncements. The Coalition was inhibited by the fact that the Cave Committee was still sitting. The Committee's initial report was considered by the Cabinet ten days after the Armistice — by which time the General Election was already in full swing. The recommendations did not go far enough to satisfy the Cabinet,[6] and the Government was not able to finalise its proposals before polling day. The broad lines of thought, however, were fairly clear, and the Government's election manifesto promised State provision for smallholdings, allotments and cottage plots for ex-servicemen, with equipment and credit on easy terms to assist them in stocking the land. The Liberal leaders could neither endorse the Coalition's programme — for many Liberals were being opposed by Government nominees — nor set forward their own policies in opposition to those of the Coalition — for many other Liberals were receiving Government support. In land policies, as on other matters, the pronouncements of the official organs of the Liberal Party were designed rather to minimise friction among the Liberals than to present a clear policy to the nation.

The Coalition won an enormous majority. The Unionists were not only by far the largest element within that Coalition, but they also formed an absolute majority of the House of Commons. The results were an unqualified disaster to the land-taxers not only because most of the Government supporters were hostile to their cause, but also because no alternative administration could be discerned on the Opposition side of the House where land-taxers had any real influence. Asquith, and every one of his principal associates, had been wiped out. The total contingent of Liberals elected without Government support was around thirty. The Labour group mustered fifty-seven; but nobody could fairly describe those men as the most luminous members of their Party.

The fate of individual land-taxers at that election is but illustrative of the general confusion. *Land Values*, organ of the enthusiasts, listed fourteen men who had sat in the old House, whom it regarded as "prominently associated with the taxation of land values". Four received Government support, and of these three were elected. Eight stood as official Liberals without Government support, and of them five were elected. One was defeated standing as an Independent Liberal; one standing as an Independent. *Land Values* also evinced special interest in the fate of eleven other candidates who had not sat in the old House. Three were elected: one each as a Coalition Liberal, a Liberal without Coalition support and a Labour man. Four who stood as non-Coalition Liberals were defeated; four who stood in the Labour interest were also defeated.

Some of the land-taxing candidates had illuminating experiences. Wedgwood, in Newcastle-under-Lyme, made it quite clear that he had no confidence in the Government, and refused to commit himself to any Party — describing himself as an

"Independent Radical". His status as a "war hero" probably played a large part in persuading both Unionist and Labour Parties not to oppose his candidature. The Coalition gave him its official support — support which not only was unsolicited, but was formally repudiated. His neighbour Outhwaite discovered that official Government support was given to an opponent from the mushroom National Democratic Party, and that the other candidates ranged against him including both a Liberal and a Labour man. The experience of Trevelyan in Elland was rather similar, although in his case the recipient of official Government support was a Unionist. P. W. Raffan, MP for Leigh, was also a strong land-taxer. He was too old to be a war hero, but he was not a pacifist either; while his statements about the Coalition were a good deal more pointed and hostile than those of Asquith himself. Yet Raffan received official Government support, and was elected. J. Dundas White, a land-taxing enthusiast of similar views but perhaps greater eminence, found that the Coalition was backing his Unionist opponent in Glasgow, and was defeated. Arthur Ponsonby, son of Queen Victoria's famous Private Secretary, was a land-taxer who had taken a pacifist line during the war. Coalition opposition was inevitable in his seat of Dunfermline; but in this case the opponent who received Government support was not only a Liberal but a noted land-taxer as well. As the Coalition Liberal was elected, the land-taxing cause in that constituency may have suffered no harm.

It soon became apparent that the situation was even worse than had originally appeared, for the relationships between the political groups in which the various land-taxers found themselves grew steadily worse. Coalition and non-Coalition Liberals very soon came to regard each other as deadly enemies. The differences between Labour and Liberal in the old Parliament had sometimes been little more than nominal; from 1918 onwards the gap between Labour and the Liberals in either group became wider and wider.

In none of the three bodies were the land-taxers dominant. From a purely numerical point of view, they might be expected to have most effect upon the non-Coalition Liberals, for six of that small band were noted land-taxers. Yet what was their influence worth, when none of the leading figures of the Party had managed to get into the House? The centre of gravity of the so-called "Asquithians" lay outside the walls of Parliament and not within; and relations between the MPs and the leadership outside the House were often far from affable.

The effectiveness of the land-taxers before the war had turned on a remarkable relationship. There was an informed electorate, whose attention had been focused again and again on questions relating to land, and who understood the main arguments. There was a substantial group of really ardent, hot-gospelling land-taxers in the House of Commons, the great majority of them within the Liberal Party. The bulk of the Government MPs, and most of the members of the Government itself, were by no means dogmatic Single Taxers; but they were not hostile in principle to any proposals for immediate action which the extremists were likely to raise. As political realists, the Government leaders and most of the Liberal MPs had been very conscious that land reform was a popular cause among the voters.

Now, at the close of 1918, all of this had gone. Most of the voters had never been involved in the old controversies; those who had been involved had had their minds deflected to other things for four terrible years.

That faith which the informed land-taxers had once had in the Liberal leadership was largely shattered. Lloyd George was a prisoner of the Unionists — although, to a degree, they were his prisoners as well. Asquith was already in his late sixties, and showing many signs of age. His energy returned in fits and starts; but it took some considerable time before he was again able to give much of a lead to Liberals, and there was certainly no evident successor among those who followed him.

Perhaps in despair, perhaps in hope, the land-taxers began to drift towards the Labour Party. Not only had Labour twice as many MPs as the Asquithian Liberals, but they had a substantial and growing electoral support, backed by massive funds. True, they had recently committed themselves to a policy in which Fabian socialism loomed much larger than land-taxing; yet it was still far from certain which of their various policies would receive principal emphasis in future. To many land-taxers, it must have seemed that the Labour Party could hardly fail to be influenced if a band of educated and informed enthusiasts, who mustered between them a very impressive record of Parliamentary experience, should decide to join it. The natural route into the Labour Party for men of middle-class origin was through the ILP, and this route was particularly attractive to those who had

174

been pacifists during the war, for they had already formed close ILP contacts.

Outhwaite was the first to go. Almost immediately after the election, he and most of his election workers constituted themselves the Hanley ILP. Very soon Trevelyan followed in the same direction. Wedgwood, in spite of the anomalous circumstances of his election, was at first disposed to work with the Asquithians. Yet when he heard Asquith speak a few weeks later, and discovered that "taxation and rating of land values and a levy on capital occupy no place in the Liberal leader's programme", Wedgwood decided that there was no place for him in the Liberal Party, and proceeded to join the ILP. A few months later, Wedgwood was followed by Dundas White, and soon by yet another former MP who had rendered conspicuous service in the past, E. G. Hemmerde. Thus, by the later part of 1919, quite a substantial group of former Liberal MPs with land-taxing proclivities had accumulated in the Labour Party.

Most of them were very far from uncritical of their new associates. Trevelyan, who found the ILP "quite enormously the most congenial organisation I have ever worked with" was the most ecstatic; but even he was driven to observe that when Labour contrived to "get hold of the government", they would "probably . . . make a horrid mess of it".[7]

Nor was the Labour Party disposed to welcome these converts with open arms. Wedgwood could hardly be deterred from joining the ILP, but admission to the Parliamentary Labour Party was a very different matter. The Labour Party's Joint Parliamentary Sub-Committee recommended that his application should be refused. Later, the Executive Committee reversed this decision, and he was allowed to join; but the reversal was far from unanimous.[8] Others had comparable experiences. Ponsonby wrote of the Labour Party that: "So long as Adamson & Co. lead them I do not see much hope. I am afraid that our gang is not at all popular with the officials. They have just turned me down for consideration in Dunfermline (my old constituency) and chosen the miners' nominee."[9]

Some of these land-taxers who had once sat as Liberals did find their way back to Parliament eventually under the Labour aegis; but a considerable number never did so. Whether Labour doubted the sincerity of their conversion, or was jealous of their ability, is difficult to discover.

A few land-taxers — of whom Outhwaite is the most famous — found the discipline or compromises of political life within the Labour Party intolerable, and departed to form a new organisation, which eventually became known as the Commonwealth Land Party, which was designed to preach land reform in its purest form. Organisations without substantial financial backing seldom have much success in British politics, and the Commonwealth Land Party was no exception. Two candidates were fielded in Stoke-on-Trent in 1931; both fared disastrously.

In the period immediately after the war, some agonising confrontations between land-taxers in different Parties were inevitable. At the Rusholme (Manchester) by-election of October 1919, a Unionist seat was attacked by both Liberals and Labour, and both of those candidates were land-taxers. Outhwaite and Wedgwood gave public support to Dr Dunstan, the Labour man; P. W. Raffan gave no less public support to W. M. R. Pringle, the Liberal.[10] The situation looked even worse when the Unionist was returned on a minority vote.

A very different position arose in the confused, but important, Spen Valley by-election at the close of 1919. Sir John Simon, the Liberal candidate, contrived to omit all reference to land taxing from his election address; while the Labour man who defeated him gave the matter some prominence.

A few months later, Asquith himself was the Liberal candidate at the even more important contest in Paisley; and the situation was different again. Asquith was by no means unfriendly to the land-taxers — while the Labour man's statements, at least at the beginning of the campaign, were positively hostile. Yet this did not deter such staunch land-taxers as Wedgwood, Outhwaite and Trevelyan from sending messages of support to the Labour candidate.

The difficulties which faced the Government itself were no less profound than those of the Opposition. At first, all seemed to be comparatively plain sailing. Prothero, Minister of Agriculture, wrote to Lloyd George that: "Land settlement for ex-Service men is a national duty, and the State must be prepared to bear a considerable part of the initial cost."[11]

No political group would dare dispute that proposition. In Prothero's view, the main demand for land would come from demobilised ex-farm labourers. He recommended a Land Settlement Bill in order to meet it. This would not make radical changes in the substantive law, but would introduce considerable administrative streamlining. Prothero's Bill was approved by the Cabinet in March 1919, and passed into law without much difficulty later in the year. The responsibility for building houses on smallholdings was passed to the County Councils. Preference would be given to ex-Service men, but the scheme would not be limited to them. This measure was accompanied by a parallel Act for Scotland. Unfortunately the schemes soon encountered trouble through the rising cost of cottage building, and in the middle of 1920 County Councils were officially urged to cease buying unequipped land for settlement where houses could only be provided "after long delay and at unreasonable cost".[12]

While the Land Settlement Bill was being considered by the Cabinet and Parliament, attention was also given to the more general question of compensation for land which had been acquired under compulsory powers. Early in March 1919, a committee was set up by the Cabinet under the Lord Chancellor, Lord Birkenhead, to examine the question.[13] The first report appeared within a fortnight; but Lloyd George's reaction was positively sulphurous: "I have received the report of your Committee on the Land Acquisition Bill with profound disappointment. The Bill was supposed to be one to facilitate acquisition of land for most urgent public purposes, speedily and at a fair price. It has been transformed into a Bill which will be represented as making sure the landlord gets a good price, that the lawyers get their pickings, and that there should be no undue hurry in completion of the transaction . . ."[14]

The public, who knew Birkenhead for his arrogance and rather cruel wit, would have been fascinated to read his grovelling reply: "I have called the Committee together again tonight . . . I have no doubt that they will arrive at conclusions satisfactory to you. I can only add that if I had been at the original Cabinet, and had the slightest means of understanding what your views were, and the grounds upon which they rested, the difficulty, such as it is, would never have arisen . . ."[15]

This particular exchange by no means ended the political machinations over the Government's land compensation proposals. A Parliamentary Bill appeared in April 1919. This proposed the establishment of a tribunal to assess compensation when land was compulsorily acquired, and laid down rules to govern its operation and procedure.

There was much playing to the political gallery. In his correspondence with Birkenhead, Lloyd George had urged the Government's sensational defeat at the West Leyton by-election (March 1919) as evidence for the need for drastic proposals. When the Bill appeared, the Coalition Liberals decided to occupy the front Opposition bench, in order to give the Government support from that unwonted quarter, and to undermine the authority of Sir Donald Maclean, who was leading the Opposition Liberals during Asquith's absence from the House. The non-Government Liberals' main criticism of the Bill was that it proposed an *ad hoc* system of valuation, instead of using the existing land valuation records as the basis of compensation.

Inevitably, the Bill was carried in the form which the Government desired; but an interesting and important point had been raised. If the land valuation which had been accumulated over so many weary years was of no use in fixing compensation — and, instead, a new and expensive device was required for that process — then could the valuation be of much use as a basis for taxation — or, indeed, for anything else? It was by no means surprising that a problem of this kind should arise. Land values had been rising rapidly in relation to other commodity values; and it was even less realistic to use the pre-war land valuation as a basis for compensation or taxation than to use pre-war assessments of (say) personal property, or income.

Five days after Maclean's criticisms were first aired in the House of Commons, the Cabinet decided that a Select Committee should be appointed to examine the land value duties, and the whole system of valuation.[16] Unfortunately, the terms of reference of the Select Committee were ambiguous. The Liberal land-taxer P. W. Raffan, and the Labour MPs who sat on the Committee, wished to submit new proposals for land-taxing. The Chairman ruled them out of order, and was upheld by the officials of the House of Commons. Raffan and the Labour men threatened to withdraw unless they were allowed to raise these proposals; while the Unionist E. G. Pretyman, and some other members of the Committee, retorted by threatening to resign themselves if the proposals were made. The question was brought before the Cabinet, who tried but failed to achieve a compromise. The Select Committee thereupon broke up, having failed to agree on its terms of reference, much less its recommendations.[17]

It is not difficult to guess the nub of the dispute. The members

178

of the Committee probably agreed that the existing duties were more or less useless; the operative question was whether they should be replaced by a thoroughgoing system of land value taxation, serviced by frequent revisions of the land valuation — or whether they should be abandoned altogether.

Soon after the Select Committee collapsed, but before the Government had taken any further action on the matter, a somewhat extraordinary resolution was carried by the National Unionist Association, chief organ of "grass-roots" Conservatism, who declared that they "regard(ed) with alarm the persistent propaganda carried on by the Labour Party and others in favour of the Nationalisation of land and industries, and desire(d) a clear declaration by the Prime Minister and Mr Bonar Law of their determined opposition to this policy".[18]

It was, of course, in no way surprising that the Unionists should oppose nationalisation, whether of land or anything else; but why did the National Unionist Association seek to raise the question in such a form at that time? At least one very important Conservative saw the resolution as "a subtle move to create an atmosphere of hostility and discontent in the rank and file of the Party".[19]

The resolution may also have been prompted by a desire to force the Government to give tangible proof of its "trustworthiness" — from the Conservative point of view — on the land question. If that was the object, the proof soon appeared.

The Chancellor of the Exchequer in the Coalition Government was Austen Chamberlain, the second man to Bonar Law in the Unionist hierarchy. In his Budget of April 1920, Chamberlain proposed to abolish both the existing land value duties and the whole valuation system. What caught the public interest most about the situation was that Lloyd George, who had introduced the land taxes and valuation in 1909, was now presiding over the Government which recommended their abolition. To the Unionist opponents of land-taxing, this confirmed their view that the whole notion had been useless from the start; while the land-taxers tended to interpret it as further evidence that Lloyd George had sold the pass to every enemy of radical thought and practice.

The Government's argument was simple, and superficially impressive. The duties were complicated and costly to administer, and their yield was slight. The valuation system existed to service the duties. Both, therefore, should be abolished.

All the old issues of 1909-10 were recalled. The land-taxers made it abundantly plain that they had supported the Lloyd George proposals before the war, not because they were enamoured of the particular duties which he proposed, but because they saw the Budget as the thin end of the wedge — as a means for securing a system of land valuation, which could later be used as the basis of a more rational, more simple and infinitely more effective system of land value taxation. In the course of the debate in Parliament, Asquith was able to throw important light both on the current arguments of the land-taxers and on the motives of the pre-1914 Liberal Government: ". . . I still believe, as my Chancellor of the Exchequer said in February 1914, in the necessity, first of all, of the valuation, and next, as a consequence of that valuation, and as a proper purpose to which it should be applied, the taxing for public purposes, both imperial and local, of the site value of land. Further it has always been to me one of the great recommendations of the valuation and taxation of land that land may be acquired by the community at the same rate and upon the same terms upon which it was taxed. The converse is even more true, that it should be taxed and rated at the same price at which the owner is willing to sell it to the community, when the community wants to purchase it. I have not changed my views upon that by a hair's breadth."

Col. Wedgwood : I only regret that you did not do it while you were in power.

Mr Asquith : We were doing it; we were on the point of doing it, in the spring of 1914 — as I have shown in the passage I have quoted — by legislation. Then came the war in August of that year which made such legislation impossible . . ."

In the same debate, Chamberlain taunted Asquith with not having been "an early or an enthusiastic convert to the principle of these taxes". To this Asquith was able to give a devastating reply by inviting the Chancellor "to apply to the Prime Minister and ask his views on that".[20]

Although yet again the Government could hardly fail to win in the division lobbies, it was remarkable how little support they received from the Coalition Liberals. The total contingent of the "Coalies" was about 130. The numbers voting in the various divisions was not always constant; but a representative sample was the division of 14 July 1920, on the motion to retain land value duties. Only eighteen Coalition Liberals supported the

Government; while thirteen of their number went into the Opposition lobbies with the "Asquithians" and Labour. Perhaps one may read some significance into the fact that all four of the Scottish Coalition Liberals who voted in the division opposed the Government, and so also did three of the five who sat for Lloyd George's own "pocket borough" of Wales. It was not wise for a putatively Liberal MP for a Celtic constituency to be seen as an enemy of land reform.

Thus in the course of 1920 it became abundantly clear that the Government could be regarded as a certain enemy of the land-taxers' cause, and that any hope for the taxation of land values must lie with the Opposition parties. The "Asquithian" Liberals were not hostile, and many of them were strong supporters; but, as time went on, the prospects of any substantial revival gradually receded. It was predictable that they would win some seats at the next General Election; but there was good reason for thinking that most of these would be in rural areas, far from the great population centres. What, then, of the Labour Party? As we have seen, a large proportion of the most prominent land-taxers had decamped to the Labour Party in the year or so which followed the Armistice. Yet there was little to suggest that the Labour Party would be likely to press the land question with the vigour which the enthusiasts desired. An assortment of Labour Party organisations at the national and local levels continued from time to time to issue statements which were designed to placate the land-taxers or the land nationalisers or both. These statements are strongly reminiscent of a church congregation reciting the Apostles' Creed; many of the faithful probably did not understand what they were saying, and might not have agreed with it if they had. In any event, the political centre of gravity of the Labour Party was rapidly moving in a different direction. Right at the end of 1920, there was an enormous upswing in the unemployment figures. During the years which followed, the incidence of unemployment was far higher than it had been in even the worst years before the war. Land-taxers could — and did — argue that land-taxing was the long-term cure for unemployment;[21] but the unemployed demanded some policy which seemed to offer quick returns. Thus the Labour Party gave more and more attention to such proposals as the Capital Levy and industrial nationalisation.

Throughout 1921 and most of 1922, the political tensions

within the Coalition grew greater and greater. At last, in October 1922, the Unionists followed Bonar Law's reluctant lead, broke the Government, and made their independent appeal to the electors. They won a comfortable overall majority. The Labour Party became, without argument, the second party of the State; while the Liberals were divided into two roughly equal groups, one giving nominal support to Asquith and the other to Lloyd George. Both among the "Asquithian" Liberals and among the Labour Party there were substantial bodies of noted land-taxers. It was claimed that no fewer than 126 MPs were "pledged to the taxation of land values".[22] Of course this did not imply that they were all enthusiasts, or would give the matter any high degree of priority. In any case, the Government was an avowed enemy. Perhaps the most attractive feature of Bonar Law's administration, from the radicals' point of view, was its incurable lethargy. Such a government would do little positive damage, although it would certainly do no good.

Notes-10

1 *Land Values*, December 1915, p. 265.
2 See, for example, J. C. Wedgwood's letter, *Daily News*, 11 September 1918.
3 Earl of Dartmouth to Wedgwood, 11 October 1916. Wedgwood papers.
4 War Cabinet 412, 15 May 1918. CAB 23/6.
5 C. Addison to Lloyd George, 27 September 1918. LG(B) F/1/4/26.
6 War Cabinet 505, 21 November 1918; 508, 29 November 1918. CAB 23/8.
7 C. P. Trevelyan to Eleanor Acland, 24 May 1919. Acland papers.
8 LPEC: Joint Meeting of EC and PP, 4 June 1919; EC, 4 June 1919.
9 Ponsonby to Wedgwood, 28 October 1919. Wedgwood papers.
10 For land-taxers' reactions, see Minutes of Manchester Land Values League, 24 September 1919.
11 R. E. Prothero to Lloyd George, 21 January 1919. LG(B) F/15/8/50.
12 Cabinet Minutes C37(20)7, 24 June 1920. CAB 23/21.
13 War Cabinet 539, 3 March 1919. CAB 23/9.
14 Lloyd George to Birkenhead, 15 March 1919 (copy). LG(B) F/4/7/9.
15 Birkenhead to Lloyd George, 17 March 1919. LG(B) F/4/7/10.

16   War Cabinet 557, 16 April 1919. CAB 23/10.
17   Cabinet Minutes C11(19)2, 8 December 1919. CAB 23/18. House of Commons White Paper 243 of 1919; *Land and Liberty*, 1920, p. 330.
18   Resolution carried 10 February 1920.
19   Sir A. Salvidge to Bonar Law, 16 February 1920. BL 96/3.
20   131 House of Commons Debates 5S, cols. 2474, 2477, 14 July 1920.
21   This view had been argued long before the war — see, for example, Wedgwood's speech at Manchester Moss Side, *Manchester Guardian*, 14 January 1909. It continued to be argued long afterwards — see, for example, the summary in *Land and Liberty*, 1921, pp. 28-9, 65.
22   *Land and Liberty*, 1923, p. 2.

11 INTO THE TWENTIES

We hold the position that the whole economic value of land belongs to the community as a whole . . . When the Labour Government does sit upon those (i.e., the Government) benches it will not deserve to have a second term of office unless in the most determined manner it tries to secure social wealth for social purposes.

Philip Snowden, MP House of Commons, 4 July 1923.

The Parliament which met at the end of 1922 pursued a policy which Government supporters called "tranquility", but which the Opposition was more disposed to describe as stagnation. Only two pieces of legislation which had any bearing on the land problem emerged, and neither of them could be regarded as of major importance.

An Act of 1896 had halved agricultural rates; the Agricultural Rates Act of 1923 reduced them to a quarter of the assessment. Neville Chamberlain (son of Joseph, half-brother of Austen) defended these proposals on the grounds that agriculture had fallen into a "desperate condition"; but as the total rate reduction amounted to less than £3 millions, Government supporters and opponents alike were unable to discover any prospect of significant improvement.

The second measure which bore on the land question arose in connection with the Finance Bill of 1923. While the proposals were being debated, an amendment was proposed by Sir William Bull — a Conservative backbencher long noted for his extreme opposition to anything remotely resembling land taxation. Under the Finance Act of 1909-10, landowners were required to supply the Land Valuation Department with particulars of sales and leases, and this obligation had not been removed in 1920. Bull's amendment proposed its removal forthwith. The Government, which was in the process of examining the valuation question in some detail, asked for the amendment to be withdrawn, and the mover was prepared to do this. With incredible ineptitude, some Labour Members insisted that it should be put to a division — with the predictable result that the amendment was carried.

One of the most interesting features of the vote was that the Lloyd Georgeite Liberals split deeply — eight opposing the amendment and ten supporting it.

Bonar Law fell ill in the spring of 1923, and was replaced by Stanley Baldwin. In the autumn, the new Prime Minister made a famous declaration in favour of Protection, which immediately precipitated the General Election. The Liberal groups reunited with almost indecent haste, and the three Parties made their appeals to the nation in what was one of the most open elections of modern times. After the poll, the Conservatives remained the largest single Party, but the Labour and Liberal Parties combined were considerably more numerous. These remarkable results produced a period of inter- and intra-Party manoeuvre, by no means all of which is completely understood to this day; but the final upshot was that Ramsay MacDonald, Leader of the Labour Party, was commissioned to form a Government in January 1924, even though his Party held well under a third of the seats in the Commons.

MacDonald showed astonishingly little tact in dealing with his Labour colleagues. That he grossly mishandled Arthur Henderson is well known. The new Prime Minister's treatment of Philip Snowden, the other senior claimant amongst Labour's "old guard" — and a noted land-taxer to boot — is less well known. A contemporary journalist, whose information seems reliable, gave a remarkable sidelight on the appointment: "You have all been wondering who(m) JRM has been relying on — if anyone — for advice in the formation of his government. No one has hit upon the fact which has been very carefully concealed. But he has gone to the worst possible source for advice and inspiration — F. W. Hirst. Last week JRM, Hirst and Lloyd George breakfasted together and went through the Cabinet proposals. JRM offered Hirst the Chancellorship and pressed him to take it. Hirst refused, in JRM's own interest, as he believed the Party would not stand the exclusion of Snowden, and it was Hirst who advised Snowden for it. Hirst has got Parmoor to come in and influenced some other strange selections . . ."[1]

This enforced inclusion of Snowden was of great importance from the land-taxers' point of view. Another famous land-taxer was also included in the Cabinet in spite of the Premier's reluctance. It will be recalled that Josiah Wedgwood had transferred to the Labour Party in 1919. In the period which followed he rose rapidly in Labour's ranks, and by the time the first Labour Government was formed he was Vice-Chairman of the Labour MPs. Dame Veronica Wedgwood, in the biography of her uncle, describes the new Prime Minister's encounter with his distinguished follower: "When MacDonald at last sent for him it was only to offer him the very minor post of Financial Secretary to the War Office. Josiah pointed out that as Vice-Chairman of the Parliamentary Party he could hardly take less than Cabinet rank. 'That is just what is so unfortunate', said MacDonald ungraciously, 'however, I will see what I can do for you'."[2]

This encounter between the Prime Minister and Wedgwood is the more poignant when one recalls that MacDonald found himself so short of talent in his own party that he was compelled to incorporate such dubious and recent converts as Lords Haldane and Parmoor in senior office.

If it were possible to guess the behaviour of a government from the known views of the MPs who sat on its benches, or were prepared to give it some measure of external support, then there would have been every reason to think that the First Labour Government would engage in a vigorous policy of land reform. One hundred and thirty-eight of the Labour MPs, and sixty of the Liberals, had given sympathetic replies to a questionnaire circulated by the United Committee for the Taxation of Land Values at the time of the election. The Chancellor of the Exchequer and at least two[3] other members of the Cabinet were committed supporters of land-taxing, not merely in the sense that they had given formal assent at election times, but also in the sense that they had been active and vigorous propagandists for the cause over many years. Few, if any, of the Labour or Liberal MPs would have been likely to provide active opposition to any initiative which the Government might take on the matter; and such initiative might well attract Liberals to the Labour Party.

As the Conservatives were considerably more numerous than the Labour Party in the House of Commons, the survival of the Government depended upon the continued willingness of the Liberals not merely to abstain from opposing the Ministry, but actually to vote for it in the division lobbies. Any government of any kind will inevitably do things from time to time which are hard to defend. Ordinary political experience shows that it is often difficult enough to persuade a government's own backbenchers to render the necessary support; to ask members of another political party to do so when they are being attacked by Government partisans in their own constituencies is too much. There was no sort of understanding between Labour and Liberal Parties as to the terms on which Liberal co-operation would be given. In addition, the Liberals were experiencing very considerable internal strains for several quite separate reasons. The Government suffered from all the consequences of inexperience; while speeches from supporters made matters steadily worse.

Thus was the Labour Government of 1924 confronted from the start with difficulties which were largely of its own making. Two notable pieces of legislation emerged all the same. John Wheatley's Housing Act greatly increased the Government's subsidy for local authority housebuilding, and proposed to extend that subsidy for fifteen years. Snowden's Budget repealed the "McKenna duties" which had been introduced in 1915 in order to save shipping space, and which had been twisted by Austen Chamberlain in 1919 into a device of Imperial Preference. The new Chancellor was also under some pressure to initiate plans for land taxing. Snowden could not introduce any relevant proposals into the Budget for reasons of parliamentary procedure. He was advised that even the restoration of machinery to collect information about land transfer would be out of order in a Finance Bill; but on the Chancellor's recommendation the Cabinet agreed that a short Bill should be introduced for the purpose. They also accepted his proposal that the Land Valuation Office "would become concerned in a new valuation of land for the purposes of new taxation".[4] Both in his Budget statement and in an important speech delivered a few weeks later in his own constituency, Snowden gave public intimation of his intention to value and tax land.

The whole atmosphere of the Parliament which met in January 1924 was bedevilled by party politics in its worst form, and this made any long-term programme impossible. Politicians played for position, for short-term tactical advantage, with little attention to the long-term interests of the community. The eventual defeat of the Government over the "Campbell case" in October 1924 reflects little credit on any of the three Parties. The General Election which followed was even more discreditable, and in its latest phases was dominated by that notorious forgery, the "Zinoviev letter". The Conservative Party won a large overall majority; the Labour Party lost a considerable amount of ground; while the Liberal Party was reduced to about forty seats.

All reasonable hopes of radical land reform of any sort could be abandoned so long as the new Parliament persisted. Some exceptionally sanguine people drew hope from the presence of Winston Churchill at the Exchequer — but the complexion of the Government as a whole could have left no doubt about the general course which would be pursued. Rather like the Unionist administrations at the turn of the century, this Government would not concede anything to the really radical land reformers, but nevertheless was willing to introduce quite substantial measures of a less fundamental character; while Ministers sometimes found themselves subjected to unwelcome pressure from their own nominal supporters who were a good deal less willing to countenance mild land reform.

The most famous land legislation of this Conservative Government was the Law of Property Act of 1925. This covered a great deal more than land; but, so far as land law is concerned, it is probably the most comprehensive statute in existence. The Act was largely a consolidating measure, and many of the important alterations in the old law which it enshrined had been proposed in the Coalition period by Lord Birkenhead, and passed into law just before the fall of Lloyd George's government.[5]

Although no radical land measures emerged from the Government, the land question was very far from dead as a political issue — particularly, but by no means exclusively, in connection with agriculture. The trade depression which affected industry and produced widespread and persistent unemployment throughout the 1920s and 1930s was paralleled by a depression on an equal or greater scale which affected many branches of agriculture. Special favours to farming, whether through "protection" or through large-scale subsidies, were more or less out of the question, because cheap food was essential for the urban population.

In this economic climate, people often adopted different attitudes to the actual proposals which were set in front of Parliament from those which they would have taken a few decades earlier. A good illustration is provided by the question of agricultural derating.

In 1896, the proposal to collect only half of the normal rates on agricultural land was regarded as essentially a favour to the landlords' interests, and a measure which conflicted with the aims of the land-taxers. By 1923, when Bonar Law's government further reduced agricultural rates to a quarter, the relative importance of site value by comparison with improvement value of agricultural land had become so small that the Government proposals represented mainly a relief on improvements rather than on site values, and the opposition of the land taxers was far less sharp. In 1929, Baldwin's government proposed to derate agricultural land altogether. By this time, some agricultural site values were literally *nil*, and cases were reported in the Press where owners were offering marginal agricultural land free, but could get no takers; overhead costs would exceed the value of any crops which might be grown. The 1929 measure was sometimes criticised in detail; but the principle behind it was practically non-contentious. On the other hand, there was no doubt whatever that urban hereditaments possessed enormous site values.

The general depression of the inter-war years was not immediately recognised as a chronic problem. In the early 1920s, it was regarded as an unfortunate economic aberration which was due to a temporary slump, and which would be overcome automatically when trade recovered. As the 1920s advanced, people came to realise that the problem would not solve itself, and they became more and more interested to discover what politicians had to offer in the nature of possible remedies.

One of the most extraordinary features of politics in the period of Baldwin's government is the rôle of the Liberal Party. In the House of Commons, the Liberals had sunk to a position of virtual impotence; yet in most economic discussions — whether on land or on other matters — it was the Liberal proposals which made the running. People might like or dislike those proposals (and some of the bitterest critics were themselves Liberals) — but nobody could ignore them.

Almost immediately after the 1924 General Election, Lloyd George was elected Chairman of the Liberal MPs. A few days later, a body of Liberal MPs, most of whom were personally hostile to Lloyd George, constituted themselves the "Radical Group", under the leadership of Walter Runciman. The Radical Group laid special emphasis on land value taxation in their pronouncements; but it would be quite wrong to consider that the division between Lloyd Georgeite and anti-Lloyd Georgeite Liberal MPs had much to do with policy. Each section included men with widely disparate political attitudes; and one of the

189

oddest aspects of the situation was that while Lloyd George was himself proposing policies of a very radical nature, some of his closest followers held views indistinguishable from those of the Conservatives.[6]

To the Liberal Party of the time, considerations of finance were no less important than problems involving personalities or policies. The official funds of the Liberal Party were practically exhausted; but Lloyd George was known to control a political fund of enormous dimensions which had been amassed in the days of the Coalition. From this fund he had made a large donation to the Liberal Party in 1923, and a much more parsimonious donation in 1924; while he continued to spend the money lavishly on economic enquiries and political campaigns which were kept firmly under his personal control. Lloyd George made the freest possible use of the leading economists of the day. Men like Maynard Keynes, Sir William Beveridge, Walter Layton and H. D. Henderson played major parts in the various Lloyd George enquiries. The reports which they produced were almost guaranteed to become the focus of great public attention.

About a year after the Coalition fell, Lloyd George set up one of these groups of experts, under the name of the Liberal Land Committee, and by the autumn of 1925 its work was complete. Lloyd George foreshadowed the Committee's rural report in a speech delivered to a crowd of 25,000 people at Killerton in Devon, in the middle of September. The venue was not without interest, for that meeting was held on the estate of F. D. (later Sir Francis) Acland, who had been one of the leading Asquithian MPs during the Coalition period.[7] Lloyd George was no man to bear grudges, and was always most anxious to turn former enemies into allies, when he respected their capacity.

Lloyd George argued that other European countries had contrived to maintain a far greater number of people on the land, proportional to their area, than had Britain. This had often been achieved without recourse to protectionist policies. If similar numbers of men could be brought on to the land in Britain, the problem of unemployment would be solved, or at least brought within manageable proportions. Lloyd George went on to argue that the traditional function of agricultural landlords as the instigators and providers of improvements had broken down, and no alternative source of capital had been developed. Ownership of land, he contended, should therefore be resumed by the State, with compensation for existing landowners in the form of an annual payment. The present tenants and their heirs should not be disturbed so long as they farmed adequately. Lloyd George distinguished this system from land nationalisation because the State would not itself farm the land. He applied the name "cultivating tenure" to the proposals. Only in special cases, such as land taken over for drainage or afforestation, should the land be set under direct State control. Lloyd George went on to argue in favour of much more active encouragement of smallholdings, and further demanded that every agricultural labourer should receive half an acre of land as of right. About three weeks after the Killerton speech, the rural report of the Liberal Land Committee was published, as a book of nearly 600 pages, embodying and amplifying Lloyd George's proposals. It was officially entitled *Land and the Nation*, but became generally known as the "Green Book".

Lloyd George's pronouncement not only attracted immense public interest, but also had an immediate effect on both of the other Parties. Each of them held an Annual Conference during the short period between the Killerton speech and the publication of the Green Book. The agenda of the Labour Party meeting included a resolution on agriculture; but before this was debated, MacDonald intervened and persuaded the Conference to avoid making a pronouncement until Labour's own committee of experts could produce an agreed programme — a task which seemed fraught with considerable difficulty.

A few days later, the Conservative conference accepted a resolution "calling on the Government to make, without delay, a definite statement on their agricultural policy, to carry such policy into effect forthwith, and with a view to the fullest use of the land for production of food and employment of labour, to take further definite steps to encourage the return of grassland to the plough".

Conservative conferences are usually unwilling to criticise Conservative Governments; but this particular resolution went very close to criticism. It derived particular force from the fact that it was moved by a delegate from the Prime Minister's own constituency of Bewdley. Whatever else Lloyd George had done, he had certainly made supporters both of the Government and of the official Opposition acutely conscious that their parties were in urgent need of a rural land programme.

Not least of the altercations were those produced within the Liberal Party. Recognising the large measure of Liberal opposition to the Green Book, Lloyd George put forward the recommendations with some caution. In a speech at Dumfries shortly after their publication, he declared that "he flung it out as a challenge for people to think about. If anybody had a better scheme, let him think it out and just as fearlessly apply it".[8]

This reticence, however, did not stop Lloyd George establishing an organisation called the Land and Nation League, and launching a great campaign, which planned to hold no fewer than 10,000 public meetings of various sizes during the following winter.[9] Lloyd George's Liberal enemies tried to persuade Asquith (now Lord Oxford) to condemn the campaign, but he refused to do so.[10]

A few weeks after the publication of the Green Book, the Liberal Land Committee's urban report — *Towns and the Land* — appeared. In sharp contrast with the Green Book, this new production (generally known as the "Brown Book") laid great emphasis on site value rating. It also advocated town planning, regional co-ordination and leasehold reform, with provisions for enfranchisement. The Brown Book caused a good deal less furore among Liberals than did the Green Book. Runciman, for example, who had just made a speech sharply critical of the rural proposals, indicated his strong approval of the urban report.[11]

Was it possible to reconcile the various attitudes on land questions which existed within the Liberal Party? The real issue lay between the line of opinion represented by the Green Book and that of the land value taxers. The point which both groups seem to have missed is that they were really trying to deal with two different problems. The Green Book attempted to meet the current difficulty of an apparent agricultural recession in an immediate and empirical manner. The land-taxers were anxious to ensure that a principle which they considered to be of universal validity should not be lost in the process. The real "inwardness" of the trouble was that many of the land-taxers were personally inimical to Lloyd George, and suspicious of everything he did; while he doubtless regarded the land-taxers as economic dogmatists who were out of touch with current problems. A very friendly obituary of R. L. Outhwaite, written a few years later, confessed that he "forgot the dole";[12] and the same could be said of many of his land taxing associates. One of the most deplorable side-effects of the Liberal schism during the Coalition period had been that very few people were in any position to serve as "interpreters" between the Liberal groups, or to facilitate a solution which would really reconcile their objectives.

At Lord Oxford's request, a special conference of Liberals was summoned for February 1926. The urban land question proved tractable. Site value rating was generally accepted, and set at the head of the policies adopted. The rather ingenious rating compromise which had been evolved shortly before the war, and echoed in some pronouncements during the first few years of peace, was quietly jettisoned.

The task of setting the rural proposals into a form which most of the Party could accept was largely achieved by Sir John Simon.[13] The original "cultivating tenure" recommendations were heavily diluted. County Agricultural Committees would be established, with compulsory powers to take over land which was badly farmed. Land might also be surrendered to these Committees in lieu of death duties. Smallholdings would be encouraged, and the agricultural worker would be entitled to his half acre. A paragraph was inserted which the land-taxers could reasonably interpret as the advocacy of rural site value rating, but which those who favoured the Green Book could equally reasonably ignore.

Neither the land-taxers nor the supporters of the Lloyd George recommendations could claim anything like a complete victory; but neither body was so seriously aggrieved that it could no longer remain within the Liberal Party. On the other hand, a few Liberal defections were inevitable. Sir Alfred Mond favoured "peasant-proprietorship"; this was equally unacceptable to both major groups, and he departed to join the Conservatives. Hilton Young, a former MP of some prominence, went in the same direction for rather different reasons.[14] At least one well-known Liberal MP, David Davies, was seriously disturbed by the policy, and although he remained within the party this led to his eventual withdrawal from active politics.[15]

Later in 1926, a series of new disputes arose over the Liberal Party's attitude to the General Strike; and as a result of these troubles Lord Oxford resigned the leadership. Lloyd George seized effective control, and proceeded to pour vast sums of money into the organisation. It is noteworthy, however, that he did not attempt to upset the Land Conference compromise, and his Land and Nation League operated in a manner which did not conflict with the official views of the party. The League, indeed, seems to have played a very large part in several spectacular and highly successful Liberal by-election campaigns.[16]

Another land policy — leasehold enfranchisement — received an important fillip from the Lloyd George proposals. In this case, actual legislation resulted. Lloyd George set up a "front" organisation called the Leasehold Reform Association. The Association's history was not an entirely happy one,[17] but early in 1927 the Government was stirred into action, and proposed its own Landlord and Tenant Bill. This would compensate tenants of business premises for improvements they had made and for the goodwill of their businesses, when their leases fell in. More contentious was the Government's provision that the tenant should be authorised to apply to a tribunal for grant of a new lease if he so desired. On that matter, trouble came from the Government's own supporters. The revolt was sufficiently serious for the Home Secretary to raise the matter in the Cabinet; but the Government dealt toughly with its own intransigent followers,[18] and secured the passage of the Bill in the form desired.

It would also seem likely that the Liberal land recommendations spurred the Government to bring forward the Smallholdings and Allotments Bill of 1926. The Bill proposed that County Councils should be required to provide smallholdings where a demand existed and provision could be made without financial loss; while in cases where a loss was anticipated, prior assent of the Ministry of Agriculture would be needed, and a Government grant of up to 75 per cent of the anticipated loss could be made. The measure was criticised from several angles, but the most serious objection was the small scale of the anticipated operation. According to the Minister of Agriculture himself, the number of anticipated new tenancies was in the region of 2,000 a year. As Lloyd George pointed out, this would hardly meet a situation where 700,000 farm labourers had no land of their own. The Bill, however, was able to pass in an essentially unaltered condition.

Not only the Government but also the Labour Opposition was impelled to take action. In the late summer of 1926, the proposals of the Labour Party Committee on Land and Agriculture eventually appeared. Land would be nationalised by vesting the freehold in the State; while landlords would be compensated by the issue of Land Bonds. Tenants would come under control of

County Agricultural Committees, who would make all provisions for long-term land improvements. Special Boards would fix the farm workers' wages, while public authorities would deal with rural housing. Although this policy required a much more detailed control over the tenant farmer than did the Green Book, there was a noticeable similarity of approach between the two documents. As in the Liberal Party, the land-taxers fought strenuously against the proposals. Land-taxing MPs, like Josiah Wedgwood and Andrew MacLaren, were conspicuous in the struggle; but, unlike their opposite numbers in the Liberal Party, they were not able to exert any noticeable effect on the eventual policies produced. The Labour Party, like the Liberal Party, was much more willing to support land-taxing in urban areas, and in April 1929 MacDonald promised that a Labour Chancellor would tax land values.[19]

The most famous of all the Lloyd George reports, the "Yellow Book", *Britain's Industrial Future*, appeared at the beginning of 1928, and was soon adopted by a Liberal Conference. As the title suggests, its principal concern was with industry rather than land, but in one important respect it bore upon land problems. A programme of large-scale road-building would be undertaken, both in order to meet obvious needs and in relief of unemployment. This programme would be financed partly out of the Road Fund and partly from "betterment" taxes on land values, which would assuredly increase as a result of the operations.

As the Conservative Government approached the end of its tenure of office, the electors could be excused for thinking that there was little dispute between the Labour and Liberal Parties over their programmes for dealing with urban land, for absorbing the unemployed in civil engineering works, or the collection for public funds of increased land values which would result therefrom. On those matters at least, the issue between them seemed to be very largely a question of "credibility", or personalities. The Labour Party's election manifesto of 1929 promised a programme of "national development" very similar to that outlined in the Yellow Book, and also declared that: "The Party will deal drastically with the scandal of the appropriation of land values by private landowners. It will take steps to secure for the community the increased value of land which is created by industry and the expenditure of public money."

The General Election of May 1929 resulted in the Labour Party becoming for the first time the largest Party in the House of Commons, and for the second time the Government of the country, although it had no overall majority. MacDonald was again Premier, and Snowden — whose land-taxing proclivities have already been noted — was again Chancellor of the Exchequer. This time, however, Wedgwood was not included in the Government.

Again, the stage seemed set for a programme of land reform which would win widespread public support. The Government Party had produced its own proposals quite recently. The Liberals, who — in theory at least — held the balance of power, had made the running on land reform for decades. Most, if not all, Labour and Liberal MPs were committed as individuals to some kind of land reform, and many in both Parties were noted enthusiasts. The popular vote of the two land-reforming parties was five millions in excess of the vote for the Conservatives. Perhaps the purists might disagree with certain aspects of the measures which would eventually emerge; but at least everyone could reasonably expect a drastic and far-reaching programme of legislation dealing with the land question.

Notes-11

1   R. T. Lang (of Sells Ltd, publishers of The World's Press) to J. C. Wedgwood, 23 January 1924. Wedgwood papers.
2   C. V. Wedgwood, The Last of the Radicals (see bibliog.), pp. 152-53.
3   J. C. Wedgwood to C. P. Trevelyan.
4   Cabinet Minutes, 29 April 1924. C28(24)1 e and f, and Appendix II.
5   Birkenhead made a striking appeal to Wedgwood for support on land-taxing grounds. See Birkenhead to Wedgwood, 13 July 1921. Wedgwood papers.
6   See New Statesman, 12 December 1925.
7   See account of speech in The Times, 18 September 1925.
8   The Times, 13 October 1925.
9   Lloyd George to Lord Oxford, 19 November 1925. HHA 34, fos. 241-44.
10 "Lord Oxford's approved draft . . .", 21 November 1925. HHA 34, fos. 245-48.
11 South Wales Daily News, 25 November 1925.
12 Land and Liberty, 1931, p. 10.

13 See Simon to Lloyd George, 12 February 1926. LG(B) G/18/2/2.

14 Hilton Young to Lloyd George, with copy of enclosure to Lord Oxford, 19 February 1926. LG(B) G/10/14/21.

15 David Davies to Richard Jones (copy), 15 November 1926. LG(B) G/5/13/1.

16 *Land News* (which also had a Welsh edition) at one time recorded a circulation of a quarter of a million copies. By the end of 1927, 7,000 speakers were receiving information, and 21 travelling vans were in operation. *Daily Chronicle*, 21 December 1927.

17 Establishment of LRA — see *Daily Chronicle*, 16 September 1926; withdrawal of Lloyd George subsidy — see *Manchester Guardian*, 22 March 1928.

18 Cabinet Minutes, 29 June 1927. C 37(27)1.

19 At the Albert Hall, 27 April 1929.

12 TRIUMPH AND DISASTER

I regret very much that the Valuation Bill is not in the Budget. . . .
I am speaking here from some sort of bitter experience of an
attempt at establishing a valuation . . . We have learnt by
experience that the only way to make a valuation of that kind
effective for taxing purposes is to make it as simple and direct as
possible. I hope that the Chancellor of the Exchequer will bear
that in mind, and that he will read the Budget of 1909-10 in
order to know what to avoid.

D. Lloyd George
House of Commons 16 April 1930

The tragedy of the 1929 Labour Government is much like that
of the 1924 Government, drawn on a larger scale. Yet there were
important differences. In 1924, the active support of the Liberals
was essential to preserve the Government from defeat; in 1929,
the Labour Party was the largest single Party in the House, and
therefore the Liberals could abstain without destroying the
Government.

As in 1924, Labour would neither seek a *concordat* with the
Liberals (until it was already too late), nor yet would the Government produce distinctive policies of its own and defy the Liberals.
The essential and crucial difference between the first two Labour
Governments, however, was the world economic situation in
which they found themselves. In 1924, unemployment was indeed
high in Britain and in most industrial countries, but it was not
rising very rapidly; while the formation of the 1929 Government
was followed within a few months by the "Wall Street crash";
and by 1931 the unemployment figures both in Britain and in
most other important countries had vastly exceeded all
precedents.

The land question in one form or another was bound to play
an important part in political relationships under the Second
Labour Government; yet the part which it did play was very
different from what could reasonably have been anticipated. A
good example of this was provided by the Government's treatment of the coal industry. The condition of that industry had

been a matter of great and universal concern for many years. The Sankey Commission which reported on the situation in 1919 was deeply divided on many of its proposals, but one of the points of agreement was that coal royalties should be collected by the State. The same proposal was made in the report, *Coal and Power*, which resulted from Lloyd George's enquiry in 1924. It was made again by the report of the Royal Commission headed by Sir Herbert Samuel, in 1926. Whether the royalty owners should be compensated or not was a matter of acute political controversy; the principle that land rights should be taken over by the nation was scarcely disputed by the various authorities who investigated the matter. There were raging disputes as to the relative blameworthiness of capitalists and workers for the industry's predicament; nobody could deny that the removal or reduction of the burden of royalties[1] would prove of general benefit.

On 2 July 1929, the King's Speech promised legislation on the coal industry, to deal, *inter alia*, with the ownership of minerals. From all this, it might reasonably be expected that something would be done about mining royalties. Astonishingly, nothing was proposed on the subject. The Government's Coal Bill took an unexpectedly long time to emerge. When it did appear, near the end of 1929, it raised highly controversial questions concerning "rationalisation" and hours of employment; yet the fundamental issue of land ownership was not touched.

No less remarkable was the Government's tardiness in applying the policies which the Labour Party had proposed on agriculture and rural land. Only after much pressure from Lloyd George were any significant steps taken to deal with the worsening situation. MacDonald was at last driven to extend invitations to the other parties to co-operate with the Government in handling the matter. In June 1930, Lloyd George gladly accepted the invitation; Baldwin, for the Conservatives, at first hesitated and then refused.

The product of this co-operation between the Government and the Liberals was the Agricultural Land (Utilisation) Bill, which appeared in November 1930. It was proposed that the Government should be empowered to spend up to £6 millions to acquire land for drainage and other purposes. The Government would also be empowered to make smallholdings available for unemployed men who were able to cultivate them, but who could not afford to acquire them from the local County Council. The Bill was welcomed by the Liberals, although the scale of operations proposed was far below that suggested in their own earlier recommendations. There was opposition from the Conservatives, and a number of amendments were advanced by the Lords. A compromise between the two Houses was effected, and the Bill eventually secured Royal assent at the end of July 1931. The Labour Government itself survived the enactment by less than a month, and the whole situation was drastically altered by its successor.

On the central and crucial question of the valuation and taxation of land values, the history of the second Labour Government was no more impressive, but a good deal more spectacular. Snowden's own wishes were well known, and these were reinforced by a petition which he received just before Christmas 1929, signed by 165 Labour and Liberal backbenchers, urging that "the taxation of the market value of all land will be included in the next Budget".[2]

The land-taxers, however, were soon disappointed, for the Chancellor made no land-taxing proposals in his 1930 Budget. He did promise, however, that the Government would introduce "forthwith" a separate Bill for land valuation. Labour land-taxers like MacLaren and Wedgwood, and also Lloyd George from the Liberal benches, criticised Snowden for failing to use the Budget for the purpose, pointing out that it was open to the Lords to block a Valuation Bill.

On 8 May, a Government spokesman indicated that Snowden hoped to introduce the Valuation Bill in the following week, and take the Second Reading the week after. The Cabinet examined the matter on 14 May, and held the same view; on "present intentions" the Bill would be introduced on the following day, and the Second Reading taken on 21 May.[3] Almost immediately, however, a snag appeared. By the Cabinet meeting of 21 May, no agreement had yet been reached between the Ministers themselves on the question of the valuation of agricultural land, and it was felt that further discussions between the Chancellor and his colleagues were necessary. MacDonald said that "owing to considerations of Parliamentary time, he was rather loath to encourage the belief that this Bill could be passed in the present Session."[4]

On 6 June 1930, just before the Whitsun recess, the Chancellor at last presented the Bill, which received its First Reading. Snowden opened his heart to Wedgwood:— ". . . It has been a devil of a job to get anything approaching agreement between rival views and even now I am sure there is much which will not satisfy you. The first trouble has been about agricultural land. Three times these clauses have been fundamentally altered. . . . The other point is the minerals. These are excluded . . . Parliamentary business is in a state of utter chaos and we shall have to drop many of our Bills or sit through to the middle of September. I am very anxious to get this Bill a Second Reading and let it go to a Committee . . ."[5]

On 25 June, MacDonald gave a list of the Bills with which the Government proposed to deal before the end of the current session. It did not include the Land Valuation Bill.

Nevertheless, the Chancellor would not allow the matter to be forgotten. At the Cabinet of 23 July, he circulated a Note concerning a revised Land Valuation Bill, which had been modified as a result of suggestions made by Wedgwood and Lord Parmoor. The Cabinet minutes record that: "Though the Chancellor of the Exchequer did not pretend that the Bill even now was satisfactory, in order to give an earnest of good faith in the matter he proposed to publish the Bill, prefacing the publication by an avowal to the effect that he was circulating the Bill for the information of Members and that he would be ready to consider any suggestions which might reach him in regard to the Bill before the time comes for its reintroduction next Session."

Snowden managed to get the Bill published on 30 July — two days before the end of the Parliamentary session. He was specifically requested by his colleagues to make his answers to questions on the subject as noncommittal and provisional as possible.[6]

For a time, the land-taxers had some real hope of at least getting the Valuation Bill properly considered by the House of Commons, even though its fate in the Lords was not likely to be a happy one. Susan Lawrence, who was both a junior Minister and the current President of the Labour Party, told the Party's Conference at Llandudno on 6 October that the Government Valuation Bill "will, no doubt, have a stormy passage through the House of Commons and the House of Lords, but I assure you it is the Government's intention to place it on the Statute Book".

With this encouraging statement, however, the Bill suddenly

stuck, as the Government changed its mind yet again. On 17 November, Snowden told the Cabinet "that conversations with leading Liberals and supporters of the Government indicated a preference for the plan of incorporating the provisions of the Land Valuation Bill in the next Budget".

The next positive step was the introduction of land valuation and taxation proposals into Snowden's Budget, which was brought out on 27 April 1931. By common consent, these provisions were regarded as the most important innovations among the Government's financial proposals. Snowden himself later explained the circumstances in which land valuation and taxation had been brought together in the Budget: "I proposed to include in the Finance Bill provisions for the necessary and preliminary step of the valuation of the land of the country and provisions for the imposition of a tax upon the valuation thus obtained . . . I proposed that the valuation should be substantially completed before the tax began to be levied. Thus the imposition would not become operative during the current financial year. I expected the valuation would be completed within a period of two years from the passing of the Bill. The tax, when it became operative, would be at the rate of 1d in the £1 on the capital land value.

"We had already been advised by the Speaker that unless a special Resolution was passed by the House the Land Clauses would fall outside the definition of a Money Bill and it would, therefore, be open to the House of Lords to reject these clauses. In order, therefore, to protect the Land Clauses against rejection by the Peers I proposed the necessary resolution a few days later for imposing tax to come into operation at a date subsequent to the expiration of the current financial year. I anticipated that such a resolution would meet with strenuous opposition from the Conservative Party, who would, no doubt, realise what its object was. When the resolution came forward I was astounded to see that the Conservatives had no comprehension of its purpose, and they confined their criticism to the general principle of a tax on land values."[7]

Even this small and experimental site value tax was not intended to apply universally. Agricultural land would be omitted, save where it had a value in excess of its agricultural worth. So also would land owned by local authorities, and land used for hospitals, churches, railways and certain other purposes be excluded. Land with a capital value below £120 would be omitted — which, in 1931 values, meant practically all working-class houses which were owner-occupied. The whole valuation would be revised quinquennially.

When the House of Commons resolution authorising the tax came to a division on 6 May, the three Parties did not split. All the Labour and Liberal MPs who voted supported the Government; all the Conservatives who voted opposed it. Very soon afterwards, however, the internal strains of the Liberal Party brought serious difficulties both for themselves and for the Government.

At this point, a brief digression is needed. Lloyd George was at that time attempting to secure some kind of *concordat* by which the Government would at least introduce certain Liberal measures, and would perhaps even incorporate Liberals in the Ministry. In return, the Liberals would give them general support, and thus relieve the Government of any serious threat to its continued existence. Some Liberal MPs, however, received a kind of counter-offer from the Conservatives, who were prepared to ensure that those Liberal MPs who would co-operate with them in bringing the Government down should not have Conservatives against them in their own constituencies. Exactly who received this offer, and whom it tempted, does not seem to be known; but the three Liberals who at this stage showed the most marked leanings towards the Conservatives were Sir John Simon; Sir Robert Hutchison — until recently the Chief Whip — and Ernest Brown, victor of a spectacular by-election in 1927. None of the three had a very large majority, and each of them had had a straight fight against Labour in 1929.

Labour had its own difficulties. Snowden wrote later that "My own Party, with a few exceptions, were not enthusiastic about the land taxation clauses, and my task in resisting unreasonable exceptions was made more difficult by the fact that some of my Cabinet colleagues were saying freely in the lobbies that I was not supported by the Cabinet . . . The Prime Minister and a large section of the Labour Party were terrified that my uncompromising attitude might lead to the defeat of the Government and to a second General Election, which they were very anxious to avoid."[8]

The large number of Labour MPs who had signed a land-taxing petition a year and a half earlier scarcely suggests lack of enthusiasm in the Party's ranks; perhaps Snowden's real complaint was that they were unwilling to countenance his "brinkmanship" towards the Liberals, and his stubborn insistence that certain features of the Finance Bill should be preserved, even though these features were by no means essential to its main objectives, and jeopardised both the passage of the Bill and the life of the Government.

The general confusion over the Government's land proposals continued. The Liberals tabled an amendment, which was to be moved on 17 June, and was designed to deal with what was called "double taxation". As the proposals stood, the holders of certain kinds of hereditaments were liable to be taxed twice when the land taxes came into operation. They already paid Income Tax on their land; they would eventually pay Land Value Tax in addition. The Liberals contended that they had supported the Second Reading of the Finance Bill because they approved the principle of the taxes; but they could not continue to support the Bill unless this matter was rectified. The position was considered by the Cabinet on 10 June. On the following day, Lloyd George declared his own Party's attitude at a meeting in Edinburgh: "As the Government's proposal stands, it is unjust. We have come to the conclusion as a Party quite unanimously — there was not a dissentient voice — that we cannot assent to the injustice of the thing as it stands. We have come to that conclusion with our eyes open, and we mean to stand by it whatever the consequences may be . . . I am told that if we insist the Government will throw in its hand. If they do that is their responsibility . . . I shall regret it, but it is for them to decide, not for us."

Both the Government and the Liberals took this matter very seriously indeed, for if all the Liberals did vote against the Government, it would probably be defeated. Anxious efforts were made on both sides to prevent this outcome, and a compromise Liberal amendment was drawn up. This was ruled out of order, but a new form of amendment was eventually produced after discussions between a Liberal lawyer on one side and Sir Stafford Cripps, the Solicitor-General, on the other. The eventual draft can have satisfied nobody, but it was passed by the House of Commons on 24 June, with the support of Labour and most of the Liberals. Four Liberals, however, voted with the Opposition.

The Liberal difficulties were made worse by the attitudes of both the Government and the Conservatives. Snowden wisely pointed out that once the valuation had been secured, it would be up to future Parliaments to decide what the tax should be. He also observed — much less wisely — that the principle of double taxation had been preserved. This led Neville Chamberlain, for the Conservatives, to declare that he had "never known a more merciless exposure than that to which (the Liberals) had been subjected by the Chancellor. So far from having their faces saved, they had them rubbed in the mud".

Snowden later reflected that: "The general tone of this debate did not reflect much credit upon any of the Parties concerned."[9]

One may reasonably ask why either the Government or the Liberals should have been so obdurate on the matter. On the Government side, there seems little doubt that Snowden himself was the most recalcitrant. He had had tremendous difficulties over land valuation all along, and was probably unwilling to allow any tampering whatever with the Finance Bill, lest some technical error should creep in and vitiate the whole structure. So far as the Liberals were concerned, they had apparently every reason both to get land valuation through, and to keep the Government in office. Why, then, did Lloyd George set everything at risk by his Edinburgh speech? The answer was really given two days after the vote in the House of Commons. Simon, Hutchison and Brown all resigned the Liberal Whip, giving as their reason the Party's behaviour over "double taxation". No doubt, Lloyd George had seen for a long time that Simon at any rate would secede on some pretext or other, and hoped that by taking a strong line over "double taxation" he would be able to hold his Party together for a few more weeks — by which time he had good reason for thinking he would be able to clinch a more or less permanent and general deal with the Government.

The Government met other obstacles as well. A fruitful source of trouble was the statutory exemptions from taxation. Innumerable bodies made impressive arguments for various kinds of land in which they had special interest to be exempted. At one point, the Opposition contrived to defeat the Government on a "snap division" concerning one of the proposed exemptions. It was not of crucial importance, and eventually the Finance Bill passed its Third Reading, on 3 July. As it could receive the Speaker's certificate as a "Money Bill", the Lords were unable to block it, and on 31 July Royal Assent was signified.

On the very day that the Finance Act became law, the report

of the famous "May Committee" was published. This showed that a grave financial deficit was anticipated. That report was the beginning of a crisis which led, a little over three weeks later, to the collapse of the Second Labour Government and the formation of an all-party National Government, charged to achieve certain economies which the May Committee, and most other people, seemed to regard as necessary.

There is little reason to doubt that the National Government of 1931 was, in its inception, a perfectly sincere attempt by the leaders of the three Parties to deal with an urgent current problem together; and that the full intention of them all had been to disband once they had done so, and to make their separate Party appeals to the country at a General Election which would inevitably supervene.

In the course of the few weeks which followed, the whole character of the Government changed beyond recognition. The Labour Party expelled those members who participated. The original Government decision to break up before an appeal to the country was reversed. A General Election was held, and not only resulted in a quite unparalleled majority for the National Government, but also gave the Conservatives an overwhelming majority over all other parties combined. After the election, the composition of the Cabinet was radically altered. Snowden — now a Viscount — moved from the Exchequer to the far less effective post of Lord Privy Seal, where he had no special *locus standi* to defend land-taxing. The new Chancellor of the Exchequer was Neville Chamberlain, one of the most bitter opponents of land reform. On the other hand, the former Labour members of the Government, and most of the Liberals, remained within the Ministry, and it was considered of some importance to avoid taking any measures which would offend them unnecessarily.

About a month after the new Cabinet was formed, Neville Chamberlain proposed to discontinue the land valuation — ostensibly on the grounds of expense. There was considerable discussion, and evidently a great deal of disagreement, within the Cabinet; but eventually it was agreed: "The the Chancellor of the Exchequer . . . should announce that for reasons of financial stringency it had been decided to suspend the Land Valuation Clauses of the Finance Act 1931, but that the decision was taken without reference to the merits of the scheme and did not involve its annulment."[10]

206

The land tax proposals next attracted attention when Neville Chamberlain introduced his 1932 Budget. The Chancellor proposed to suspend the Land Value Tax projected for 1933-4, but not to repeal either the tax or the system of valuation. Opponents of the Government predictably criticised the recommendation. The Government was also attacked from the other side. In the Committee Stage of the Finance Bill, a Conservative MP, Lt-Col Acland-Troyte, proposed an amendment to repeal both the tax and the valuation altogether. Not the least savoury aspect of the debate which ensued was that Acland-Troyte's view was strongly supported in the Commons by George Lambert and in the Lords by Lord Strachie — who had both recently broken from the Liberals. The most weighty contribution came from Stanley Baldwin, who was virtually acting as joint Premier. "Had this been a Tory Government, we should have repealed the Statute . . . What is the present effect of this Statute? It is a Statute in coma. For this Parliament there can be no prospect at all of there being a land tax or land valuation, so that apprehension ought to be removed . . . Do you think that I, going about the country as I did and knowing the force of Lord Snowden's speeches and broadcasts in helping to win seats which we should never have won, was going to say to them, 'Oh, no, now we have got a big Tory majority, much bigger than I expected, out you go.' Not much . . . We can accept neither a repeal of the Act nor the insertion of the Amendment."[11] The amendment was pressed to a division, but the Government Whips were imposed against it, and it was heavily defeated.

By the time of the 1933 Budget, the situation had changed in several respects. Lord Snowden and the Liberal Ministers had at last resigned from the Government, although several former Labour Ministers (who were called "National Labour"), and several former Liberals ("Liberal Nationals"), remained. A strong Committee of MPs who were anxious to secure the removal of the offending clauses had been established. An amendment to the annual Finance Bill to that effect was signed by 204 supporters of the Government, and about 300 MPs were eventually associated in a move to secure either Government support for the Amendment or a free vote — which, of course, would come to the same thing. Baldwin met the Members concerned, and his arguments were similar to those of the previous year. He told them that the Cabinet had unanimously decided against the removal of the 1931 provisions from the Statute Book — adding that "he and his Conservative colleagues felt that the ungrudging loyalty with which their Labour colleagues had supported other features of the policy of the National Government did call for mutual consideration."

Neville Chamberlain spoke to the meeting in the same vein, and the Members agreed to withdraw their amendment. It was noted, however, that "the Committee will continue to press the urgent considerations calling for the repeal of these taxes whenever the opportunity to do so may legitimately arise."[12]

Thus for another year did land valuation and the land taxes wait in limbo. Their existence on the Statute Book, however, presented a continuing irritant to a large section of the Conservative majority. The following Budget, in 1934, again made no proposals to alter the situation. Quite astonishingly, when the Finance Bill appeared, it was proposed by the Government that the valuation and taxation should be repealed. By what test the Ministers could justify the retreat which they thus made from the strong line taken in the previous two years is difficult to understand. MacDonald's own explanation, given in the course of a public correspondence with A. W. Madsen, secretary of the United Committee for the Taxation of Land Values, seems peculiarly inept: ". . . A Government which was determined to 'take drastic and energetic steps to put into operation the taxation of land values' would have to proceed to legislation, as the clauses that have been in suspense for years, largely owing to amendments which the Chancellor had unwillingly to accept from both Liberals and Conservatives, were not sufficiently full to enable a great deal to be done."[13]

On the motion for the inclusion of the repeal clauses in the 1934 Finance Bill, the House divided on purely party lines. All the Conservatives, with their National Labour and Liberal National associates, supported the repeal; all the Liberal and Labour MPs opposed it.[14] The overwhelming majority, of course, lay on the Government's side, and the Bill eventually passed into law in the form proposed. The manner in which the land taxes were eventually destroyed can have given little satisfaction even to their most inveterate enemies. It was a dreary end to a tremendous saga.

For the remainder of the 1930s, the chief preoccupation of

statesmen lay at first with industrial unemployment and later with international questions. Arguably, the land problem really stood at the root of both of these issues; but whether this be true or false, most men did not see things that way.

Rural land questions were not so much settled as thrust aside. The spirit of the Government's policy towards agriculture in the 1930s was essentially contractionist. When industry secured "protection" in 1932, the farmers were bluntly — and officially — told that "any (agricultural import) duty, to be effective, would have to be so high as to cause an immense intolerable rise in the price of the commodity . . ."[15]

Thus did the farmers get the worst of all worlds. They were now required to pay duties on things which they needed to import, while their own products were unprotected.

This policy of contraction was seen in other places as well. The Agricultural Marketing Act of 1933 imposed severe penalties on those who dared to produce too much food. There seemed some sign of a change when the Agriculture Act of 1937 authorised Exchequer grants for certain kinds of improvements, and for grain production; but an important speech delivered by the Prime Minister, Neville Chamberlain, on 2 July 1938 made it clear that the Government did not propose to give any substantial boost to agriculture, even in view of the threat of war and blockade.

Specifically Scottish questions were treated in a similar way. The Scottish Department of Agriculture decided in 1933 that many of the smallholdings created under the Pentland Act of 1911 were uneconomic, and began to move in the opposite direction — towards large, consolidated holdings.[16] Thus there was little encouragement for anyone to take up a career in agriculture, and those who were already there tended to drift into the towns. Some farmers were able to make a success of livestock rearing, but most men saw little hope for agriculture either in the present or in the foreseeable future.

The story of the land question in the urban areas was markedly different, and much attention was focused on London. In 1934, the Labour Party won control of the London County Council. This victory was immensely important for the *morale* of the Labour Party, which had suffered such a disaster at the General Election three years earlier. Herbert Morrison, who was the principal figure among the Labour group on the LCC, was evidently determined to make the Labour administration of

London so successful that it would greatly assist the Party's revival on a national scale. A vigorous attack was made on a number of problems; but our concern here is with the vociferous demand which was raised for the right to levy rates on the basis of site values. In 1936, the LCC petitioned the Government for legislation to that effect. When the request was refused, the Council decided to promote a private Bill. For technical reasons this had to be withdrawn, and on 15 February 1939 Morrison — by then also a Member of Parliament — brought a motion under the "Ten-minute" rule for leave to introduce a public Bill. The proposal was predictably defeated by the large Government majority, but it attracted considerable attention. Land Value Taxation was certainly by no means dead as a public issue, and there was good reason for thinking that when and if the Labour Party became again the Government of the country, some positive action would be taken on the matter.

Then came the war. As in 1914-18, emergency legislation gave the Government special powers to acquire property for wartime purposes. Subsidies for food production were applied on a much larger scale than in the 1914 war, and were eventually continued into the post-war period. As in the First World War, a Coalition was eventually formed, and policies of post-war reconstruction were devised, which — it was hoped at the time — all parties might later accept.

A special problem arose because the scale of bomb damage in Britain was incomparably greater than it had been in the earlier conflict, and this damage inevitably presented great opportunities for land speculation. Oliver Marriott, in his book *The Property Boom*, describes the methods of one of the land "developers": "Generally he would ring an estate agent the day after a particularly heavy bombing raid. 'Take off your coat, roll up your sleeves and go out and buy,' he would say. 'Did you hear the bombs last night? There must be some bargains around this morning'."[17]

Wartime restrictions on building were largely relaxed in cases involving bomb damage, especially where structures became dangerous as a result of that damage. Considerable discretionary powers resided with public officials, who were occasionally amenable to direct bribes, or at least to the "generosity" of interested parties. It soon became clear that any town planning which might be projected after the war could well be vitiated by the activities of such gentlemen. On 29 December 1940, the Government announced the establishment of a Committee, under Mr Justice Uthwatt, to consider what action should be taken, while the war was still being fought, to prevent the work of post-war reconstruction being impeded through land speculation.

The Uthwatt Committee's interim report appeared in the summer of 1941, and its final report a year later. The latter proposed distinct policies for urban and rural areas. Future development within the towns would only be allowed with State permission. In built-up areas, public authorities would receive compulsory purchase powers over any land which might be required for planning or other public purposes, and compensation should be based on the value of that land on 31 March 1939. The compensation value for the whole country should be assessed, and a General Compensation Fund to that amount should be created, which would then be divided between claimants.

The Government now had to decide to what extent it would follow the Uthwatt proposals, and how to implement its policy. Great difficulties were encountered, and long delays resulted. Early in 1943, a Ministry of Town and Country Planning was established "to secure consistency and continuity in framing and execution of a national policy in respect of the use and development of land throughout England and Wales". By October, the Minister was able to assure local authorities that the Government had accepted the principle that all land in areas of extensive wartime damage should be acquired by public authorities, and at a compensation figure not exceeding the 1939 value.

Much further delay now ensued, and it is not difficult to guess that differences of opinion within the Government played a large part in producing that delay. Eventually, in the middle of 1944, the Government set out its plans. A Town and Country Planning Bill was issued — although, in spite of its name, this was only designed for certain urban areas. A White Paper was also published, providing the Government's view on the Uthwatt Report and the modifications which were considered necessary.

The Town and Country Planning Bill of 1944 was concerned both with areas of extensive bomb damage and with slums. Local planning authorities were invited to submit redevelopment plans to the Ministry. If these were approved after a public inquiry, the local authority would receive compulsory purchase powers. When the Bill came before Parliament, much further difficulty was encountered over the question of compensation, and at one point Churchill intervened in the debate and threatened to drop the whole Bill. Eventually agreement was reached to the effect that (with certain exceptions) the basis should be the 1939 values. The Bill then proceeded to enactment without much trouble.

The Coalition Government's White Paper did not lead to legislation, but it is of interest as a link between the original Uthwatt proposals and the measures which were adopted after the war by the Labour Government. The Coalition proposed that development should only be authorised when specifically approved by the planning authority. When such permission was granted, the landowner should pay a "betterment charge" corresponding with 80 per cent of the increased value of his land; while if permission were refused, he should be entitled to compensation for loss of development values as they had existed in 1939.

At the General Election of 1945, the Labour Party won a massive overall majority. The new generation of Labour leaders had received experience of major office in the wartime Coalition; but most of them were mainly interested in industrial nationalisation and the extension of what was called the "welfare state". Herbert Morrison was Lord President of the Council, and many regarded him as the natural successor to Clement Attlee, the new Prime Minister; but there were not many other senior members of the Government whose interest in land questions had attracted much attention in the past.

The man apparently best placed to give practical effect to his views on land matters was Lewis Silkin, the new Minister of Town and Country Planning. Town Planning was of immense public interest, and radical changes were assuredly required. Silkin did not have a seat in the Cabinet, however, and his proposals were bound to be influenced by the Uthwatt Report, which had acquired a considerable *mystique* in the public mind. In January 1947, Silkin brought forward the Government's Town and Country Planning Bill, which attempted a broad-fronted attack on the whole future course of land development.

The Bill proposed that, as from an "appointed day", no further development of land should be permitted without consent of a local Planning Authority. In certain cases, a landowner would have a right of appeal to the Minister concerned, who could modify the Planning Authority's requirements. The landowner was authorised to continue to use the land in its current manner without interference. When permission to develop was granted, the landlord would be required to pay to a new body, the Central Land Board, a "development charge of such amount (if any) as the Board may determine". The principle of assessment of development charges would be decided by the Minister, but the charge would not exceed the estimated increase in value deriving from the development. In a number of cases — such as most alterations to existing buildings, and the repair of war damage — no development charge would be levied. Owners who considered that their land possessed a "development value" on the "appointed day" would be allowed to submit claims for compensation to the Central Land Board. A fund of £300 millions would be set up, which could be used in satisfaction of these claims — compensation taking the form of negotiable Government stock. This particular Bill applied to England and Wales only, but a similar Bill for Scotland followed a few weeks later.

The aim of these Bills was thus to collect any increase in land values which might arise in the future as a result of actual or prospective developments. The £300 million compensation fund would ensure that those whose land was "ripe" or "ripening" for development did not suffer so far as their present interest was concerned. Any increase in land values arising without an alteration of use would remain with the landlord; and a landlord who proposed to keep his land in its current use would not be disturbed, even though there existed a great demand that that land should be set to some more profitable function.

Long before the Bills were published, the general intentions of the Government were known to the Parliamentary Labour Party. On 15 July 1946, no fewer than 167 Labour MPs signed a Memorial to the Prime Minister, protesting against the form of the proposed measure, and enclosing two reasoned memoranda on the subject.[18] The Uthwatt proposals were strongly and directly confuted by the memorialists. They contended that if the development charge were substantial it would be likely to inhibit development; that the scheme would not collect all kinds of land value increments; that it would not extinguish speculation; that great sums of public money were being given away unnecessarily to landowners; that the scheme would be costly to administer. The need for general land valuation was firmly stressed.

Something like half of the available members of the Parliamentary Labour Party were thus subscribing their names to a document wholly in the spirit of the pre-1914 land-taxers, and completely contrary to the intentions of the Minister. It is difficult at present to say how and why such an impressive array of arguments and men was unable to deflect the Government from its proposed course. We may guess that one of the reasons was that the leading members of the Government had been involved in the production of the 1944 White Paper, and could not easily abandon the Uthwatt proposals.

Just as the decisions of the wartime Coalition seem to have determined the general line which the post-war Labour Government would take, so also do they seem to have inhibited the Conservative Opposition which had been similarly involved. The chief Conservative spokesman was able to criticise the Bill for "haste, inconsistency and vagueness", and could shrewdly observe that the sum of £300 millions looked like the result of bargaining with the Treasury; but he was in no position to deliver any kind of fundamental attack on the Bill's provisions. Some Labour critics objected to the compensation fund, and other features of the Bill, in the spirit of the Memorial which they had delivered to Attlee. The Whips, however, were put on; the measure was forced through, and the "Appointed Day" was set at 1 July 1948.

Almost at once, the weaknesses of the Town and Country Planning Act of 1947 began to appear. Long before the Third Labour Government had left office, they had been forced to accept modifications. In June 1950, and again in the following month, the Government announced types of development on which the charge would not be levied.

In the autumn of 1951, the Conservatives were returned to office. Early in 1952, Harold Macmillan, Minister of Housing and Local Government, told the Commons that the total sum received in development charges in the three and a half years which had elapsed since the "appointed day" was but £8.6 millions, with a further £4.9 millions set off against the compensation fund. The revenue which the charge was producing was negligible; the disincentive to development was massive. At last, in November 1952, the Government announced its intention to abolish both the development charge and all further claims on the £300 million fund; although the full apparatus of planning control would be retained. Little more than a perfunctory protest could be made by the authors of the 1947 Act. The development charge perished almost without regret;^{iv} a remarkable monument to the failure of leading statesmen to make a proper study of land economics.

*　　*　　*　　*

Thus far, the author has attempted not merely to record events, but to try to get behind those events and understand the real causes. This is exceedingly difficult when primary documents are not available, and may easily descend into idle speculation. Even the story of the Town and Country Planning Act will probably require considerable revision when the relevant Cabinet papers are opened, and the private documents of statesmen of the period become more generally available for inspection. It is best, therefore, to leave our detailed chronicle at this point.

It would be quite wrong, however, to imagine that the land problem has in any way diminished in interest during the more recent period. In 1967, for example, the Labour Government set up a Land Commission with very wide powers of compulsory acquisition. That Commission was abolished three years later by the Conservatives, but a further Labour Government has since brought out a Community Land Bill which is at present (autumn 1975) before Parliament. That particular question is evidently by no means settled. The radical alterations of leasehold tenure which took effect at the beginning of 1968 is a further reminder that statesmen cannot, and will not, neglect the problems presented by land. A great deal more will need to be done, as and when the documents become available, to unravel and understand the events which have already occurred.

Notes-12

1 Mineral royalty values, unlike ordinary land values, are wasting assets. Nevertheless, the two kinds of values are similar in the respect that neither derives from the activities of the landowner.
2 Wedgwood to Snowden (copy), 23 December 1929; see also Snowden to Wedgwood, 24 December 1929. Wedgwood papers.
3 Cabinet Minutes, 14 May 1930. C 27(30)4.
4 Cabinet Minutes, 21 May 1930. C 28(30)8.
5 Snowden to Wedgwood, 7 June 1930. Wedgwood papers.
6 Cabinet Minutes, 23 July 1930. C 44(30)12.
7 Viscount Snowden, *An Autobiography*, ii (see bibliog.), p. 905.

8   Snowden, *op. cit.*, p. 915.

9   *Ibid.*, p. 911.

10 Cabinet Minutes, 7 December 1931. C 85(31)2.

11 House of Commons, 26 May 1932.

12 *The Times*, 31 May 1933.

13 MacDonald to A. W. Madsen, 14 May 1934; published in Press shortly afterwards.

14 Division 270, 5 June 1934.

15 Oliver Stanley, Under-Secretary for Home Affairs, at Clifton, 15 October 1932.

16 John Brown, "Scottish and English Land Legislation 1905-11", *Scottish Historical Review*, 1968, vol. 46, at p. 85.

17 Oliver Marriott, *The Property Boom*, p. 60.

18 Copies of both memoranda, the letter to the Prime Minister and the list of signatories, are included in the R. R. Stokes papers.

19 The modern 40 per cent Development Levy is assessed on the difference between capital value before and after permission to develop has been granted.

13 COMING OFF THE FENCE

*For if anyone, seeing justice, be willing to proclaim it, to him
will far-seeing Zeus grant happiness.*

Hesiod, *Works and Days*, 280-1

Land is, beyond all comparison, the most valuable asset in the
United Kingdom. An estimate published in spring 1974 declared
that, in the previous two years, the value of that land had risen
by more than £50,000 millions — equivalent to the entire gross
national product (Christopher Booker and Bennie Gray, "Blueprint
for a land tax", in *The Observer*, 24 March 1974). Assuming that
capital value is twenty times annual value, the collection of that
increase alone would produce a revenue of £2.5 thousand millions.
There is no apparent reason for distinguishing between old land
values and recent increments; and it is fascinating to speculate
what the true annual value of land in the country may now be.
There can be very few economic questions which are not influenced
to a greater or lesser extent by the value of land. Although it is
seldom possible to predict what course events will take, it is
possible to assert with confidence that the "land question" will
be of recurring interest in the future.

What has bedevilled statesmen of the past when dealing with
the land question has been their failure to examine the fundamental rules of economics, and try to anticipate and avert future
difficulties in the light of those laws. All too often, problems
relating to land have been ignored until they have become so
critical that the treatment which would have done most towards
dealing with the root of the trouble has become impossible. This
was well shown by the Irish Land Act of 1881. In the circumstances of the early 1880s, there was very little that politicians
could do, except to grant the "Three Fs" — even though it was
evident to many contemporaries that this measure would in some
ways actually prejudice a permanent solution. It was futile at the
time to argue whether the "Three Fs" were desirable or not; the
practical choice before statesmen was whether they would come
as a result of parliamentary action, or whether they would be
seized in circumstances of chaos, bloodshed and ensuing famine.

217

The criticism which may properly be levelled at the men of the time is not that they did less than their best in the actual crisis, but that they had failed to think seriously about the problem of Irish agrarian poverty in the years and decades which preceded the crisis.

A good modern example of just the same kind of failure to anticipate and avert trouble is provided by the background to the Town and Country Planning Act of 1947. The problem here was not how to head off famine and revolution, but how to preserve rural amenities; how to prevent objectionable urban development; and how to ensure that publicly-created land values should be returned to the community. Yet, just as the statesmen of the 1880s could not achieve a long-term solution of the Irish rural problem because no one could go behind the peasants' preoccupation with the "Three Fs", so also were statesmen of the 1940s unable to escape from the trammels of the Uthwatt Report. If the third Labour Government had been capable of listening to the friendly criticisms of its own backbenchers, then it would almost certainly have proved possible to devise a scheme which would have achieved the common object of Ministers and back-bench critics. Instead, all criticism was overborne; the expedient which the Ministers forced down the throat of Parliament was never a success by any test at all, it was finally swept aside a few years later.

In our own time, there are signs that similar situations may be building up; that chronic problems relating to land may be developing an acute character, and that measures may be introduced which are more connected with the attractions of some slogan than with a real understanding of causes and effects. Indeed, one could point to several aspects of the land problem which are likely to become acute at almost any time.

It is all too easy for men to take refuge in convenient slogans. We have seen abundant examples where people have been confused by rhetoric— their own rhetoric, as well as the rhetoric of others — over expressions like "land nationalisation", which have been used in the past, and are still used to this day, in wildly different senses. An attack on the land problem is not something to be bodged and fumbled in a hurry amid a cloud of political excitement by men whose main preoccupation is with other things; that attack needs to be prepared carefully and quietly by men who have really thought through the economic and social implica-

218

tions and likely consequences of what they are trying to do.

There is no reason why this attack on the land question should be partisan in the ordinary political sense. A very large number of the past disputes derived from the fact that for one body of people the word "landowner" signified a wise and generous improver; for another body of people the same word signified a rapacious and predatory creature whose sole interest was the acquisition of rent. Landowners of both kinds doubtless existed; most landowners were probably something between the two. In any event, the rôle of the individual landowner has been so enormously eroded over the past century that this particular dispute is for all practical purposes dead. There is no need for "right" and "left" in politics to strike up attitudes of defence or attack, or to go on fighting nostalgically these old battles.

There is, indeed, no good reason why the modern supporters of various brands of "capitalism" and "socialism" should not discover an exceedingly wide measure of agreement over what needs to be done. There are two fundamentally different kinds of value associated with real property: site values, which derive little or nothing from the activities of the owner; and improvement values which stem from the activities of the owner and those operating under his control, or his predecessors in title. The socialist, who wishes to increase the proportion of value collected by public authorities for public purposes, would be well advised to commence with those values which do not derive from the activities of the owner, rather than those values which do. The great disparities of wealth and poverty are far older and more universal than "capitalism", and may surely be mitigated by ensuring that all men should have access to values created by the community, which in most societies have been arrogated by a few to the exclusion of the majority. The upholder of capitalism or free enterprise, on the other hand, would be well advised to switch the burden of taxation, so that it does not inhibit production or deter people from useful activities. The great bulk of modern taxation does serve, to a greater or lesser extent, to penalise and therefore to deter productive effort; whereas a tax imposed upon site values cannot discourage production — indeed, it will encourage the most productive use of land.

The author does not dissemble his own conviction that the taxation of land values would be a most valuable measure, which would in the long run satisfy many of the apparently conflicting

219

wishes of very disparate people in politics. Insofar, however, as the author hopes to impart some political message (and what historian does not?), the one which he seeks most strongly to bring out is not the wisdom of some particular measure, but rather that those who in the future will come to deal with economic problems should perceive how vast damage has been done in the past, and may well be done in the future, because people have been so obsessed with a welter of urgent problems that they have failed to look closely enough at the underlying principles involved in the ownership and use of land.

The land problem changes in shape, but not in substance. The quantity of land cannot be significantly increased; and without land no man can live. An unsatisfactory land system will produce innumerable distortions in the workings of the economy — just as a disease affecting one organ of the human body may produce innumerable malfunctionings elsewhere, which the layman may not readily perceive to be connected with the original illness. Statesmen have dealt with effects, but they have done little to deal with causes. Until these causes are treated, no one may properly inscribe "The End" to a book such as this.

BIBLIOGRAPHY

1 Official Papers

Cabinet Papers (Public Record Office, London) (CAB)
Census Reports (British Museum, London)
Parliamentary Debates
Royal Commission Reports (British Museum, London):

1881:	Into workings of Landlord and Tenant (Ireland) Act 1870 (Bessborough Report) C2779, xviii
1884:	Into the condition of the crofters and cottars in the Highlands and Islands of Scotland (Napier Report) C3980, xxxii
1887:	On the Land Law (Ireland) Act 1881 and the Purchase of Land (Ireland) Act 1885 (Cowper Report) C4969, xxvi
1890–1:	Western Highlands and Islands: Second Report.
1896:	Land in Wales and Monmouthshire C8221, xxxiv C6242, xliv

2 Archives

Beaverbrook Library, London
Bonar Law (ABL)
David Lloyd George (1st Earl Lloyd-George) (LG[B])

Bodleian Library, Oxford
H. H. Asquith (1st Earl of Oxford and Asquith) (HHA)
Sir Antony MacDonnell (Lord MacDonnell of Swinford) (Mac-
Donnell)

British Museum, London
A. J. Balfour (Earl Balfour) (AJB)
Sir Henry Campbell-Bannerman (C-B)
Sir Charles Dilke (Dilke)
W. E. Gladstone (WEG)
1st Marquis of Ripon (Ripon)

Christ Church College, Oxford
3rd Marquis of Salisbury (S)

Labour Party, London
Labour Party Executive Committee Minutes (LPEC)

National Liberal Club, London
Election Addresses

National Library of Ireland, Dublin
Isaac Butt (Butt)
James Bryce (Viscount Bryce) (Bryce)
Davitt Letters
D. R. Daniel
William Haley
T. C. Harrington
J. F. X. O'Brien
William O'Brien
C. S. Parnell
J. E. Redmond

National Library of Scotland, Edinburgh
J. S. Blackie (Blackie)
Master of Elibank (Lord Murray) (Elibank)
5th Earl of Rosebery (AR)

National Library of Wales, Aberystwyth
T. E. Ellis (Ellis)
Thomas Gee (Gee)
Glansevern Collection (A. C. Humphreys-Owen) (Glansevern)
David Lloyd George (1st Earl Lloyd-George) (LG[NLW])
Stuart Rendel (Lord Rendel) (Rendel)

Scottish Record Office, Edinburgh
William Ivory (Ivory)
9th Marquis of Lothian (Lothian)

United Committee for the Taxation of Land Values, London
R. R. Stokes

University of Birmingham
Sir Austen Chamberlain (AC)
Joseph Chamberlain (JC)

University of Edinburgh
Scottish Liberal Association, Minutes etc. (SLA)

University of Newcastle upon Tyne
*Sir Charles Trevelyan (CPT)
*Sir George Otto Trevelyan (GOT)

Private Collection
J. C. Wedgwood (1st Lord Wedgwood) (Wedgwood)

3 Periodicals

Annual Register
Christian Socialist
Daily Chronicle
Daily Herald
Daily News
Freeman's Journal
Glasgow Herald
Inverness Courier
Irish Times
Irish World
Justice
Labour Leader
Land and Liberty (continuation of Land Values)
Land Values (continuation of Single Tax)
Liberal Magazine
Liverpool Daily Post
Manchester Guardian
Morning Post
North British Daily Mail
Northern Ensign
Orcadian
Rossshire Journal
Scotsman
Shetland Times
Single Tax
South Wales Daily News

---

*Copies only seen by author.

Star
The Times
Westminster Gazette

4 Books, articles, etc.

(Books published in London unless otherwise indicated)
Abels, Jules: *The Parnell tragedy* (Bodley Head, 1966).
Arensberg, C. M.: *The Irish countryman* (Macmillan, 1937).
Argyll, 8th Duke of: "Land reformers", *Contemporary Review*, 1885, pp. 470-79.

Barker, Michael: *Gladstone and Radicalism : the reconstruction of Liberal policy in Britain 1885-1894* (Harvester Press, 1975).
Beer, Max: *History of British Socialism* (2 vols; Bell, 1919).
Bettany, F. G.: *Stewart Headlam* (John Murray, 1926).
Blackie, J. S.: *The Scottish Highlanders and the Land Laws* (Chapman & Hall, 1885).
Blatchford, Robert: *Land Nationalisation* (Clarion Pamphlet No. 26, 1898).
Blunt, W. S.: *The Land War in Ireland* (S. Swift & Co., 1912).
Brown, John: "Scottish and English Land Legislation 1905-11", *Scottish Historical Review*, 46 (1968), pp. 72-85.
Buckland, Patrick: *Irish Unionism I : The Anglo-Irish and the new Ireland 1885-1922* (Gill & Macmillan, Dublin, 1972).
Buckland, Patrick: *Irish Unionism II : Ulster Unionism and the origins of Northern Ireland 1886-1922* (Gill & Macmillan, Dublin, 1973).
Bund, J. W. Willis: *Law of compensation for unexhausted agricultural improvements* (2nd edn, 1883).
Burn, W. L.: "Free Trade in Land: an aspect of the Irish question", *Transactions of the Royal Historical Society*, 4s, 31 (1949), pp. 61-74.
Butler, D. and Freeman, J.: *British Political Facts 1900-1960* (Macmillan, 1963).

Cameron, Charles: *The Skye Expedition of 1886* (National Liberal Federation of Scotland, 1886-7).
Cameron, James: *The old and new Highlands and Islands* (James Cameron, Kirkcaldy, 1912).

Chamberlain, Joseph (preface): *The Radical Programme* (Chapman & Hall, 1885).

Clark, G. B.: *A plea for the nationalisation of land* (Bennett Bros., 1882).

Clark, S.: "The social composition of the Land League", *Irish Historical Studies*, xvii, 68 (1971), pp. 447-69.

Cobden, Richard: *Speeches on questions of public policy*, ed. John Bright and J. E. Thorold Rogers (Macmillan, 1870; T. Fisher Unwin, 1908).

Cole, G. D. H., and Postgate, R.: *The Common People, 1746-1946* (Methuen, 4th edn, 1949).

Crowley, D. W.: "The 'Crofters' Party' 1885-1892", *Scottish Historical Review*, 35 (1956), pp. 110-26.

Curtis, L. P.: *Coercion and conciliation in Ireland 1880-1892* (Princeton U.P., N.J., 1963).

Davies, John: "The end of the great estates and the rise of freehold farming in Wales", *Welsh History Review*, 7 (1974), pp. 186-212.

Davis, Peter: "The Liberal Unionist Party and Irish policy 1886-1892", *Historical Journal*, xviii (1975), pp. 85-104.

Davitt, Michael: *The fall of feudalism in Ireland* (Harper & Bros., 1904).

Day, J. P.: *Public administration in the Highlands and Islands of Scotland* (University of London Press, 1918).

Derby, 15th Earl of: "Ireland and the Land Act", *Nineteenth Century*, 1881.

Douglas, Roy: " 'God gave the land to the people!' " in A. J. A. Morris (ed.), *Edwardian Radicalism 1900-1914* (Routledge & Kegan Paul, 1974), pp. 148-61.

Douglas, Roy: "Labour in decline 1910-14", in Kenneth D. Brown (ed.), *Essays in anti-Labour history* (Macmillan, 1974), pp. 105-25.

Douglas, Roy: *The history of the Liberal Party 1895-1970* (Sidgwick & Jackson, 1971).

Edinburgh Review (unsigned): "Men, sheep and deer", vol. 106 (1857), p. 467 ff.

Emy, H. V.: "The Land Campaign: Lloyd George as a social reformer 1909-14", in A. J. P. Taylor (ed.), *Lloyd George : Twelve essays* (Hamish Hamilton, 1971), pp. 45-68.

English Land Restoration League Reports.

Ensor, Sir Robert: *England 1870-1914* (Oxford U.P., Oxford, 1936).

Gardiner, A. G.: *Pillars of Society* (James Nisbet, 1913).

Garvin, J. L.: *Life of Joseph Chamberlain* (Macmillan, 1932 *seq.*).

George, David Lloyd, and others: *Coal and Power* (Hodder & Stoughton, 1924).

George, Henry, sr.: *The Irish Land Question* (D. Appleton & Co., NY, 1881; later republished as *The Land Question*, Robert Schalkenbach Foundation, NY, 1965, etc.).

George, Henry, sr.: *Progress & Poverty* (D. Appleton & Co., NY, 1880; Hogarth Press, 1953, etc.).

George, Henry, Jr.: *The life of Henry George* (Heinemann, 1900, etc.).

Gwynn, Denis: *Life of John Redmond* (Harrap, 1932).

Hadfield, A. M.: *The Chartist Land Company* (David & Charles, Newton Abbot, 1970).

Hammond, J. L., and B.: *The village labourer 1760-1832* (Longmans, 1911, etc.).

Hanham, H. J.: "The problem of Highland discontent 1880-1885", *Transactions of the Royal Historical Society*, 5s, 19 (1970), pp. 21-65.

Haslip, J.: *Parnell* (Cobden-Sanderson, 1936).

Healy, T. M.: *Why Ireland is not free* (Dublin, 1898).

Howard, C. H. D.: "Joseph Chamberlain and the 'Unauthorised Programme'", *English Historical Review*, 65 (1950), pp. 477-91.

Hunter, James: "The Gaelic connection: Highlands, Ireland and Nationalism, 1873-1922", *Scottish Historical Review*, 59 (1975), pp. 178-204.

Hunter, James: "The politics of Highland land reform 1873-1895", *Scottish Historical Review*, 53 (1974), pp. 45-68.

Hyndman, H. M.: *The record of an adventurous life* (Macmillan, 1911).

Kee, Robert: *The Green Flag* (Weidenfeld & Nicolson, 1972).

Kellas, J. G.: "The Crofers' War 1882-8", *History Today*, xii (1962), pp. 281-88.

Kellas, J. G.: "The Liberal Party in Scotland 1876-1895", *Scottish Historical Review*, 44 (1965), pp. 1-16.

Land Enquiry Committee Report (Hodder & Stoughton, 1913-4).

Land Nationalisation Society: Pamphlets, 1881 *seq.*

Lawrence, E. P.: *Henry George in the British Isles* (Michigan State U.P., East Lansing, Mich., 1957).

Leasehold Enfranchisement Association: 1st Annual Report, 1885.

Liberal Industrial Inquiry: *Britain's Industrial Future* (Liberal Summer Schools, 1928).

Liberal Land Committee: *Land and the Nation* (Hodder & Stoughton, 1925).

Liberal Land Committee: *Towns and the Land* (Hodder & Stoughton, 1925).

Lynd, H. M.: *England in the 1880s* (Oxford U.P., Oxford, 1945, etc.).

Lyons, F. S. L.: *Ireland since the Famine* (Weidenfeld & Nicolson, 1971).

Lyons, F. S. L.: "The economic ideas of Parnell", *Historical Studies*, ii (1959), pp. 60-75.

Lyons, F. S. L.: "John Dillon and the Plan of Campaign, 1886-1890", *Irish Historical Studies*, 14 (1964-5), pp. 313-47.

Lyons, F. S. L.: *John Dillon* (Routledge & Kegan Paul, 1968).

MacAskill, Joy: *The treatment of "land" in English social and political theory 1840-1885*, Oxford B.Litt. thesis, 1959.

MacCarthy, Justin: *Ireland since the Union* (Chatto & Windus, 1887).

Mackenzie, Alexander: *History of the Highland clearances* (A. & W. Mackenzie, Inverness, 1883).

Mackenzie, Alexander: *The Isle of Skye 1882-3* (A. & W. Mackenzie, Inverness, 1883).

Mann, Tom: *The programme of the I.L.P. and the unemployed* (Clarion Tract No. 6, 1895).

Marriott, Oliver: *The property boom* (Hamish Hamilton, 1967; Pan, 1969).

Mitchell, B. R. and Deane, P.: *Abstract of British Historical Statistics* (Cambridge U.P., Cambridge, 1962).

Moody, T. W.: "Michael Davitt and the British Labour movement, 1882-1906", *Transactions of the Royal Historical Society*, 5s (1952), 3, pp. 53-76.

Moody, T. W., and Beckett, J. C. (ed.): *Ulster since 1800* (First Series, BBC, 1954; Second Series, BBC, 1957).

Morgan, K. O.: *Wales in British Politics 1868-1922* (University of Wales Press, Cardiff, 1963).

Morgan, K. O.: "Gladstone and Wales", *Welsh Historical Review*, 1 (1960-3), pp. 65-82.

Morley, John (later Viscount): *Life of Gladstone* (Macmillan, 1903, etc.).

Morris, A. J. Anthony: *Radicalism against war 1906-1914* (Longman, 1972).

Murdoch, John: *Autobiography* (manuscript, Mitchell Library, Glasgow).

O'Brien, William: *An olive branch in Ireland and its history* (Macmillan, 1910).

Orwin, Christabel, and Whetman, Edith: *History of British Agriculture 1846-1914* (Longmans, 1964).

Parnell, Anna: *The Land League : the story of a great sham* (manuscript), National Library of Ireland, Dublin.

Pelling, Henry: *Origins of the Labour Party 1880-1900* (Macmillan, 1954).

Prebble, John: *The Highland clearances* (Secker & Warburg, 1963).

Probyn, J. W. (ed.): *Systems of land tenure* . . . (Macmillan, 1870, 1881, etc.).

Rees, Thomas: *History of Protestant Nonconformistry in Wales* (J. Snow, 1861).

Richard, Henry: *Letters on the* . . . *condition* . . . *of Wales* (reprinted from *Morning and Evening Star*, 1866).

Savage, D. C.: "Scottish politics 1885-6", *Scottish Historical Review*, 40 (1961), pp. 118-135.

Savage, D. C.: "The origins of the Ulster Unionist Party 1885-6", *Irish Historical Studies*, xxi, 47 (1961), pp. 185-208.

Saville, John: "Henry George and the British Labour movement: a select bibliography, with commentary", *Bulletin of the Society for the Study of Labour History*, 5 (1962), pp. 18-26.

Shearman, H.: "State-aided land purchase under the Disestablishment Act of 1869", *Irish Historical Studies*, iv, 13 (1944), pp. 58-80.

Skeffington, F. Sheehy: *Michael Davitt* (Fisher Unwin, 1908).

Skidelsky, R.: *Politicians and the Slump* (Macmillan, 1967).

Snowden, Viscount: *An autobiography* (2 vols, Nicholson &

Watson, 1934).

Solow, Barbara: *The land question and the Irish economy 1870-1903* (Harvard U.P., Cambridge, Mass., 1971).

Taylor, A. J. P.: *English History 1914-1945* (Oxford U.P., Oxford, 1965).

Thompson, E. P.: *William Morris* (Lawrence & Wishart, 1955).

Thompson, F. M. L.: "Land and politics in England in the 19th Century", *Transactions of the Royal Historical Society*, 5s, 15 (1965), pp. 23-44.

Thomson, Malcolm: *David Lloyd George* (Hutchinson, 1948).

Wallace, A. R.: *Land Nationalisation : Its necessity and its aims* (Trübner & Co., 1882).

Wallace, A. R.: *My life* (Chapman & Hall, 1908).

Watson, R. Spence: *The National Liberal Federation 1877-1906* (Fisher Unwin, 1907).

Webb, Beatrice and Sidney: *History of Trade Unionism* (Longmans, revised edn, 1920).

Wedgwood, Dame C. Veronica: *The last of the Radicals* (Cape, 1951).

Westminster Review (unsigned): *Landed Tenure in the Highlands*, vol. 34 (1868), pp. 277-300.

Westminster Review (unsigned): *The land question in England*, vol. 38 (1870), pp. 233-62.

Winder, G. H.: *British Farming and Food* (City Press pamphlet, 1953).

Woods, R. A.: *English social movements* (Swann Sonnenscheim & Co., 1892).

INDEX

232

General Elections: (1868) 97;
(1874), 27; (1880), 29; (1885),
31, 50, 53, 67-8, 72, 98; (1886),
56; (1892), 115; (1895), 117;
(1906), 134-6, 141; (Jan., Dec.
1910), 148; (1918), 171-2;
(1922), 182; (1923), 185;
(1924), 187, 189; (1929), 195-
6; (1931), 206; (1945), 212
General Strike (1926), 193
George, Henry, 43-9, 51, 66, 72,
106, 111-14, 117-18, 134-5,
145
George, D. Lloyd (Earl Lloyd-
George), 42, 99, 102-3, 134,
138, 141-5, 155-6, 170-71,
174-80, 185, 188-91, 194, 198-
9, 204-5
Germany, 144
Gladstone, W. E., 21, 29, 32-4,
42, 47-8, 50, 54-6, 61-2, 78,
86, 99, 114-17, 124, 136, 142
Glasgow, 47, 71-2, 113, 117-18,
135, 139, 162, 173
"Glasgow Bill", 139
Glendale, 64, 67, 90
Glengarry, 61
Gordon, General C. G., 26
Gorst, (Sir) John, 66
Goschen, George (Viscount), 55
Goulding, K. A., 149
"Green Book", 191-2, 193, 195
Gregory, St, 111
Grey, Sir Edward (Viscount), 146-
7
Ground Game Act (1880), 42
Ground Rent. See Land Value
Taxing, Site Value Rating
Guild of St Matthew's, 45
Gwynedd, 97

Habeas Corpus, 31
Haldane, R. B. (Viscount), 114,
186
Hanley, 157-8, 165, 169, 175

Harcourt, Lewis (Viscount), 144
Harcourt, Sir William, 61, 67, 70,
116-17, 144
Hardie, J. Keir, 115
Harrington, T. C., 77
Harris, Isle of, 89
Hartington, Marquis of (8th Duke
of Devonshire), 25, 35, 50, 55-
7, 77, 83, 120
Hawick, 112
Headlam, Stewart, 45
Healy, Bishop, 80-81
Hemmerde, E. G., 156, 175
Henderson, Arthur, 185
Henderson, H. D., 190
Herbista, 88
Hesiod, 217
High Peak, 146
Highland Clearances, 61
Highland Land Law Reform As-
sociation, 64-6, 91, 111
Highlander, 61, 65
Hirst, F. W., 185
Holbourn, J. G., 117
Holmfirth, 116-18
Holywell, 98
Home Rule, 53-6, 70, 76, 78, 99,
124, 136, 164
Horsham, 159
Housing, 159, 160, 162, 165, 187,
210-11
Housing Act (1924), 187
Housing and Town Planning Bill
(1909), 147
Humphreys-Owen, A. C., 17, 101
Hutchison, Sir Robert (Lord),
203, 205

Illingworth, Percy, 160, 164
Independent Labour Party, 72,
118, 174-5
Inverness, Invernessshire, 61, 64,
67, 69, 71
Irish Church Act (1869), 24-5
Irish Labourers Act (1906), 136

234

Irish Land Bills, Acts: (1870), 25, 82; (1881), 32-5, 51-2, 55, 68, 70, 78, 82, 125, 217; (1887), 78-9, 82; (1909), 137-8
Irish Land Question, 45, 47
Irish Local Government Board, 85
Irish National Land League. See Land League
Irish National League. See National League
Irish National Party, 27-32, 53-6, 76, 83-4, 115-16, 119-20, 135-6, 141, 148
Irish Republican Brotherhood, 77
Irish Times, 26
Irish World, 28-9, 36, 44
Ivory, Sheriff W., 63, 67, 87

James, Sir Henry (Lord), 55
Jones, Rev. Evan (Pan), 98
Jones, Rev. Michael Daniel, 98

Kennet, See Young, E. Hilton
Kerr, Hugh, 88
Keynes, Maynard (Lord), 190
Killerton, 190
Kilmainham Jail, 34-6
Kilmuir, 66
Kinsale, 62
Kyle of Lochalsh, 91

Labouchère, Henry, 53
Labour Party, 115-16, 135-6, 146, 148, 155-6, 162, 170-79, 181-7, 191, 194-206, 209-10, 213-14
Labour Representation Committee, 135-6
Labour Representation League, 18-19
Labourers (agricultural), 23, 40-41, 53, 97, 103, 106, 122, 159-60, 165, 191, 194
Ladies' Land League, 34-5
Lambert, George (Viscount), 207
Lanarkshire, N. W., 117

Lancashire, 164
Land Acquisition Bill (1919), 117-18
Land Bank, 150
Land Bonds, 194
Land Campaign (1913-14), 160-66
Land Commission (1965), 215
Land Courts, 34, 36
Land Enquiry Committee, 158-66
Land and Labour League, 18, 107
Landlord and Tenant Bill (1927), 194
Land League (Highland). See Highland Land Law Reform Association
Land League (Irish), 28-36, 44-5, 63-4
Land League (Welsh), 99, 101
Land and the Nation. See "Green Book"
Land and Nation League, 192-4
Land Nationalisation, 45-6, 106-7, 118, 161, 163, 191, 218
Land Purchase, 33, 52, 55-6, 68, 83-5, 106, 124-30. See also Ashbourne Act, Balfour Act, Wyndham Act
Land Question, 45
Land Reform Union, 46
Land Restoration Leagues: English, 46-7, 106-7; Scottish, 47
Land Settlement Bill, Act (1919), 175-6
Land Tenure Reform Association, 18
Land Tenure Bills, Acts: (1895), 121; (1906), 138
Land Value Taxing, 112-15, 117-19, 136, 139, 142-6, 149, 155-8, 169, 172-7, 180-82, 192-3, 203-10, 219, 220
Land Values, 172
Land War, Irish, 26, 36, 40, 60
Lands, Ministry of, 159, 166

236

237